22:44 OUR
HIDDEN GIFT

22:44 OUR HIDDEN GIFT

FIND THE WAY TO DISCOVER YOUR OWN

TRICIA L. LA BELLA

BALBOA.
PRESS

A DIVISION OF HAY HOUSE

Balboa Press books may be ordered through booksellers or by contacting:

Balboa Press
A Division of Hay House
1663 Liberty Drive
Bloomington, IN 47403
www.balboapress.com.au
1-(877) 407-4847

ISBN: 978-1-4525-1068-2 (sc)
ISBN: 978-1-4525-1069-9 (e)

Because of the dynamic nature of the Internet, any web addresses or links contained in this book may have changed since publication and may no longer be valid. The views expressed in this work are solely those of the author and do not necessarily reflect the views of the publisher, and the publisher hereby disclaims any responsibility for them.

The author of this book does not dispense medical advice or prescribe the use of any technique as a form of treatment for physical, emotional, or medical problems without the advice of a physician, either directly or indirectly. The intent of the author is only to offer information of a general nature to help you in your quest for emotional and spiritual well-being. In the event you use any of the information in this book for yourself, which is your constitutional right, the author and the publisher assume no responsibility for your actions.

Any people depicted in stock imagery provided by Thinkstock are models, and such images are being used for illustrative purposes only.
Certain stock imagery © Thinkstock.

Printed in the United States of America

Balboa Press rev. date: 07/11/2013

PREFACE

The past years have led to some major changes in my life.

In 2006, I had a personal experience with cancer. It was the event that changed my life. It led me, in 2007, to commence work as a life coach.

During that time, I went on a personal mission to explore my own life, learning how to tackle the constant challenges, disappointments, and difficulties. The strength, understanding, and comfort I gained prepared me for what lay ahead.

In 2011, my husband was diagnosed with stage IV mantle cell non-Hodgkin's lymphoma. His diagnosis came only a few weeks after my dad passed away unexpectedly. In that moment, it felt like our world had turned upside down once again.

As you would expect, there were ups and downs and highs and lows throughout this experience. But nestled among them were some amazing gifts. I'd like to tell how we found them and how they enabled us to embrace the time with love and spirit.

This is our story.

CONTENTS

PART

THE MACK TRUCK

This section describes our ups and downs over a few tough years. It gives a more detailed account of the treatment and journey along the road to my husband's cancer recovery. It is our unique story, but it is not unique. We all have a unique story. For my husband and I, our predominant story revolved around our experience with cancer. That was our "Mack truck"! But whether it's illness, loss of a job, loss of a partner, sadness, personal challenge, financial crisis or difficulty, a tragic event, or separation, it seems we are all facing something.

CHAPTER 1

WHEN YOU KNOW SOMETHING'S WRONG

When you get that gut feeling (from who knows where?), just go with it! You'll look back from the future and understand what it was all about.

For many months, I had a nagging feeling about Steve's cough.

"You better get that cough checked out," I'd say regularly.

He'd respond with a roll of the eyes that declared, *You're nagging and worrying for nothing.* He'd assure me he'd had it looked at and it was just a lingering cough from a virus.

The thing was, he *did* have a virus with a cough residue last year and again this year, but it seemed that it never really cleared in between.

In addition to the cough, I had a feeling that he just wasn't the same. What did I mean by that? Well, it was difficult to define, but I sensed he was in some sort of struggle—a struggle where the thought of taking on new things seemed too difficult.

When I made suggestions to do or go somewhere different—with a "Let's check out . . ." or "Let's . . ." or "Why don't we . . ."—he wasn't interested. In fact, he seemed slightly irritated by the idea.

We began building our beach house at Maslins Beach in January 2011 (it had already been put on hold when I was diagnosed with cancer back in 2006), and although we were both excited about the project, I noticed he lacked the energy and drive to deal with many aspects of the building. Fortunately, as he pointed out, I was working part-time and did have the time to take them on. Still, I felt that something wasn't right.

I remembered thinking how tired and "full" he must have been. I questioned whether that was normal, or whether he was abnormally drained. I had that ongoing sense that something was going on, but nothing stood out.

When we finally got the keys to the beach house in July 2011, Steve was so excited and proud. He had worked hard all his life, and to finally build the house meant great times ahead with family and friends. It was a time in our lives when work was supposed to slow down a little. But that's not how it was.

We found that time to work on the house didn't just arrive out of thin air. There was already plenty to do with our Highbury home, not to mention work commitments, so there was only a limited amount of time for work and pleasure at the beach house.

Sensing the difficulty, I did what I could to organize all the bits: blinds, carpets, floors, furniture, appliances, decorations, sundries, and so on. Steve would say there was no point in him doing it because "the boss" (that's me, apparently) would have the final say anyway. I suppose there was in fact some truth to that, but in the past he would still have come along to give his ideas and get involved.

It seemed that there was one thing after another that stopped Steve from doing things. He had problems with his back. The last time his back "went out" was when he went surfing with his cousin's husband and good friend who also enjoyed the surf. That was about six months earlier. It was sad that the very thing he loved caused him problems. In fact, he would say that since he turned fifty, everything seemed to have fallen apart! First his knee stopped him from playing indoor soccer, then the other knee stopped the social tennis he loved, and then his back stopped him from surfing. No matter how much therapy he underwent, he always seemed to struggle with his back.

Then it was time to do the more physical aspects of preparing the house: cleaning windows and outdoor areas, scrubbing floors, gardening, moving furniture. His back stopped him from tackling many of the jobs that needed doing at the beach house. He felt that nothing was moving, but at the same time, he knew he wasn't up to it.

Steve was a hairdresser with his own business, and he was still working harder than ever on the hairdressing floor. At his age, many hairdressers were doing mainly management rather than the hair work, but Steve really loved that part and found it hard to let it go. So he found himself doing it all—managing and doing hair—and it was getting harder and harder.

About four years earlier, we'd had the biggest surprise when our son Dion told us that he wanted to drop out of university (where he was studying physics and maths) and begin hairdressing. We were really shocked by this—he had never shown any desire to be involved in that profession. Unsure of his motives or if it was going to be right for him, we honoured his request and sent him off to hairdressing school.

We were pleasantly surprised at his natural ability and talent for the work. He'd always wanted to manage a business, and we began to think there could be a chance for him to help his dad in the future. But that would be a long time off, because he was still quite fresh at the trade.

So the jobs at the beach house remained, but that was OK. There was no need to rush. I have learned that time frames are all self-induced, and if you can't, you can't. Not that Steve liked that concept. Jobs not done frustrated him. He was a worker and kept going until the job was done, so this didn't feel comfortable for him. He was so happy when his back improved, and he listed the many things he intended to do that weekend.

But soon after, he was hit with a virus and felt quite fatigued by it.

He wasn't happy to be stopped again. In all his forty or so years of working, there weren't many days when he didn't go to work. He had a very strong work ethic. In fact, even if he was sick, he felt he could and should go to work. I sensed he thought it weak if you didn't operate like he did. He could never understand why people didn't work through "minor" illnesses. But this illness did seem to stop him from pushing through in the way he was used to.

Because of his illness, jobs remained undone. Luckily, the internal aspect of the house was completed enough for us to spend nights there. That was great—we got a taste of how it felt to switch off and relax. Steve began to talk about his intention to cut down a day a week in February to gain some time to enjoy the beach house and life in general. I changed my work schedule to ensure we would both be together for a few days each week.

That new plan was the start to our slowing down.

Even though we had a plan, I had an overwhelming feeling I was moving against the grain, as though a tide was pulling me in another direction. It felt like a knot in my stomach, but I couldn't explain the reason.

My fiftieth birthday was coming up in October, and I had always said I wanted a big celebration with my friends and family. It was the five-year anniversary of the all-clear for bowel cancer, so it was to be a double celebration. But somehow, I resisted getting things organized. My daughter and niece kept asking when I was going to organize my invitations and other things that were needed. I felt a resistance that I couldn't explain.

Was it that I just didn't want to turn fifty? No, that wasn't it, because I've never had a problem with my age. But for some reason, it was difficult to actually set a date. Nothing seemed to flow. In the end, I decided on a date and swiftly put a few things into place.

I didn't know why, but it still felt all wrong.

It was near the end of August 2011 when my mum phoned, telling me that my dad had just been taken to the hospital by ambulance. The ambulance officers weren't sure, but they said the severe pain in Dad's back could have been his heart, and they weren't taking any chances. We rushed to the hospital and were mildly relieved when the emergency-room doctor suggested Dad had pneumonia and required antibiotics and an overnight stay.

The next day, he had a CT (computed tomography) scan and a suspicious mass was spotted in the upper lobe of his left lung. Although nothing was confirmed, it meant a process of further investigation was ahead. During the next two weeks, he underwent biopsies and tests, and it took another two weeks to confirm that the mass in his lung was in fact a carcinoma.

From there, we went through a roller coaster of emotions. We discovered from the PET (positron emission tomography) scan that while the tumour was malignant, it was contained in the upper left lobe, which meant a successful surgery and he'd be cured.

It was amazing watching my dad take the news and deal with the process. I'm not sure if it was denial or amazing acceptance, but whatever it was, he tackled it brilliantly. He continued his volunteer work, which included bus driving and helping prepare weekly lunches for the "oldies" (as he termed them) at the Italian Village, until a few days before he was to be hospitalized.

When he explained to his family overseas what was ahead, he repeated what he was told by the surgeon—he would have his left lung's upper lobe removed and remain in intensive care for about twenty-four hours. By the second or third day, he would be walking around, and he would be home in about seven to ten days. He reassured them it was "nothing"—I'm not sure if that was to help him or them, or if he really believed that.

On September 26, the morning of the operation, my mum, sister, and I stayed by his side until he was ready for his surgery. Our goodbyes and good-luck wishes betrayed a glimpse of the awful possibility that any surgery brought—that he might not make it through. It was a deeply emotional moment.

Immediately after the operation, we were to get a phone call from the surgeon to let us know how the surgery went. He had estimated it would take two hours to complete, so when after three-and-a-half hours we hadn't heard from him, we naturally started to feel a little anxious.

When the call came with word of a successful surgery, the other details seemed distant to my ears. They decided to keep him in an induced coma for twenty-four hours—a little longer than usual because his body did struggle because the tumour was wrapped around his pulmonary artery. Amazingly, the surgeon painstakingly chipped away at the tumour with utmost precision. We later learned it was like scraping tissue paper from the artery. One slip and it would have been over.

We were OK with the induced coma, as the doctors reassured us it was standard procedure after such an operation. Watching him in that state, however, was painful. The tube that went down to his lungs seemed to cause him a lot of problems, and he just didn't seem to be coping very well. Days passed with him still in the induced coma. He faced an onslaught of challenges, including a pneumonia infection, a heart attack, and a procedure to insert a stent in his coronary artery. They later learned it had a 90 per cent blockage, so we were amazed he survived the surgery.

It was like a nightmare had unfolded.

My parents' fifty-fifth wedding anniversary came while Dad was still in his coma-induced state. We tried to make a special night for Mum by having everyone over for a dinner. We toasted both of them and hoped for a better celebration when he was well.

It ended up taking seven days to see him out of intensive care and into high-dependency. The doctors (as were we) were amazed and relieved when he pulled through. It only took a day or two to see he was on his way back. His humour and wit were amazing. He seemed in the best of spirits—he could hardly believe he'd had the operation.

Many things made him laugh and feel happy. Geelong beating Collingwood in the AFL grand final was the most significant. He joked with the nurses. When one nurse asked if he was "finished" (with his dinner), he promptly replied, "No, I'm Polish!"

When Mum tried to help him perform his much-needed deep-breathing technique with cues of "in through your nose, out through your mouth," he promptly reinforced his understanding of the technique by repeating "in through your nose, out through your arse!" My son, who had been visiting at the time, couldn't believe how "in form" Dad was, and together we laughed and felt relieved that he was back.

At that point, I felt confident he was going to be OK, so I made the decision to go ahead with the birthday celebration that I had reluctantly planned. He wanted me to have the party, as did my mum (they were both party people and enjoyed a celebration). So I confirmed with everyone that it would go ahead, even though I was still struggling with what he had just gone through.

I didn't have much enthusiasm or desire. It was more like, "I'll do it, but my heart is not feeling very comfortable with it." Steve, my sister, and I worked like bullets, once the decision was made, to prepare for the event. That was the Tuesday before the party on Saturday.

Then something changed.

Dad seemed a little agitated and unsettled, and we suspected an infection. He had been moved quite swiftly from high-dependency to the ward, and both my sister and I felt it was too soon, as his stats were not stable. But that was what the doctors decided.

The next roller-coaster ride had begun. Within two days, he was back in intensive care with an infection. The doctors reassured us that he could get past this next obstacle, but it would require very strong doses of antibiotics. Dad was keen to get up and out of bed to come to my birthday. The doctors thought he was delirious, because they weren't aware there was to be a party. Days melt into one when you are in intensive care, but Dad knew it was Saturday morning, October 8, and it was the day of the party. The doctors were amazed at how clear he was, given his situation. My sister and mum promised Dad a double celebration together with his own birthday that was coming up on October 22. He was happy with that.

So my birthday celebration went ahead.

It was good to see Mum have some joy, for we had spent the last three weeks at the hospital dealing with the ups and downs of Dad's recovery. It was great to have all my friends and close family there to celebrate my birthday and five-year remission.

We all sent Dad lots of love and best wishes for his recovery. While it was a great party (so said the guests), it was a blur to me. I was there but not there. My heart was feeling pain and worry for what was happening with my dad.

Steve knew how difficult it was for me to go ahead with the party. He witnessed the emotional outbursts each night after I returned from the hospital. Steve knew the close bond I had with my dad and how it was breaking my heart to see him so ill.

It's amazing how wonderful Steve was, and how much strength and support he gave me during that time. He just knew what to do. He would comfort me and encourage me to express all my emotions. He would just hold me while I poured out my heart. I felt his heart was breaking too. He looked strained and tired, but despite that, he was my rock and nurturer.

We were at the hospital each day and did our best to bring something special to Dad during this time. We played his favourite music (he was a choir member and had an appreciation for opera), surrounded him with beautiful healing essences, and brought loving touch to his body with a gentle massage to his swollen and bruised arms. It was all we knew to do in the given situation. We spoke to him as though he could hear our words, and we expressed our love for him and our sadness for what was happening.

Dad passed away on October 24 following many complications post-surgery: infection, aspiration pneumonia, kidney failure, and septicaemia. We all felt, however, that his soul had left his body two days earlier, on his seventy-ninth birthday. That was the day the hospital phoned for us all to be there. It seemed at that point he had already left.

Fortunately, Dad had been induced into a coma at the end, so he didn't endure the physical suffering associated with each of the complications. Unfortunately, his loved ones endured the emotional pain of watching him leave. Although he may not have been consciously aware during that time, I'm sure he would have felt the magnitude of love and comfort we brought to his final moments. They were moments to be treasured.

It was a couple of weeks after the funeral, while my sister and I took some time off at the beach house, that Steve decided to help erect a fence at his dad's place. Together with our brother in law, he set out to nail, hammer, and construct. It was the day after an evening of visitors who were at our house giving condolences for Dad's passing. It was hot and humid, and Steve was feeling quite dehydrated.

Toward the end of the construction, Steve helped out by climbing the ladder to drill into a section of the fence that the others couldn't reach. He only managed to do four screws before he felt quite faint and woozy. He made his way to the lounge, which was significantly cooler, and put his feet up to recover. Everyone insisted he get himself checked out. Despite being able to explain why he felt the way he did, he decided it was time to go to the doctor for a check up.

As soon as the doctor saw Steve, he said, "You're anaemic."

The doctor did routine blood tests, and anaemia was confirmed. From there, they did the usual series of tests to determine why the red-blood-cell count was low. I made the booking with the gastroenterologist for the following week, otherwise the next available time wouldn't have been until January.

Steve was not happy about taking time off just before Christmas, as that was the salon's busiest time of year. Everyone wanted their hair done for Christmas, and Steve didn't want to let anybody down. I insisted it was important to get moving on things straight away. This took some convincing.

The colonoscopy and endoscopy were all clear, and while I'd normally think that was great, I was even more concerned. What was causing his low levels? The gastroenterologist wanted to repeat the colonoscopy and do another test that involved a small camera being inserted into the intestine, and that was to happen over the next few weeks. But something made me feel they were off track with things. The cough, the red bloods cells, the back, the lack of drive—what else could it mean?

Friends started to express their concern about his pale colour and change in energy, and I began to feel it was more than something subtle. I remembered and drew upon how a wonderful doctor looking after Dad when he was in intensive care acted on things as they appeared. This doctor didn't wait, he dealt with things. I was not going to wait.

I contacted Steve's doctor and expressed my desire for Steve to have a CT scan straight away. It needed to be on Monday, which was his usual day off; he wouldn't have agreed to taking another day off during Christmas week. It was my daughter's birthday that day, and we were to have her birthday celebration at our house that evening. It was going to be an after-dinner event, so there wasn't too much preparation involved. We could fit in doctor's visits, blood tests, and scans quite comfortably.

When we returned to the doctor at four p.m. after the series of tests, I sensed something wasn't quite right. The doctor told us there and then that they found lymphoma. We questioned whether it could have been anything other than that, perhaps a parasite causing a mass of lymph nodes in his stomach to enlarge? The doctor didn't think so, but of course anything was possible. We held on to this possibility until lymphoma was actually confirmed. We both cried anyway.

Needless to say, the night of my daughter's birthday was tough.

We decided not to say anything to family and friends; they all just needed a happy night after the difficult months we had just experienced. The day after the birthday, we told them what the doctor had suggested. Everyone was numb, including us. I tried not to go anywhere in my mind until we knew for certain what we were dealing with. That, however, proved to be very difficult.

A week later, we saw the specialist who seemed to think, from the scans, that Steve had a slow-advancing follicular non-Hodgkin's lymphoma (NHL). If that was the case, he explained, in many instances they did no treatment initially; they watched its progress and only when necessary did they treat it. He also mentioned the slight possibility that it was a more aggressive type of NHL. That being the case, he said Steve would need very harsh and intense treatment that would require four to six months off work completely—but from the scans he felt more confident it was the slower form.

We couldn't believe what we were hearing. We had until then held on to the possibility of it being a parasite, but that seemed out of the picture now. Was it all real? It was like in a moment my body, mind, and spirit separated. I was in my body listening, talking, and breathing, while my mind was in a distant space trying to make sense of it all, and my spirit—the part of me that connected with my inner knowing about this amazing and beautiful life—seemed a lifetime away.

I launched into action to do what I could do. I felt it was up to me to step up and get a handle on how we could tackle things. Steve already had so much to process with the news of what was happening in his body. He didn't need extra stress or worry.

As much as possible, I thought about how things could work if he did need time off. We thought it best that I visit his parents to explain what was happening and what may lie ahead. It meant Steve didn't have to face his parents at that point when he so emotional and shell-shocked.

I reassured Steve that everything would be OK. I could see a basic plan of how to tackle things if he needed time off work, but at that point we had our hopes on it being the less aggressive form.

It was that night when I let my emotions in on the scene. Tears of love and compassion bolted through my body, causing a massive release. I'd never cried so deeply. It needed to happen. I think I cried for all my held-in grief from Dad and possibly everything in my life. Surprisingly, once all the tears and wails had left my body, I felt calm and ready to continue.

I think I heard Steve's cries as well that night. Somehow, we needed to do this alone. I'm not sure why I didn't want to share my tears with him at first; perhaps to keep him from sensing my fear or me from sensing his. Any way it didn't take long until we sobbed in each other's arms, and the unspoken magnitude of our love for each other was expressed.

A few days after Christmas, Steve had a biopsy to confirm the type of NHL. From there, we would know the exact nature of the treatment. It was a tricky procedure.

He said it was the most unusual sensation when the needle penetrated the layers of skin and muscle near his liver to reach the nodes in his upper abdomen. I was amazed at his composure through the procedure. He was already showing courage and strength for what he had to endure.

CHAPTER **2**

THE "FIRSTS" ARE
THE HARDEST

You can never really know the pain of losing people very close until it happens. Keep them close in your memories by maintaining their life story and the mysteries that surrounded them.

Christmas was always going to be hard. I had heard it so many times before from people who had lost loved ones: "You feel it on special occasions and the 'firsts'"—first Christmas without them, first birthday, first Easter.

I had lost friends, aunties, uncles, and acquaintances, but never an immediate family member. It wasn't until Dad passed away that I actually felt the deep pain of loss. Before that, my understanding and talk must have been from a distance. Not that distance was a bad thing; distance brought a different perspective, which was often useful. However, distance could be cold, theoretical, and conceptual. I realized distance had protected my heart. When I lost my dad, however, there was no chance of avoiding it. I was in that space where deep intense emotions are felt.

I have since created a bridge between the two—distance and heart, the points I flitted between often at the beginning. Sometimes I was in my heartfelt emotions and sobbed uncontrollably, and sometimes I was at a distance with perspectives that kept my sorrow at bay.

Overall, I found that feeling loss at that level changed how I experienced life. It added another layer to "me" and how I responded to things. It added a layer that was more sensitive and real. I could feel both sad and happy at the same time. I recognized that one didn't make way for the other; the two coexisted in my world.

To tell you the truth, the loss of my dad was more painful than I ever imagined it would be. I'm not sure why it had such an impact. Was it because I wasn't expecting it? Or because I witnessed such a difficult final process? Or that I didn't do enough? Or because it was the first of my parents? Or because I loved him so much? Or because I felt I hadn't captured all I wanted to know about him? Or the reality that I'd no longer have our weekly chats? Or that there was a lot still to say? Or that I realized how hard and yet how easy it was to die? Or that I was sad for what he would be missing? Or that I was sad for what I would be missing? Or that this would happen again and again in my life? Or all of these?

Whatever it was, it was hard. Fortunately, to parallel these sad and difficult moments, there were many others to comfort and pull me from the sadness.

The day of Dad's operation, my daughter Danielle confirmed she was pregnant. Even though it was very early to announce, she felt she needed to let her *nonno* know as soon as possible (she was blessed with a strong intuitive nature). It was in the first couple of days when he came out of his coma that she broke the news. He was so happy. He rubbed her belly and was so proud that he was to be a *bisnonno* for the first time! Humorously he asked, "How did that happen?" We all laughed. He joyously told the doctors and nurses about the news. The fact that he knew about his great-grandchild brought me comfort.

There were other things that gave my mum, sister, and I comfort during that most difficult time. We felt many were signals of the greater divine's presence throughout the time of his passing. Some might call them coincidences or good fortune, but they felt like more than that.

My dad was not a very religious man; spiritual yes, religious no. He was a firm believer in the greater God or whatever you'd like to call it, but he did not agree with the all the man-made constructs of the church. He supported those who did well in the day-to-day—that was his religion.

Fortunately, such a person looked after Dad while he was in intensive care—a male nurse, Brett, who Dad trusted and felt safe with and who cared for him on many days in the ICU. You could see he was happy when Brett was around. On Dad's last day on earth, amazingly, Brett was on duty. It was certainly apt that it was Brett who bore witness to his passing.

Knowing that Dad was in his final moments, Brett (who *was* a religious man) offered to contact his local parish priest for Dad's final blessing. He explained this was a wonderful priest for such things. While grateful for the offer, we had already organized someone from the local cathedral. That priest, however, because of last-minute sickness, could not attend, so the cathedral organized another priest who was just able to fit it in before he departed overseas.

As Father Devine walked in to provide the most beautiful words for Dad's passing, Brett's face lit up. He was the local parish priest Brett had intended to call. It felt right to have Father Devine for this blessing.

It felt just as right to have a picture of Padre Pio on the front cover of the memorial card we prepared for Dad's funeral mass. Padre Pio's name, for some strange reason, was mentioned quite regularly by different people during the final days before Dad's passing. While we didn't think too much of it at the time, when it came to choosing a picture for the memorial card, an image of Padre Pio (that I had searched for many weeks earlier) appeared on my phone. It seemed to come from nowhere. We all agreed it was significant, so we chose his image for the card.

Padre Pio of Pietrelcina was a recent saint of Italy. We had known about him for a while. This came about when my mum did her family tree and discovered that we were distantly related on her mother's side. Apart from that, he bore no significance in our lives . . . or so we thought.

It was a couple of weeks after the funeral when Mum needed something from my dad's wallet that she discovered a very old and worn out prayer card with the image of Padre Pio and his healing prayer. This man must have been important to Dad. We all felt comforted that Dad was well looked after.

The week before Christmas, my mum and sister returned to the intensive-care unit at the hospital to give thanks and best wishes for Christmas. They met up with the wonderful doctors and nurses and, fortunately, Brett. His young son had been very sick during the time of Dad's illness and had become even more critical. Brett informed them that one night, he had decided to pray to Padre Pio—his significance in our life then unbeknownst to him—for help, and it was not long after that his son made a good recovery.

Coincidence or not, we took comfort in this strong Padre Pio connection.

You see I have come to take note of instinctive feelings and coincidences. There were so many over the years. They often guided me.

In June 2011, for example, I got a strong feeling about a work situation. It was while in my lecturing role at TAFE SA (Technical and Further Education South Australia) that I went with my feelings to begin changes that were needed for a new course in 2012. Usually we would commence the course changes toward the end of the year, November and December. For some reason, this urge arrived in June, so I followed it. I was working at a ferocious pace to restructure, redesign, and reproduce all that was needed. What was my rush?

I had learned from past experience that these feelings made sense down the track, so it was wise to just go with them. By the time Dad was diagnosed in mid-September, much of my work was completed. This enabled me to spend the next six weeks or so by his side with my mum and sister. I took the time off work to be fully present at this challenging time. I started to make sense of the urgency I felt earlier.

By the time I returned to work, which was a couple of weeks after dad's funeral, I was still on track to complete the work needed for the next year. Naturally, things did not feel the same. I was grieving. I pushed forward but felt a nagging discomfort. I thought to myself, *This is natural after what we've experienced with Dad*. It was quite a traumatic process. But it didn't take long before I knew I was dealing with something more: Steve's health.

So at a time when I was meant to be grieving, I was pulled into a new chasm that felt even more treacherous. It's difficult to express how I felt. Was it numbness, shock, fear, disbelief—maybe all of them? What I did know for sure was that I had to shift my focus away from Dad and toward Steve and the journey ahead.

I could feel I had moved Dad into the distance. It wasn't intentional. I think it was a protective mechanism to cope with the enormity of everything. I felt sad, even bad, that the daily ritual of lighting a candle at the picture memorial corner I had set up at home was left behind.

The ritual I had established to honour Dad had already fallen away. As I walked past his picture, the pain of my loss and my inability to feel all the unexpressed emotions was unbearable.

In the small pockets of time when I could view his picture and connect with him, I would cry. I found this to be helpful.

At the same time when I was meant to be rejoicing about becoming a first-time grandmother, I was divided by so many other things. Even though it was my first Christmas without Dad, the real grief of these "firsts" seemed to have been suspended. I had a scary feeling that there would be a huge release during the next festive period. But fortunately, along with the pain was the joy of a new baby who was due to arrive in May.

Pleasure and pain to its extreme—all at once.

But among it all, I also felt gratitude. I was both grateful and relieved that Steve seemed to be coping well. You can't predict how someone will take the news until it happens. I was amazed, proud, and in awe of the strength and attitude he displayed in the early phase of his diagnosis.

As I sat back, I realized we were in the midst of a major change. Life as we knew it was never going to be the same again. The universe had placed us away from the usual life roller coaster and positioned us to tackle something much bigger and more important.

I knew from the start that no matter what, I wanted be with Steve every step of the way and engage the lifestyle change head on. I was keen and ready to do all that was necessary if he had to face a challenge. If needed, I would reshuffle my priorities and focus on what was most important, and that was getting Steve through his illness.

CHAPTER **3**

YOU SEE, WE'VE BEEN HERE BEFORE

When something really challenging arrives in your life, it gives you the chance to take a good look at what you can do differently. Unless we have challenges sometimes, we just sit idle in a way that is actually quite damaging.

Before I tell you more about Steve's health crisis, I want to backtrack and share the story of my own. Back in 2003, Steve and I began to make some lifestyle changes. Up until then, we both had crazy busy routines that left little to no time to really enjoy life together. (I'll talk about that a little later.) Feeling stressed, depleted, and quite dissatisfied, we made the decision to change things up. This, however, took time to put into practise. During the following years, we made a few changes, but there was a long way to go.

It was on a long weekend in June 2006, while Steve was in Sydney for Hair Expo (an annual event where hairdressers around Australia gather for an expo and the winners of a photographic competition are announced), that I had a couple of days of not feeling well.

I was supposed to take part in an annual olive-picking event at a friend's, which I was really looking forward to, but just as I was about to leave, packed picnic basket in hand, I had a bout of diarrhoea. While this might not be the nicest of topics to discuss, I thought it worthwhile to let you know a little about the details. It had often been the case, since I had my children, that a "volatile" bowel action like this would cause a slight bleed from the haemorrhoids I gained during childbirth, as many women do. This had happened on many occasions, but something told me this time I needed to follow it up.

My doctor suggested I wait until the haemorrhoid blood ceased and then do the standard faecal test to just check that everything was OK. Waiting until the blood had passed would be the normal thing to do. However, something told me not to wait, and instead, I allowed blood in the sample. So sample 1 contained the haemorrhoid blood, but by sample 2 and 3 there was no evidence of blood.

As expected, the doctor phoned to inform me that blood was found in the first sample, with sample 2 and 3 clear. It was a good sign that the second and third samples were clear. That really suggested that all was actually OK. It was protocol, however, to follow up with a specialist when blood was evident, so that is what I did.

In the meantime, Steve and I were well and truly on our way to another change. We decided we were going to have a holiday together overseas. In the past, we had been overseas, but it seemed most of the trips were related to our respective jobs or careers. Steve had visited many countries with hair-industry conferences, and I went to others that were linked to my work or to Danielle's dancing, which was a big part of her life growing up.

We were scheduled to depart on October 3, 2006, for a trip to Europe. My sister, who had never been overseas, and a friend from work were also coming along. My sister-in-law was going to be taking my mother-in-law and father-in-law for their maiden trip, so at some point we would all be there together for a wonderful meet-up.

On September 6, I had a colonoscopy that the specialist had booked during our initial consultation. At first, he thought it wasn't needed. I was fit—an aerobic athlete from way back and still in good health and fitness. I had no family history or other outward signs. I might normally have gone along with avoiding such a procedure, especially knowing that sample 2 and 3 were clear, but something kept saying, *You've got to follow this up.*

It's a good thing I did. Immediately after the procedure, the doctor broke the news to Steve and me. There was a tumour located in the lower section of my bowel that would require immediate surgery.

Shock . . . everything in that moment seemed surreal.

After the immediate shock, I went into business mode with questions and discussion on how we were going to tackle things. How long had the tumour been there? Where was it? Did it look like it had spread? What was the best way to get rid of it? What was the next step? I'm not sure where my clarity came from.

Steve took it a little differently. I suppose he hadn't had the same nagging feeling, so this was a complete shock and blow to his system. He looked pale and overwhelmed and nearly collapsed in his chair. Tears and pain covered his face. In that moment, I felt his heart open with love for me, and I felt so comforted.

I felt in that moment that life would never be the same. I felt OK with it—I wasn't sure why, but a distinct sense of relief arrived. Perhaps it was relief that my very busy life was about to change forever. Is that what my heart and soul were yearning for?

The night I was diagnosed, in the stillness and silence of my bed, something strange happened. It was as though in that moment I found a feeling of bliss and peace. I felt connected to something eternal, and for some reason I felt I was going to be absolutely OK. I'm sure that night helped me prepare for the days ahead.

Needless to say, our overseas travel plans were cancelled as I undertook further tests and prepared for surgery. During that week I had scans, and I'll never forget when the scan results came back clear—the cancer didn't appear to have spread to the other organs of my body. It felt as good as winning the lottery! It helped me remain positive in the days leading up to my operation. Eleven days after the initial diagnosis, I had bowel surgery.

After my surgery, I knew things had gone well. I don't know how I knew, but I did. I didn't have to look for the colostomy bag that I had been measured for prior to the surgery (the doctor thought it might be needed because of the location of the tumour). Immediately after waking up from surgery in intensive care, my first words were, "Everything is beautiful!"

It was a further eleven days after surgery that I arrived home. The next six weeks were dedicated to getting stronger. I had lost at least eleven kilograms and was very weak. During that time, I also needed to make some important decisions about the next phase of my treatment. Chemotherapy or no chemotherapy?

I began to wonder if the whole experience was my lesson in making big decisions. I was born under the sun sign of Libra, and all my life, people—me included—would laugh at my inability to make decisions, a commonly noted trait of Libras. I would always see the pros and cons of both sides and often found myself on the fence.

So I was about to make what felt like one of the biggest decisions of my life, and there was no clear-cut solution. My tumour was, as the surgeon explained, "just a B stage," which meant it had just left the bowel wall but hadn't shown up in any lymph nodes. One school of thought said chemotherapy was necessary in case the cancer had made its way out of the area, while another school thought it not necessary. Great—now it was up to me to decide. It would have been so much easier if there was little doubt as to the action to take, but that was not so.

During the six weeks after surgery, I embarked on a naturally evolving journey of self-discovery that helped me make my final decision about treatment.

First came the journaling. I didn't plan to journal; it just happened. For our trip, I had purchased a journal that had a cover with sketches of the Eiffel Tower and other amazing landmarks. It was sitting on the bench waiting to be used, so I picked it up and began to write, "Well this was meant to be about the first day of my trip to Europe—but for now, that is not meant to be."

And it went on from there. I became very close with my journal—I explained what had happened throughout each day and my feelings and thoughts about things. There was a lot going on, so there was a lot to write. I didn't hold anything back; it seemed important to be honest. I rarely read over the journal entries I made, but it was instrumental in helping me reach a better understanding and come to a completely new way of living.

It was interesting how the nature of my journaling evolved. Initially, it was a list of actions and events that took place. In time, I also found myself expressing frustrations or things that disturbed me. After a while, my own patterns and the way I dealt with and responded to things seemed to jump out at me. I began to look more at *me* rather than all those things outside of me that I usually saw as the problem.

So instead of seeing others as wrongfully loud, I saw myself as sensitive. Instead of seeing others as critical, I saw myself as resisting feedback. Instead of seeing others as overly talkative, I saw myself as intolerant. I began to find the yang to balance the yin and create a less biased reality.

I got quicker at catching myself out when I got upset or frustrated with Steve or other things. I began to notice what I couldn't let go of. I questioned why that was so. What did it say about me? What was my point? What makes it right that I have my way?

I began to feel how much inner discord I had held on to and learned through honest response to the challenges—ways to settle my body and gain a feeling of balance. I was amazed at how differently I began to see things. I began to laugh at myself for my previous stubborn and self-centred view.

I had given up on thinking that someone outside of me could make things right. I realized it was up to me to get my body and mind in the right frame of mind to get better. There was so much I had to let go of for this to happen.

I slowly found myself more willing to challenge things. I used confronting questions and perspectives to shake myself out of a pattern of control and manipulation. Not that these were intentional. I found most humans used these patterns for survival.

This realization also helped me not only forgive others but feel a deep empathy as I realized their patterns too were unconscious strategies of survival. I certainly softened my approach to those I once struggled with. I understood that we all had our own way of dealing with things, including my illness. I realized it was not possible for me to understand where others were coming from—there could be so many reasons for their actions or lack of action, most of which were unconscious to them and me.

Some people just didn't know what to say or do during this time. Others did. Usually the simplest thoughtful things were the most powerful; a very important lesson for me. I learned it wasn't personal—it wasn't about me. It was about them and their own lives.

I recognized how, in the past, the energy of certain words, tones, and looks penetrated to my inner self. I would get affected by what I was receiving. I began to see it all as merely energy and slowly learned ways to engage that energy differently. It was as though the moment I was aware of this energy heading my way, it became disabled and bypassed me. In time, I could feel my own personal energy had increased, as I was not wasting it on unnecessary, unhelpful things.

I started to take ownership of what to engage with and what to bypass. This was a useful tool when I began to seek out alternative approaches to support me after surgery. I approached a few different naturopaths to identify some suitable strategies for healing during this period. Amazingly, I found that some of them just didn't feel right for me. I sensed some were using fear tactics: they would explain how I would only survive if I did as they suggested. Others offered practically everything that had been linked to curing cancer, which seemed overwhelming to me.

I knew when I had found the right support person. It felt right in my body and heart (wow! a very new approach for me). She was collaborative in her approach and placed the power in my own hands, which felt right.

I took the time to meditate and develop a quality breathing rhythm that brought a sense of calm and peace. I had glimpsed something powerful the night of my cancer diagnosis, and that inspired me to continue with that practice. It was in my stillness that I became very clear. I began to see how hoodwinked I had been, making decisions out of fear and ignorance.

I recognized how fear played out in me and the things I did. It often arrived in repetitive head talk, overwhelming emotions, ego games, and fanciful stories. I started to know when the fear arrived; my head would be filled with *I couldn't do that because . . . it shouldn't . . . what if . . . .* I would then consciously challenge these messages until I found a clear, peaceful, and powerful place.

My thoughts and beliefs on how to heal changed dramatically during that time. I was feeling healing benefits just from the new approaches I was adopting. I began to read true stories on self-healing, all of which supported my own discoveries. My body was cleansing itself on the deepest level. I began to recognize how my mind—although powerful in my day-to-day functioning—was very vulnerable. It could be sabotaged to think I was something that I wasn't and to play games that kept me away from my true inner knowing.

I was feeling life very differently—I had a deep compassion for everyone and everything and felt completely content and at peace with myself. The more I connected with this new me, the more confident I was that my body would heal. As days went by, my decision about chemotherapy became clearer. I was still open to opinions, but interestingly, many were laced with fear or framed by unsubstantiated claims rather than being positive or constructive.

There could be no guarantees either way, but I realized that if I chose not to have chemotherapy, I would be the main contributor to my well-being. I would be taking ownership of my own health, and this would be ongoing throughout my life. That felt right for me. I had already come a long way in my new learning, and I was feeling the internal benefits.

In fact, as time went on, I discovered more ways to access powerful healing. I noticed the power of conversations and events that were happening around me, in which someone gave me a name of a person that led to an insight or information that from there led to another insight or understanding. I would look back on this and marvel at how it evolved, and recognize that I was in a place to listen, respond, and act on the things that felt right to do.

I was beginning to realize the importance of other people in my own life progression. The more open I became to this, the more I received. Everything in each day was potentially a gift when I was open to it. I was beginning to have a very new relationship with other people in my world. Everyone was important—I loved what I was gaining, especially from those I least expected it from.

There were so many instances where I happened to chat with someone on the street, in the shopping line or wherever I was, and somehow they gave me some information I was looking for. I began to wonder how this magic occurred and if it had always been there. I realized I had never been open or listening in that way. I started to write about the coincidences and significant findings in my journal and found that the more I tuned in to them, the more they would arrive.

I remembered a time when I heard about the concept of seedling cancers. I wondered what this actually meant and if bowel cancer was considered one. Within the week, a program on television gave me the answer to my question. Seedling cancers were described as those more likely to spread a large number of seeds to other parts of the body. The report said that bowel cancer was not a seedling cancer.

I was beginning to read my own intuition. I'd often just feel something was the right thing to do and go with it. These intuitive feelings came in handy. One day, I started out to go to the butcher's to get some meat for dinner. Without realizing it, I travelled in a different direction and landed at a butcher I don't usually go to. Curious as to what that was about, I drove past the butcher I normally purchased from and found that the shop was closed for the day for renovations.

It didn't take long before I understood how to read the play. It all felt perfectly in tune. I was beginning to live in conjunction with everything around me, and this certainly felt different from my previous life approach. But let's face it, I was far too busy to do any of this before.

So the time drew near for me to make a decision about chemotherapy. During the morning appointment, I needed to inform my specialist of my decision—but I still wasn't fully sure. (Yes, that indecisive trait even popped up that day!) I was still going over the two medical opinions that were given. My surgeon said chemotherapy wasn't needed for my stage of tumour; his partner, who I saw on several occasions, suggested it was.

I decided in that moment that I would have the treatment, which was considered more of a safeguard against the cancer returning. By the time I travelled to the oncologist to finalise arrangements, though, I'd changed my mind. I realized my decision had come from angst in my gut—from fear. When I slowed things down and accessed clarity from deep within, I found my true answer. I would not be having chemotherapy.

Although disappointed, my family understood it was my decision, and for that reason, they were OK with it. They had been so wonderful during this challenge. They wanted what was best for me. They all made sacrifices and helped in a way I was so grateful for. Steve was there for me in a way I had never experienced before. Danielle was a rock and kept me strong. Dion showed me all his love. Mum and Dad showed their confidence that everything would be OK. My sister spent each and every day by my side, helping out in whatever way she could. She had taken a long service leave to go on her maiden overseas trip but found herself caring for me instead. As I made my decision, I sensed their fear, but I knew that would go away in time.

For someone who in the past found it hard to come up with a decision, I was absolutely confident and certain about what I had chosen. It was then up to me to uphold my new ways and live out the decision with confidence.

In the beginning, this brought some challenges. When the time came for me to return to work, I noticed how easy it was to fall into old patterns. I kept as connected as possible with what I had learned about keeping my body, mind, and spirit in a healing environment.

I sought ongoing inspiration from a wonderful network of health professionals, spiritual beings, family, and beautiful friends both old and new. I revisited the lists of reasons why I didn't choose chemotherapy when any doubt entered my mind. I continued a daily practice of meditation to still my mind and find a centred and peaceful state. I continued to journal insights and realizations as they arrived.

I didn't want to return to those busy crazy life patterns, but I could see how easy it was to creep back if I wasn't careful. I was thankful for the time I gave to myself to find something powerful within.

Needless to say, when Steve received the gift of a personal journal from a client at the start of his own health problems, I couldn't help but smile and be grateful. I remembered what a blessing my own journal was to me, and I knew it could offer something wonderful for him. He was actually very grateful for the gift and decided he would write his journey.

CHAPTER 4

A CHANGE IN LIFE DIRECTION

As your life situation changes, so do you—your passions, wants, and needs. It is a path to discover your hidden gifts. Just because you always have doesn't mean you always have to.

It was during my time of healing from cancer that I decided to change my career. I had been involved in the fitness industry for many years. I started out as a fitness instructor, and was later an aerobics competitor and a fitness lecturer. I always had an interest in health and wellness, and in 1998 I studied health counselling.

My cancer experience, however, had me yearning to do more in the helping area. I wanted to share my personal findings and expand concepts of health and wellness beyond the physical domain. Over time, I'd seen many fitness people overdo training, become obsessed with their diet and their bodies, and be quite miserable. That was not what I called a "health and wellness" approach to life.

I could see the gaps. I wanted this to be the focus of my work and life. I felt it was time to direct my future into what was most meaningful to me.

So for what seemed like the first time ever, I began to create a new life. I had a thirst for learning. I studied a broad range of concepts: coaching, breathe therapy, NLP (neurolinguistic programming), spirituality, EFT (Emotional Freedom Technique), quantum bioenergetics. My mind expanded as I internalized new concepts. I felt I was waking up to the world of possibilities. It seemed as though in my past life, I had no influence. This was now my choice, my way, and under my direction and influence.

In 2007, I established Rhythm of Life coaching as a base to commence my work. I had formulated so many concepts, and I wanted to express them. As my views grew and my self-awareness expanded, so did my approach.

In the past, I would have waited for things to be "just right" before I commenced with a venture, let alone a business. But I had come to understand there was no such thing as *right*. Perfect was just as it was. Perfect was allowing things to grow and shift in accordance with the ever-changing environment. I realized having things in order one day didn't mean they would be in order the next. So it was perfect to just get started and allow things to change as needed.

Going in without a formal plan or strategy was very different from my previous way of operating. My new approach was to read the play and act as it unfolded. If I was open, listening, and fully present, I would make the most appropriate decisions at the time. Of this, I was confident.

Steve asked what I was doing one night when I was jotting down an insight I received during a meditation. He was amazed when he read my entries, and he encouraged me to record them on the computer. Later he suggested I put them together into a small book. Normally I would have rejected such an idea, because I thought I couldn't write. I realized as I voiced this old belief about myself that it was another of my past-life *I can't* messages that was deceiving me. I decided I would gather the insights, and it didn't take long before a small book, *A Thought in Time*, was produced.

Things appeared with such clarity when I kept still. The messages were simple. I felt life and earth as if we were connected as one. It was no longer *me* as an isolated, separate being. To love meant to love it all. Empathy and compassion grew in my heart. They actually felt familiar, but I wasn't sure from where.

This was the most authentic I had ever felt. I wasn't scared to show who I was. The courage I needed to face the cancer helped me to find courage in all things. It seemed like the first time ever.

In time, I jotted down more and more concepts, and then a program unfolded. It wasn't long afterward that I ran the first version of Find the Way. This was a collection of concepts, activities, and perspectives that brought together the whole of my understanding on how to live the life that I felt was intended for us. It was from these perspectives that I approached life.

I loved running the programs and working with people. I find it hard to describe what I actually did. I didn't work in a rigid framework of coaching or counselling but rather drew from all my work and life experience to generate an opening for people to find their own way to master their life. This meant I threw away traditional rules on how I "should be" working with people and trusted what naturally unfolded in the exchange of our energy. I learned to listen in different ways; I observed, sensed, and intuited to capture messages beyond the words and stories that often camouflaged a deeper hurt.

It was my own personal experience with compassion and unconditional love that prepared me to work in this way. It was important to connect with that before I worked with anyone. I found this to be the key to real connection and great outcomes.

I knew that just by being myself, I was bringing something powerful to others. It was something I hoped others would also discover—they just had to be themselves and value and love that. We had much to give each other.

This feeling was a world away from where I spent much of my young life. Apart from the usual complexities and insecurities that naturally arrive in childhood and teenage years, I grew up in the '70s and '80s as the daughter of an Italian immigrant. My dad came to Australia with only a suitcase of clothes and a violin, but he brought along many old customs, traditions, and ways that were different from the Australian way of life. Our society was still searching for ways to integrate and appreciate multicultural influences.

Like many others during that time, I looked for ways to balance the cultural contradictions that existed in my world. I wanted to be like everyone else at my school and in my community, and I connected so much more with those Australian ways. I didn't want to bring Continental-style sandwiches to school when others had Vegemite. Rather than being known as Patrizia Lucia, which was on my birth certificate, I used "Patricia," and that was later reduced to "Pat" with school friends and then "Tricia," the name I have used since my early adult years. I disconnected from all that my heritage had to offer.

As an adult, I realized what I had missed out on. I hadn't even learned the language, and oh how I wished I had when it came time to travel. When my dad arrived in Australia, he was without any family—they remained in Italy. He had decided he wanted to become proficient at speaking English and because of that didn't speak Italian in the home. Hence, I never learned.

I became more and more curious about my family overseas, but it wasn't until after my illness that I finally revisited them and got to know them better. They were all such beautiful people, doing some amazing things: restaurateur, chef, artist, scientist, shop owner, mother, father, caregiver. It was also a time of getting to know my dad and mum. I felt proud of who I was and where I had come from. It motivated me to learn as much as I could about their lives. I came to see my parents as amazing people for their life story, not just their role as parents. I empathised with the hardships they both endured.

Mum's challenges were different but nonetheless there. Her parents too were of Italian origin, but she was born in Australia. She endured a tough upbringing by parents who were workers of the land, and that brought its own hardships. I realized she must have endured even more challenges living as a migrant during her younger years. I came to see both my parents in a different light. Relative to their experiences as youngsters, my own experience seemed much less troubled.

When I began to love who I was and how I came to be, it changed how I embraced everything. Nothing and no one looked the same, not even those I loved and thought I knew. When I saw others trapped in hardship, I yearned for them to discover a simple truth that could set them free too. I felt that no matter how trapped or entangled one was, there was always a way out.

I observed my own life and shared it with others. I wrote fortnightly posts on the website I had created at the start of my business to connect me with people. I'd find that in every small thing that happened, there were beautiful big realizations if I took the time to see. That was powerful for me, and I loved sharing it.

My work helped with the upkeep of my self-care. I was passionate about maintaining what I'd gained during the time of healing from my illness, but I was only human. I was a creature of habit and found that in time, I had entwined good life practice in old restrictive patterns. I realized getting stressed about upholding a better routine served no purpose—and in fact was probably more detrimental. I also noticed how easy it was to find myself mindlessly in old patterns of mind without even being aware.

I became more and more curious about how we (as a society) were ever going to shift the momentum from a fast-paced mindless direction to a more centred, nurturing, and mindful existence. I felt we needed to for our survival as a race, and I became the guinea pig in my own experiment. My curiosity had me looking at myself. When I succeeded, I noted how I did it, and when I slipped up, I noted how it happened. I began to see the common themes and traps that surrounded the ups and downs. I discovered some useful ways to shift to a better place.

My experience informed the reshaped program that I began to run for whoever was keen to attend. Before long, Steve came along to the program, and he actually enjoyed it. The program was quite practical, which he liked. He found he could apply some of the things to his own work and life. Interestingly, the biggest thing that stood out for him was the acronym PATIENCE. I'll explain more about it in Part 3, but briefly, PATIENCE stands for **P**erspective, **A**wareness, **T**houghts, **I**ntention, **E**motion, **N**onsense, **C**larity, and **E**scape. These were areas he felt he struggled with.

My work helped me develop some personal tools that came in handy in my day-to-day reality. I was coping so much better with the ups and downs that arrived in the normal ebb and flow of life. I felt calmer, clearer, and more confident to manoeuvre through the challenges that arrived in many forms: strong emotions, wayward thoughts, and unwanted situations or events.

I focused my energy more wisely. I discovered it worked so much better not to fuel the negative things. I redirected my focus to gain fruitful outcomes, which meant letting go of things I once spent lots of time fighting over. Some of my deep patterns and tendencies were moving out of my body. It felt new and different; and quite frankly, it felt like a relief. I was no longer wasting energy proving or defending but rather creating what it is I wanted—usually peace and connection.

I thought that rather than trying to make Rhythm of Life grow, I would plant a few seeds and count on a natural flow of growth. If people were meant to see me, they would find me. If I was meant to share something, the thought would come and the vehicle would arrive. When the signs and signals told me no, I didn't go there. In the end, it was a language that made sense to me. It was my way of going about things, and I was happy with that.

From the outside, no one would have known there was a big shift taking place within me. It was only me who could feel the difference in how I was experiencing my life. Sometimes I felt a little like an alien, because I didn't enjoy the talk and walk that I once got involved in. I preferred immersing in different things that had become more important to me. So although life was different, it felt great.

Life felt even better at the end of 2007 when Steve and I went on the holiday that was meant to take place twelve months earlier. After my cancer experience, the trip felt even more special. I valued every moment of every day. I had grown in my capacity to appreciate and was very grateful for that. It felt wonderful.

I was directing my life in a way I had never done before. I was beginning to go for things that I once wouldn't even attempt. I had more courage and understood there was only one chance in this here-and-now life to do so. I used my heart and spirit to guide me, and I watched out for when my ego stifled me.

I was beginning to understand how and why I had not faced life this way before. This was all new to me. I finally felt brave enough and able to do things in a way that felt right. This led to many changes in how I went about work also.

Before long, Steve came up with the idea of converting our unused garage into a room to work from. It took a few months for tradesmen to transform the room, but before long, I was working from home. Change had become something I was more comfortable with—a big difference from my past life, in which I sought comfort in familiarity.

I had become far more flexible. I would thrive on finding ways to a new solution, even with the most seemingly unimportant things that caused turbulence in the day-to-day. I knew what was most important, and I would put that first. I realized nothing at all was permanent. I could change this up at the last minute if I needed to, and I was prepared to do it.

I was able to let go and release more easily than ever. In the past, I would be riddled with guilt over letting people down, so I would try to put everyone else's happiness before my own needs. I discovered I could do it differently and it would still be OK. I learned a different approach to handling what landed on my doorstep. I was riding the life wave differently.

Many waves of ups and downs arrived. Someone close went through an ugly break-up with a partner, a few dear friends endured miscarriages, and I lost a dear auntie and friend to cancer. Somehow I felt more equipped to handle these things—but more importantly, I knew how to get out of my comfort zone and be there to help in some small way.

I did some things I would never have thought to do in my past life, such as spend a good deal of time in open conversation with a friend who was in the final stages of cancer. This was greatly appreciated by her and her partner. I don't know if I would have had the confidence or heart to do that before.

Around the time when Dad got ill, I decided to stop running my weekly meditation classes. I felt I needed to be around for what was going on. Little did I know, I was needed for that and more.

It was time to change . . . again.

CHAPTER **5**

THE MACK TRUCK

When you receive a knock—feather, brick, or Mack truck—take the time to listen. Hidden within may be clues that are telling you to stop and look.

It seems that most of us needed to be hit by the emotional equivalent of a Mack truck before we make much-needed changes to key areas of our life—health, work practice, relationships, family, finances. Sometimes we need it to happen over and over again before the message actually arrives.

When I look back at both Steve and myself, I see us in the same way— waiting for the Mack truck. We were both caught in the same traps as many people in our age group. From the outside it looked like we were just Type A personalities. It was hard to know, though, if it was a personality type or a condition that we had developed from living mindlessly in a fast-paced society, constantly fitting in more without realising we were already overdoing it. We hardly took the time to nurture or care for ourselves in the way it was needed or had the space to really take in life's small treasures.

I remember way back to around the year 2000, when Danielle was in her later years of high school and Dion was at that age where he loved to participate in all sports. Danielle was still heavily involved in dancing, and most evenings we were either at Norwood for ballet or at a sport for Dion. *That in itself was taxing.*

On top of that, I was working full-time at Regency TAFE during a time when big changes were in progress. Their systems were changing from a curriculum course approved at a local level to training packages that were approved at a national level. It required a lot of work and focus to transition to that new approach. *That in itself was taxing.*

I was also coaching and coordinating the coaches for the school aerobics at Danielle's school. This took place a couple of mornings a week as well as some weekends. There was a lot of organizing to do—costumes, music, and extra rehearsal. *That in itself was taxing.*

Having finished my university studies in health counselling, I had a great opportunity to implement some of the learning at the Next Generation Club Adelaide. It was a time when the tennis club had been converted to a fitness and lifestyle club, and there was a lot of fine-tuning needed in relation to systems, protocols, procedures, staff, and practices. I was appointed to help get these in order. It was a challenging role, and I needed all my skills and knowledge to succeed. I loved how it expanded my organizational, creative, and management skills. *That in itself was taxing.*

Doing all of these things at once somehow seemed quite manageable . . . or that's what I thought I felt. To tell you the truth, I probably didn't know how I felt. Being that busy, I couldn't feel my body or spirit too closely. My mind wouldn't let me. It just told me to keep going. It showed me how to become more organized to fit even more into my schedule. I had no time for soft things like *feelings*. The adrenalin from this approach kept me "up," and I didn't want to let go and lose momentum.

At the same time, Steve was undergoing much the same sort of overload. He was running a hairdressing salon in North Adelaide and had started a partnership with a couple of others in a hair-product company. This partnership also went on to purchase another salon. His life was full, day and night. During the day, he worked in the salon, and in the evenings he was involved with partnership meetings and the hands-on making of the products. Then on the weekends, he would do his salon business.

As you can probably tell by reading this, it was a very busy and taxing time. Steve was also out of touch with how he felt. Amazingly, he could see it in me and I could see it in him, but we couldn't see it in ourselves. We both thought we were OK, it was the other who was out of balance. We were each as blind as the other.

We probably needed each other in some way, but there was little left in us to give. On the surface, our life and relationship looked fine. We were just busy people doing what everyone did at this stage of life. But was that really fine or the thing to do?

I think we were both beginning to feel the distance between us. It's amazing how the distance slowly crept in. It was very subtle. I was tired and strained and needed nurturing, and I found it hard to nurture. The same applied to Steve. Both of us seemed unable—or unwilling—to budge.

I remember the day this changed. It was when a mini Mack truck smacked into us.

I had arrived home from one of my usual days—early morning training sessions with the school teams, then off to TAFE for a busy and complex day, then off to Next Generation to conduct meetings and organize and plan for the many things that were needed to gain a better operation, then . . .

Well, then I was to *supposed* to go home to start on dinner, do the household chores, and support the kids with their after-school activities. However, the only thing I managed to do was walk through the front door. I stood in the entrance and realized something was very wrong. Instead of going into action with all that needed to be done, I stood frozen—unable to sort out what to do. The thought of preparing dinner seemed confusing, and quite frankly, I couldn't seem to get it coordinated. The only thing I could manage to do was to get into bed and lie very still.

I had hit my limit, something I never believed existed. I had heard about others having breakdowns or not being able to cope, but I never thought it could happen to me. For the first time, my mind couldn't sort out what, when, or how at its usual rapid speed. I could only lie there and hope that in time I would slowly come back.

During that time, I remember clearly the message that hovered in my heart: *things have to change.*

I can't remember how long it took for me to come back, but it seemed like a couple of hours. That night, after I slowly regained my capacity to think, I made the call to end my work at Next Generation. That decision was powerful on many levels. I felt instant relief, because it had already created some space in my mind. It also brought comfort to Steve, who had been very worried about me for a long time.

It's amazing how nothing changed if nothing changed, but much changed if something changed. This was how it felt for us. We began to talk much more honestly and openly about how our lives were going. We agreed we both needed to do things differently—and that was just what we planned to do.

I remember the night we went on a dinner date and began to plan how we would go about changing things. We talked about what he really wanted to do for the next period of time—and when Steve took the time to dream, he realized he wanted a new salon in the city where he could focus on his creativity and service his clients. Over the next few years, this became his priority, and he chose to leave the partnership and focus solely on his new salon vision.

We had made the break from our roller-coaster ride and slowly regained closeness in our relationship, which was very comforting. We had taken the first step toward getting off the ridiculous treadmill we were on. But things didn't change that quickly.

We were used to running on adrenalin, and the addiction to adrenalin didn't just go away. Sometimes things seemed just as stressful, even though we were doing less. When we finally had the time to relax, I noticed that we weren't very good at it. I realized that the adrenalin and stress hormones in my body weren't only there because of the busyness. My state of mind played a big part in how my body felt.

We had changed some things in our physical environment, but there was still so much more to learn about looking after ourselves and each other. I started to dabble in meditation and commenced reading books about the relationship between the mind and body. It came in handy when I was really struggling to find some inner calm.

I recall a time when, as a family holiday, we travelled by car to Melbourne for the Australian Open Tennis Championships. It was when Steve was around his peak of zero tolerance, and I was at my peak of sensitivity. Unfortunately, Dion was going through what normal teenage boys go through (that painful stage), and Steve found his humour and attitude nearly intolerable. I remember some of the yell-fests in the long car ride. We both still had some serious work ahead to find our calm and clarity with the kids and each other.

It was around this stressful period that my bowel tumour began to form, according to the pathology. Whether it was the cause or not, I felt my body was not in a healthy environment to fight it. Our life felt toxic, and that would not help my immune system fight effectively.

Although we had both made attempts to settle our bodies, minds, and lives, we still had so much more to discover and learn. When a bigger Mack truck arrived in the form of my cancer, we learned some more. And then Steve's cancer slowed us down again.

This Mack truck would force us into territory that pushed limits. We had lots more to discover.

CHAPTER **6**

THE FIRST CYCLE OF
CHEMOTHERAPY—PART A

We learned about Part A of the treatment; we learned a lot about how to approach it. Being informed was valuable.

New Years Eve 2011 was pretty low-key. We had both families at our Maslins Beach home, which was nice. For so long, we'd looked forward to sharing our beach house with family and friends, but not under these circumstances. We managed to enjoy some nice food and a couple of walks and outings before Steve went back to the specialist on January 3.

On that day, the specialist confirmed the results of the scans: mantle cell non-Hodgkin's lymphoma. That meant it was more aggressive than we first thought and would require more intensive treatment. Not the news we wanted to hear. It seemed each time we saw the doctor, the news got worse. Steve was now required to have a bone-marrow biopsy to determine the actual stage of his cancer.

On January 4, Steve worked his last day in the salon. It was an emotional day for everyone. Steve had been hairdressing for thirty-eight years, and he loved it—the clients, the staff, and the work. From the next day on, each client would receive a personal letter sharing the news of Steve's illness and his need to take six to eight months off work to undertake treatment. Because of the intensity of the treatment and the depletion of his immune system, he would become very fatigued, and the risk of infection would be high. Everyone agreed that whatever was best for Steve was the way to go. Between my son and the staff, the salon would continue without him.

On January 10, the specialist confirmed that based on the bone-marrow biopsy, Steve's cancer was at stage IV, with about 50 per cent of the bone marrow affected. We had suspected that to be the case from what the specialist had told us about mantle cell, but until we had confirmation, we still had hoped for something better.

Waiting for the bone-marrow result had been hard. The doctor planned to call us with the stage results, and we jumped out of our skin each time the phone rang. The doctor finally told us what we already knew in the back of our minds. That was such a weird thing. Once we knew the outcome and we weren't waiting anymore, we didn't seem to feel as bad. So in many ways, waiting felt worse than knowing. And that's how Steve explained it—he just felt better knowing. And I could see that for myself. His anxiety and stress, which had him unsettled and feeling sick, disappeared nearly instantaneously after the call.

I have had that thought before about waiting. I was a victim of it in my past fast-paced life because that is what I tended to do. I tended to wait for the next thing and the next and rarely found myself "in" what I was in.

During my own health recovery, I recognized my own "waiting" discomfort signals and learned how to slowly get myself back to the here and now. It took time and mind focus, and I still needed practise. I got better at allowing things to unfold in their own time and found it was much easier on me when I did. When I wasn't attached to every moment with that apprehensive feeling, I didn't feel paralysed or frozen but rather more productive and useful.

I felt I brought a bit of that past learning to the time before Steve's first hospital treatment. I organized pyjamas, dental-hygiene products, and other things he needed for his stay. I got updated on his food and wellness requirements. I sorted our personal affairs and those of the business and prepared the house for the time ahead.

We have two beautiful dogs who are more like children—spoiled children! (Steve kept reminding me that it was all my doing, but I'm not sure about that.) Their behaviour patterns and routines had to change. No more sleeping on our bed or sitting on the lounges; the highest level of hygiene was required to minimize infection.

So as well as doing regular hand-washing and using antibacterial gels, we made sure there was no fur on general surfaces. At first the dogs complained with their usual whines and cries, but it didn't take long before they knew the new rules. Our dogs were amazing—they seemed to know that something wasn't right and did what they were told. That was unusual for them. They seemed to know that we needed comfort and support—and that's what they brought.

On January 15, 2012, Steve celebrated his fifty-sixth birthday. It was both nice and sad—nice that he got to celebrate before the chemo started, but sad that the next day he would start his treatment. I felt Steve's apprehension and fear in the silence that lingered in his birthday-cake wish. The look on his face told the story. Many tears followed.

The next day, we headed to Calvary Hospital for the first cycle of his treatment. It's funny: up until then, I had only vaguely searched out information about the treatment. All we knew was that he would be hospitalized for one week, followed by two weeks home to recover before he would start the treatment over again. This would continue for between six to eight cycles.

Everyone in the family approached this time before treatment differently. Steve was content to have a chat with two people who had gone through similar experiences—a family acquaintance and a salon client—and were both now in full remission. Apart from that, he was happy to hear the good perspectives we presented to him about his illness and treatment.

The children did it differently. Dion had done Internet searches and found a large amount of information about the latest treatments and what they involved. He needed to know the background and what was ahead. Danielle talked it out with others who had been through the treatment or knew of someone who had. She didn't delve too deeply with the Internet search.

We received some great information from a friend whose nephew had gone through similar treatment, so that was useful in later discussions. We found that some talk and information was good, but after a while it got overwhelming. Somehow it felt better to allow things to unfold a little first rather than do too much upfront stuff.

I figured we would find out about the treatment in time, and that's what we did on the first day of his schedule. After registering at the front desk at the hospital, we were ushered to his room in St. Helen's ward. It was a dreary ward and room. We later discovered that nothing had been done to improve it for a long time because of the major renovations that were due to commence within a few days of our arriving.

It didn't feel like the warmest of greetings. We waited once again, for about twenty minutes, until a nurse arrived and explained what would be happening for the day. We were handed a treatment protocol, and Steve was told he would start the Part A cycle that day. There was a lot to take in, but we were reassured we'd slowly get to know the process. And quite frankly, slow and progressive was the best way to not get too ahead of ourselves.

We had hoped to speak to the specialist before the treatment, but the nurse wasn't sure what time he would arrive. His usual routine was to see hospital inpatients later in the day after he finished consulting outpatients at Kimberley House. He had a heavy schedule in his consulting rooms, so we understood the reason for his delay. We were previously outpatients, and I remembered how grateful we were at our first consultation when he gave us the time to explain and answered our questions. We found him to be a generous man with his appointments, so this double-shift routine would be very taxing.

At the time, however, we both thought how much nicer it would have been to have a warm and fuzzy welcome. But it was more about business; simple gestures of comfort were not to be. Overall, the nurse, Laura, did a great job when you consider all the constraints of her work situation.

During the six months of treatment, I knew it was important to approach things with a good attitude and focus on embracing rather than embattling. I remember as we walked toward the entrance of the hospital, we laughed as we claimed it to be our new third home for the next six months or so. We needed to look for what was good about this time rather than wallow in what was bad about it. So the fact that the nurses were lovely, he could walk around if he wanted, he was in a private room with his own bathroom and window and his own music, DVD player, and flowers—all these things were beautiful. And the fact that we would be together making the most of each day and taking the greatest of care of each other was even more beautiful.

The specialist actually came in a little after the nurse and explained the treatment more fully, which we were grateful for. If you want to know about the Hyper-CVAD protocol and drugs involved, read this next paragraph; if not, you have permission to skip ahead.

Steve would start with Part A of the protocol, alternating Part B on the next cycle and repeating over the next four to six months. Part A was to start with mesna, a drug used to protect the bladder from the effects of the particular chemotherapy drug that was to follow. It would be infused over a two-hour period for immediate protection from the cyclophosphamide (the name of the chemotherapy used for this protocol) and then infused for the next two days during the chemotherapy. Cyclophosphamide would be given twice daily in doses infused over three hours, morning and evening. Each morning before any treatment, dexamethasone and Kytril, the important anti-nausea drugs that helped make the process at least bearable, would be administered. Mabthera, another important support therapy, would be given on the third day before another chemotherapy drug, doxorubicin, and vincristine on the fourth day. And to end, twenty-four hours after the final chemotherapy drug was administered, a Neulasta injection would be given.

In theory, it sounded straightforward, but Steve was very anxious not knowing how his body would feel and respond to the harsh chemicals. He had heard so many stories about how sick you get from the chemotherapy, and to make matters worse, he read Lance Armstrong's *It's Not About the Bike* a couple of weeks before the start of his treatment. A friend recommended he read it for inspiration, but I'm not sure if it served that purpose.

Chapter 6 was particularly tough for Steve. It described Lance's tough battle with the toxic effects of the chemotherapy—in much detail. "Chapter 6!" Steve would randomly call out with apprehension in the days leading up to his own treatment. Despite the specialist reassuring him that the drugs had since improved—especially in the anti-nausea area—he needed to find out for himself.

Before the treatment, Steve had a small procedure under general anaesthetic to insert a PICC line into a vein that travelled from his upper left arm to just above his heart. Through this device, drugs and blood would be given and blood would also be taken. The instant line into the bloodstream meant he avoided being pricked and prodded excessively.

The first day of treatment went quite well. He felt no sickness or discomfort and was quite happy with that. When the specialist came to see him that night, Steve told him he felt like a fraud because he felt pretty good. The doctor laughed at his comment but affirmed he would feel the effects after the treatment had finished.

We took the time to ask questions about what was going on, especially when we saw nurses gown up and wear protective glasses each time any chemotherapy drug was administered. The doctor explained that the drugs were designed to enter the bloodstream and kill cancer cells, but not to make contact with skin or eyes—hence the protection. I felt more comfortable sitting opposite the chemotherapy stand.

In time, Steve came to name that stand Fred, because it was his constant companion. He was attached to it 24/7; his only reprieve was when showering. Each time he wanted to move from the bed, he would disconnect Fred from the power source and walk it to wherever he needed; fortunately, it had a battery backup. He was encouraged to walk as often as possible to keep up his strength and circulation. He enjoyed moving away from the confines of his small room and did small walks a couple of times a day. It was also a break from the very uncomfortable bed and pillow. We eventually brought his pillow from home to help make sleep a little more bearable.

It was on one of his walks around the hospital that we bumped into an ICU (intensive-care unit) doctor who had only a couple of months earlier treated Dad at another hospital. His face expressed an understanding of how difficult it was for us—first Dad, then Steve going through treatment. He did however give good reports about the treatment for Steve's particular cancer. That was comforting.

Days two and three were quite good for Steve. From there, though, his energy lessened and the effects from the chemotherapy crept in. He found it more and more challenging to walk around and spent more time in bed.

On day four, he was to have the first of his Mabthera treatments. A nurse would supervise the infusion in case he had an allergic reaction, which was common. As he started the treatment, I could see he was not feeling too well. Within half an hour, it was evident that his body was adversely reacting to the treatment (vomiting, shaking, and agitation), so it needed to stop immediately.

The doctor informed us that next time, he would start the week's treatment with the Mabthera, as this would help Steve cope better. He also said it would be infused more slowly to increase the chance that his body would accept it. We were hoping this would be the case, because the Mabthera treatment was known for its positive enhancing effect on the Hyper-CVAD treatment. We crossed our fingers for next time.

Steve went on to complete his last two chemotherapy drugs but felt quite depleted and unwell from the Mabthera reaction the day before. He stayed on in the hospital an extra day, which meant the nurse was able to give him the Neulasta injection to stimulate his white blood cells. We also learned he needed a blood transfusion because his haemoglobin levels were very low. We were concerned. It sounded serious. They reassured us this was a common thing and likely to happen again.

It was great to get the reassurance about these things. For us, everything was uncertain. What was normal, what was risky, what was a problem? We were slowly establishing a framework for the many aspects of this protocol. We felt from this first week that it was not going to be a straight line but rather an up and down, meandering process. It was good to acknowledge this early so we didn't lock into any rigid expectations that would lead to disappointment.

One thing I learned from Dad's situation was that our bodies are unique and respond differently on any given day. I realized it wouldn't always go as predicted, and that was absolutely normal. I also learned there was a lot that could be done to get the body back on track. This learning helped me to stay positive and find a healthy perspective for the minor setbacks experienced throughout that first week of treatment.

This was not always easy to do. A lot of people around me struggled with it. They would worry or question the implications and the *what ifs*. I found that staying too long in this space was damaging. It was important for me to move on to a better outlook and attitude as quickly as possible. Dwelling on worry was fruitless. I didn't give it much energy or attention. I disengaged quickly from this type of conversation and brought my focus back to what in the here-and-now would make the day better for Steve and myself.

The moment Steve stepped away from the hospital, the intense fatigue and sickness set in. Up until then, drugs had kept the nausea at bay, but he was now on his own with a packet of Maxolon. By the end of that day, we were experiencing the chemo side effects we had been warned about—nausea, fatigue, and overall feeling yuck!

Steve took the Maxolon to curb the nausea, as was recommended. It didn't take long before Steve was vomiting violently. "Chapter 6" came to his mind, and he wasn't happy! Was this really going to be how he responded to the treatment? We were both feeling very overwhelmed by the effects. I phoned the hospital for advice, and they suggested we increase the Maxolon. We continued with this until something didn't seem to add up. Steve started to have some effects that weren't listed on the handout given to us by the hospital listing all the possible problems. It was very useful because it helped me differentiate between normal and abnormal.

Steve started to feel quite agitated and vague, and this later turned to slight hallucinations. We knew he was going to have some spaciness, but it seemed more than that. After talking to a friend about the Maxolon, I realized it could have been a reaction to that drug, not the chemotherapy. We discovered that to be the case, and after a different anti-nausea drug, Ondansetron, was prescribed, Steve improved nearly immediately.

I got a taste of how "switched on" I needed to be throughout the process. That night, I slept on the lounge where I could see and hear him in the bedroom. We felt it was best he slept alone so he could move freely in the bed without restriction. It would also minimize the risk of me passing on any germs through the night and ensure I was close enough to help him out if needed. When the side effects settled down, I slept in the spare room and managed a more comfortable sleep.

We had a system. I placed a bell that I'd previously used for meditation sessions by his bedside. When he needed me for something, he would ring the bell. Sometimes I would jump out of my skin when the bell went off, but it did the trick. We came to laugh about the bell in time.

The hardest part when we first left the hospital was how to know what was considered normal and OK to manage at home. We soon accepted there was no normal—there was just how his body went. I observed and regularly asked how he was feeling. I would ask him to describe the sensations or rate the pain or energy level. We found that useful because it set a baseline for the side effects and his health in general on certain days after his treatment.

The other thing we watched was his temperature for any sign of infection. An infection for someone who was immunosuppressed and going through chemotherapy couldn't be managed at home. I needed to be vigilant. I had seen things change very quickly with Dad and understood the importance of not taking anything for granted. If something didn't seem right, I needed to follow my instincts and act.

Within three or four days after coming home, Steve slowly climbed back from total fatigue and depletion. He then took small steps to rebuild his strength. The only commitment each week between treatments was to have his PICC line dressing changed and have blood taken to check if he needed a transfusion.

The week after the treatment, he was still extremely low, but by the second week when he had more energy and felt more alive we travelled to Maslins Beach where he really got to relax and recover in the beautiful beach air and surroundings. We were very fortunate that the house had been completed in time for his healing process.

All in all, it was not too bad a start to the process. Apart from the rough beginning, Steve tolerated the effects with a great attitude. While at his weekly PICC line dressing, he had a quick chat with the specialist about the presence of that same persistent cough. The doctor prescribed some antibiotics, and within a few days there was no sign of it.

During the remainder of our time at Maslins Beach, we did lots of things together. We sang, read, walked, ate, and watched DVDs. We enjoyed friends and family, and we stood still from our usual busyness. Steve played guitar, and we both sang our hearts out. Steve spent time downloading old favourites. We reconnected with some of the most beautiful songs.

We had time to appreciate the lyrics from some of the most talented songwriters of all times—Neil Diamond, Cat Stevens, Paul Simon, the

Beatles. In fact, it was the words of Paul Simon's "Sounds of Silence" that resonated so deeply that it inspired me to share this journey.

We also read novels, which for Steve was a new experience. He had never been still for long enough to read in the past, but he had found a calm and open place within that helped him appreciate many types of books.

Although Steve's fatigue limited the amount he could do, we still managed to get out for some beautiful, very short strolls along the beach. We had never before watched a whole TV series, but now we managed to do that with *Mad Men* and *The Tudors*. We really started to slow right down.

Apart from organizing a few work-related things, we spent most of our time focused on the some quality day-to-day living practices. There was something really nice about doing it together.

CHAPTER **7**

WHAT COMES
FROM ADVERSITY?

**In adversity, you are forced to face up to what you
may never have thought you could. When you do,
you discover strengths and qualities that you may
only have seen or thought possible in others. It
becomes your way of knowing more about yourself
and others. It can lead the way to challenging some
of your old beliefs.**

Opportunities arrived in different ways. In the past, I believed they were
from good things. However, since my own health incident, I saw many
worthwhile opportunities come from difficulty and adversity.

Whether we acknowledged it or not, we were affected when someone
in our network was ill or had problems. It didn't matter how busy or
preoccupied we were with other life matters, there was a silent connection
that always existed in the thoughts and feelings we held. When people
heard about Steve's illness, the strength of this connection was evident.

I witnessed some special things. From the moment letters went out to
clients and the word about Steve's condition was on the grapevine, he

received an overwhelming number of well wishes. The messages and thoughts had a great impact on Steve. The stream of cards, emails, calls, and letters somehow filled a gap.

His isolation from the public made these messages even more important and meaningful. Each helped him feel part of people's lives, and he was truly comforted by their words. Some were funny, some were comforting, some were encouraging, and some were simple—but all were appreciated. Steve recorded in his journal the name of every person who made contact. I'd love to mention and acknowledge everyone at this point, because everyone played a role during that time.

Steve was especially humbled by messages from those he hadn't seen for such a long time or staff he had employed years before or people he never thought would care or show concern. Some people responded immediately when they heard the news while others did it later, often after they built up the courage. Some handled conversation with heart and strength, others with uncertainty and fear. It didn't matter how they did, it was the fact that they *did* that mattered.

Some people had to overcome their own personal fears and insecurities to make contact and extend their best wishes. I saw this as an opportunity Steve's illness gave to others. It made them step outside of their own comfort zone to make contact. It may have been something they wouldn't have done in the past.

People would often tell Steve they didn't call before because they didn't know what to say. Steve would put them at ease and chat freely and honestly with them, in a way that made them feel really good about making the call. He told them how much he appreciated the contact and encouraged them to do so again. He was showing them how to handle it all.

Some people engaged in the most generous and kind acts to lift his spirit. It was clear that Steve meant so much to people and had their utmost respect. It was nice that he experienced that.

One of the most uplifting acts was a video produced by our dear friends Harold and Josie, along with their son, Shannon. They gathered birthday and get-well wishes from many hair-industry people. People didn't have much time to put in their submissions, but Harold and Josie managed to collect many inspiring contributions for the surprise.

Much care was taken to hide the happy fifty-sixth birthday video on the menu of the TV box that I organized as his birthday gift. On the morning of his birthday, I encouraged him to check out how the box worked, and it was then he discovered the surprise. The video began with Harold's message of support and motivation for the difficult time ahead. Many others followed.

Steve was blown away by the effort that was taken to produce the video, but also by the messages themselves. Many people from the past had taken the time to voice or write a message, which totally amazed him. It was as though he was hearing his own eulogy. It was a special moment, for it is generally rare to hear in our lifetime the heartfelt thoughts and feelings of others.

The video brought him to tears. They were good tears, tears that needed to flow. I sensed he was beginning to realize the enormity of what he was about to endure. I felt he also realized how much people cared about him.

I began to see how people showed care differently. Care for some was to stay away. They saw distance and space as a valued thing. Others, however, needed to connect with acts or words of kindness. And so many people responded in that way. We understood that even a small gesture like sending a card took a lot of effort—purchasing the card, obtaining the address, and sending it off among the events of an already busy life was a significant act.

For many, it was not a once-off. They regularly made some sort of contact. Steve appreciated that because the treatment went on for such a long period of time. I noticed that while Steve loved to hear from people, he would often tire from repeating the same information about the medical side of his situation. That also got difficult for the salon staff. They found it hard to keep up with the questions from clients who rightfully wanted to know about Steve's progress.

Josie had mentioned in passing about her friend who wrote a blog to communicate with friends and family during her cancer treatment. I knew immediately this would be a great thing to set up for Steve. Anyone interested in Steve's progress could read the blog and keep updated with the details.

On January 30, the first blog post on Steve's progress was published. It turned out to be so valuable and worthwhile. It helped people understand what was happening and also provided an outlet to contact him if they wished.

I marvelled at how something so simple could reduce so much stress and effort. We could still communicate with friends and clients without the emotional recounting of events. That was important, because we already had plenty of emotional things to cope with.

We were learning ways that were best for Steve going through the treatment as well as for me doing the caring. We both started to notice what and who didn't feel right for us. I made some decisions about what I would keep and what I would walk past. I felt Steve did the same in some way.

It wasn't an easy thing to do, but it was important. It wasn't worth getting upset by the comments or actions of others. I knew it wasn't intentional when people made comments or actions that weren't helpful. It was usually because they weren't aware—and I'm sure there were times when I did the same.

Nonetheless, it was necessary for the sake of self-preservation to let things go and not follow up on them. If someone told a story about a person who got their cancer back after being in remission, I chose to let that story go. Or when someone kept dwelling on the drama or misery of Steve's situation, I chose to steer that person off course. Or when I felt my energy being drained, I chose to walk away. It was a time when we chose to put ourselves first so we could be in the right space for the things we needed to do.

It was something we both struggled with. We were not used to putting ourselves first. We found it physically and emotionally difficult to do. At first, it was a challenge, because we were both so independent and responsible. We were used to doing things for ourselves and others, not the reverse. It didn't take long, however, before we realized it was essential to accept help if we were to stay healthy throughout. Our time for grieving was shared with time for caring and loving.

What was most difficult for Steve was that physically, he wasn't able to do the usual things around the house. I took on some of the smaller things like taking the rubbish out, sweeping outside, and watering the plants, but there was a lot of heavy gardening that needed doing. It was Steve's dad who took on this role. He was from the old school—very fit and strong, and very capable in the garden even at eighty years of age. He loved the garden, and he loved even more that he was helping Steve out.

Steve found it hard watching his dad do the work. But for his dad, it didn't seem so hard. He did it with ease and great technique. His back straight and his movements smooth, he made every task seem easy. He just knew how to do it. It was something he had done all his life. It said something about the value of physical, intense work. He was an amazing help—the garden and house stayed well-cared-for, and this released any need for worry.

That's what we all did. We worked together to take on what was needed so Steve didn't have to worry that things would decline. While I took on the bookwork for the business and my son took on the management of the salon, the layers of people in our circle supported us. My mum, Steve's mum, my sister, Steve's sister, Danielle, and our close friends all helped out—ironing, shopping, preparing meals for the freezer and meals to bring to the hospital, and most importantly, providing a caring and listening ear.

Some weeks were especially taxing, and I knew help was critical. I had experienced that fragile breaking feeling in the past during my crazy days, so I knew the feeling. Times when I didn't get a lot of sleep and took a lot of trips to the hospital and back home in between to make dinners (Steve couldn't eat hospital food after the first cycle in hospital), I was running on adrenalin, and with that came a feeling of total depletion by the end of the day.

My good friend Anna, also a life coach, kept me on track. She was well aware of the adrenalin trap, where you're totally oblivious to your real feelings and state. I stayed mindful of this and, at the end of each day, did a meditation where I slowed down my body and breathing to tune in to what was really happening within. I knew this was too big for me to be stubborn, or a hero, or a martyr. I learned to say yes to offers of help. When the offers came, it actually felt like a relief.

Some offers were particularly thoughtful. Anna opened her house to me to cook Steve's meals, since her place was only five minutes from the hospital—as opposed to mine, which was twenty minutes on a good day, but with the magnitude of roadworks being conducted along North East Road due to the preparation for the desalination water pipes was more like thirty to thirty-five. Anna also baked Steve's favourite cake (you can find the recipe in the back of the book), and it came in so handy many nights when he felt peckish and needed something to lift his spirits.

Another friend offered to walk my dogs when I didn't have time, and while I never took advantage of that offer, it was comforting to know it was possible. Another friend, who was supposed to have travelled with us on our cancelled overseas trip in 2006, just turned up on my doorstep with soup. She had been a great support during my own illness, and there she was again.

There were many more stories of thoughtfulness and support. I realized how powerful it was when people offered concrete suggestions and ways to help. It planted ideas that I wasn't able to generate on my own. When I was in caring mode, I found my head couldn't think in that way.

The offers meant there was always a backup in case of an emergency. They also meant that although we were alone on many days, we never felt isolated. We felt comforted and cared for.

Asking for help was a little different, but I did at times when I knew it would benefit Steve and his well-being. I could see my own patterns and vulnerabilities surface. Why was it so difficult to ask? That was a great thing for me to ponder and delve into more deeply. This experience gave me another opportunity to confront my own vulnerabilities. It peeled away another aspect of me that I had come to love and humour. It was cathartic. I acknowledged this about myself without judgement or defensiveness, another step in my own healing and personal well-being.

I'm not sure where I got the impression I could or should do it all myself. Was it one of those deeply engrained beliefs that needed to be challenged? *I'm strong enough to do this alone. I'm not worthy if I don't.*

This is how it should be. Others might see it as weakness. Others can't do it as well.

Whatever it was, I threw it away and asked for help and support when needed. I knew that some of those deeply engrained beliefs resulted from an accumulation of everything that had happened—everything I had been told, thought about, felt about, seen, experienced, and decided upon in my past. There could very well have been many distortions and misunderstandings among them all, so I was ready to try something new.

I came to see asking for help as a strength rather than a weakness. I realized that even when I thought I was doing it alone, it was just an illusion, because I was never alone. No matter what I did, there was a whole team of people riding along and doing their part to support us on the way. It deepened my own gratitude for everyone around me, and that was a powerful thing to feel.

We were all growing in different ways. We were all extending our personal qualities. During these difficult times, I learnt to allow the emotion, the outcry, the frustration, the hurt, and the sadness. It was not time to try to make anything right, for there was no *right*—there was just what needed to be expressed. It was a great lesson for me in compassionate non-judgemental surrender.

This is what Steve gave me during the six-week period of my dad's illness. I remembered how wonderful it felt to cry freely, unload, and express whatever was on my mind. He did it with loving arms around me and with tenderness. I learned a lot from him, and I endeavoured to give him the joy of that same emotional freedom.

I felt we were both doing our best with what we knew. We cared for each other emotionally and also engaged in some quality practices for our health and well-being. It felt like a good start to this long process.

I realized that no matter how we did it, the process would move on, but if we did it with love and lightness it would feel much better. I felt because we shared the same outlook, we were helping each other stay on track with a caring, healthy, loving approach. We chose to supplement treatment with good food, fun times, hearty singing, and an ear to listen.

But it wasn't always fun and light. There were many awful moments: vomiting, needles, head spins, reflux, diarrhoea, constipation, nausea, weakness, fatigue. During these times, it was a matter of keeping the focus on just what was needed. I did what I could to help—brought the bucket, rubbed his back, got the tablets, prepared some juice.

Steve didn't linger in the memory for too long afterward. When he finished vomiting, he would just be grateful that he felt better. When he was so fatigued that he could only sleep in bed, he would just be grateful when he could sit up and chat. He never wasted good moments going over bad ones.

This approach made it bearable for me. I was so grateful for that. We could laugh and find good moments relatively easily. The more good moments, the more we forgot the bad ones. It's amazing how quickly we adapted. The sunset walks, the singalongs, laughter with friends, and so much more—we both knew how to be totally in the pleasure of the good times.

The bad moments, however, felt as intense with emotion as the good ones. I was on the lookout for when Steve's body wasn't coping with the toxic after-effects of the chemo. My body was on regular alert.

There were times when Steve was very, very unwell. In these moments, he would meditate to get his body back to health—focusing, he called it—while I vigilantly watched for signs that he might need the extra support of the hospital. During those times, I felt I was holding my breath to find the silence needed to see clearly.

Those times were like storms that we had to ride out. I had to be switched on to read the play moment by moment. I only got one chance to survive a ferocious storm, so quality decisions were essential. It was when decisions really counted.

I couldn't postpone a decision or take too much time to ponder. In a storm, minutes mattered, not days or hours. Action couldn't be delayed. Observe, decide, act—no waiting to see what his temperature would be in the morning or letting his cough ride out or assuming the hallucinations were part of the side effects of the chemotherapy. Action, action, action. Get into my body and out of my mind to check, ask, phone, talk to, research, measure, or go to the hospital.

This was one of the most significant things I learned when Dad went through the final phase of his life in intensive care. Because his body was put under immense strain and disruption, its homeostasis was vulnerable. Things changed and became unsettled very quickly—temperature, blood pressure, oxygen, and blood levels. He had to be observed and checked and constantly supported, because his body couldn't always find its own way back. Sometimes disruptions to the homeostasis were just far too great, and sadly, as in Dad's situation, the road back was impossible.

But I thank Dad for what I gained as I watched the amazing team in intensive care. The experience helped me appreciate the physical and emotional demands of the caring role—and most importantly, to never take anything for granted.

CHAPTER **8**

CYCLE TWO—PART B

We learned about Part B of the treatment, and we learned a lot about how to approach it. Once again, when you have a bit more understanding, you know what to expect—and sometimes that helps.

By the time the second round of chemotherapy was due, Steve was actually feeling quite good. We had just spent the week at Maslins Beach. Steve was told by others who had been in similar situations that he would find it hard to go back to treatment, since he was just starting to feel better. I can't imagine how hard that must have been.

On Monday, he packed his bag again, ready for another week of treatment. It seemed we were doing a lot of packing and moving between our three locations. It was, however, travelling without the holiday that I must say felt quite tiring.

Travelling to the hospital for the next cycle, Steve felt just as apprehensive as the first time. He was to undertake the Part B cycle of the Hyper-CVAD treatment, which involved all new drugs with different side effects and many unknowns. We had read a little about them and the side effects, but once again, until Steve felt them for himself, he remained unsettled.

This paragraph is for those who would like to know about the treatment and the drugs: Part B would start with an infusion of sodium bicarbonate to prepare Steve's body for the chemotherapy. His body needed to be at a pH level of 8 before they could commence the methotrexate (the first of the chemotherapy drugs). He also was given the dexamethasone and Kytril each morning before any chemotherapy was administered. Methotrexate would then be infused for two hours, and then for twenty-two hours for two days. On the third and fourth day, he would receive the leucovorin that was designed to help flush the methotrexate from his body—before he could go home, his blood needed to show that the majority of methotrexate had left his body, otherwise it could cause damage and infection. On the third day, he would also be given the chemotherapy drug cytarabine. This drug was known to cause dryness of the eyes and mouth, so he was to receive eye drops and a preventative mouth treatment. As with Part A, he would require a Neulasta injection twenty-four hours after the completion of his chemotherapy. As well as that, he was booked to have the Mabthera treatment that he reacted to the first time. They were going to infuse it over twelve hours rather than six to minimize the risk of another reaction, and do it on the first day before any other chemotherapy. It was very important for the long term that he tolerate this treatment, so we were certainly feeling apprehensive about his response.

Fortunately, Steve was fine with the Mabthera this time. Apart from the treatment being slow and boring, he coped well, with no side effects or reactions. It was a great start to the week. We were all thrilled that this could now be a regular start to his Hyper-CVAD regime. I provided a text update to family and close friends to inform them of the success, as they too were keen to know the step-by-step progress. In this way, we never felt alone. Our closest people were with us all the way, and it was comforting.

On Tuesday, he commenced the Part B routine. As with the Part A, Steve felt quite good for the first day. The most difficult thing to cope with was the frequent toilet stops. It was very important that his weight remain constant with this round of chemo. The chemo was particularly harsh, and it was imperative that they check his urine for blood and fluid retention.

Three times a day, they would weigh him, and the dose of diuretic they gave would be determined by how much over his start weight he was. This was to ensure that his pH level remained alkaline and his organs were coping. The more over his weight, the more diuretic needed, the longer the five-minute toilet stops lasted. One kilogram over his weight meant two milligrams of diuretic, which meant half an hour of five-minute toilet stops. Two kilograms over meant four milligrams of diuretic, which meant one hour of five-minute toilet stops. Three kilograms over meant six milligrams of diuretic, which meant an hour and a half of five-minute toilet stops. Steve would dread the weigh-ins because he knew exactly what they meant. He became progressively worn out by all those toilet stops.

Wednesday morning came, and on that day I had an appointment with the salon staff as well as a stop to fix the temperature meter in my car. My car had been in need of a lot attention from as far back as when Dad got sick. The clutch, temperature gage, air conditioner, headlights, windscreen wipers—my car seemed to mirror the myriad of ills I was facing in my life! By the time I arrived at the hospital that day, the nurse was about to administer the cytarabine. It seemed he was on to that chemotherapy drug quite quickly, but we didn't know any better.

He ate his lunch, and it was clear that the food offered by the hospital was not going down very well. He looked uncomfortable, and we both thought that perhaps the food was a problem. It wasn't long after, however, that we realized the morning nurse had forgotten to give him the anti-nausea preparation that was required daily before the start of treatment. This meant he had received two very powerful chemotherapy drugs without any help for the harsh side effects.

That morning he had chatted with Harold and Freddie, another friend, and was looking forward to their visit that afternoon. By the time they arrived, however, Steve was vomiting violently from the mishap with the anti-nausea preparation. I greeted the visitors at reception and let them know there was a change in plans. Steve thought he'd be all right to chat for a moment, so they walked to the room. He got as far as "hello" before the uncontrollable urge to vomit surfaced again. Our friends made it out of the room just in time.

They later told us the vomiting could be heard all the way down the corridor, and I can believe that. It was like the motion started from Steve's feet and built up an intensifying roar as it came out of his mouth. Even the doctor, who happened to be just down the corridor, and the nurses thought it quite impressive.

Anyway, it didn't take long after that to administer some relief and get him back on track. I was concerned. I had a feeling that the extra stress on his body would make the treatment even more difficult. Chemotherapy alone was stressful enough. I worried about the implications for when we went home.

The specialist reassured us it wouldn't happen again, and that apart from major discomfort, it wasn't a problem. It was while I was in discussion with the specialist that Steve made the decision that he would check all the drugs and processes himself in the future. The doctor agreed there was no harm in that, because at the end of the day, everyone was human and humans did err from time to time.

The incident helped me realize that there were many parts to Steve's road back to health. It wouldn't be just the treatment that cured him. It would be the utmost care and attention in many areas: the drugs, the administration of the drugs, the pain and nausea relief, the food, the love, the communication, the attention, the rest, the personal care, the sleep. Everyone and everything played an important role in the process. And it needed to be a team effort, with others stepping in when and if required.

From that moment on, Steve made it his business to learn the names of all the drugs and the routine for their administration. He checked and double-checked, because he never wanted to feel that sick again. At the end of the day, it just needed to be right, and it didn't really matter who ensured that it was. No point in waiting to blame someone later when you could've avoided it in the first place. This was an important approach to take throughout.

Freddy returned later that night to find Steve in good spirits and feeling much better.

After that incident the side effects of the chemo seemed to arrive much sooner. Steve was very fatigued and flat when we left the hospital. I did the usual—collected the car and drove to the entrance to pick up Steve and take him home. He looked very pale and weak, but he was able to take in, with much appreciation, the beautiful blue sky and the breeze on his body. It's amazing how the hospital stay enabled him to really appreciate the simplest of beauty. It was wonderful to see.

We had a different routine after this cycle, unlike the first time when the Neulasta was administered in the hospital. We had the choice to administer the injection ourselves at home or to go back to the hospital the next day for the nursing staff to do it. I was happy to learn how to administer the drug, because I felt it would make things easier. Steve wasn't quite comfortable with me doing it at this stage. He felt better with the nursing staff administering it.

It was evident the next day, however, that what may have seemed a simple task of going to the hospital for a quick injection was not so simple at all. The fatigue and nausea had set in, and the thought of the trip was painful for me watching, let alone him doing. Somehow we managed to get there, and we soon found the nurse's station. To the nurses, a small wait meant nothing, but for Steve it was a major discomfort. Somehow he managed to keep himself focused enough to receive the injection and get back to the car. It took so much out of him that day. We decided he would not do that again.

The side effects of Part B were very different from Part A, and included mouth thrush, ulcers, diarrhoea followed by constipation, and reflux. While it probably wasn't related, Steve's cough retuned. He managed all of these problems quite well with the appropriate medication. The usual after-effects of fatigue, weakness, and overall low-grade nausea also presented.

I discovered something about Steve that I probably knew before, but it didn't seem to matter as much then. When he had a bee in his bonnet, his drive was unstoppable. Steve and the salon team were entering a Schwarzkopf photographic hairdressing competition, and the application needed to be sent that week. While he knew we could organize it, there was a part of him that wanted to do it for himself. Trouble was, he didn't have the energy to do it, and he felt absolutely terrible. I'm sure he drew on adrenalin to make it happen, and I knew exhaustion would be the by-product of that. It was the Wednesday after we arrived home that the application was completed, and we headed to Maslins Beach for his recuperation.

It was very clear, however, that he was struggling more than the same day of the last cycle. I was concerned about the cough. I did my usual regular temperature checks and noticed by Thursday that his temperature had risen to 37.5 degrees Celsius. He had just eaten, just slept, just . . . . I heard my thoughts and my excuses, and I snapped myself into action. I phoned the doctor but had to wait for his call back.

In the meantime, I purchased a refill of the antibiotic the specialist had given us after the last cycle, in case Steve needed it again.

The specialist finally phoned and did recommend the antibiotics again. If Steve's temperature went past 38 degrees, though, he would need to be hospitalized. For the next twenty-four hours I took his temperature regularly. It remained under 38, which suggested the antibiotics had worked. A good sign.

That Friday evening, Danielle and Jordan arrived to spend the weekend with us. Jordan had hired equipment to paint the fences, and we were looking forward to seeing them. After a beautiful evening meal that we ate outdoors on the balcony, we noticed that Steve looked flat. His temperature was under 38, although by the time he went to bed it was only just under. Both Danielle and I were concerned. Steve did his usual "I'll be all right," but we didn't listen to that. Although his temperature never did reach 38, Laura, the oncology nurse at the hospital, said to bring him in, because it seemed his temperature wasn't going down.

We arrived at Calvary Hospital at midnight. His first temperature reading was 36.8. Wasn't that always the way? They informed us that temperatures did fluctuate quite significantly, and it was good that we brought him in.

As it turned out, the next day's blood results indicated that he not only had an infection, but his haemoglobin, platelets, and white blood cell counts were very low. He was a very sick boy!

Steve received intravenous antibiotics, blood, and platelets for several days until he was back to a suitable level. It took until Wednesday to recover. On that day he was released, so he managed to have some quality time at home before the next cycle was due. He was just so relieved to be free and back outside in the beautiful light of day.

It was amazing how he pushed past the bad times and immersed himself in feel-good activities. Those few days felt wonderful. We started to watch episodes of *The Tudors*, which consumed many hours. It sparked an interest in the royals and their history. We enjoyed the most glorious weather at the beach, and once again the most beautiful sunsets.

The process was certainly a roller-coaster ride, and we needed to appreciate the parts that were enjoyable. That was so important; otherwise, it could feel even worse than it actually was. It was great to see him feel well again . . . just in time for the next cycle that loomed close by.

Second round down. Well on our way.

CHAPTER 9

CYCLE THREE— PART A AGAIN

When your life seems jumbled, create a pattern to find some comfort and security. When you do, life in that moment can seem a little more predictable and a little easier to cope with.

Our new pattern of life started to become familiar. I cleaned up at Maslins Beach, we returned to Highbury, I did the bookwork for the business, Steve packed a bag, and we ventured into the hospital on a Monday morning for the next cycle of chemotherapy. I realized it was important for me to establish routines quickly so as to create familiarity. Without routines, life felt jumbled. When the routines and patterns were confirmed in my mind, I felt more secure and comfortable about things.

This time, he would have Part A in room 101 in St. Helen's ward. This part of the hospital was still in the midst of massive renovations, so we were surprised they took us to that area. Fortunately, the room was the furthest from the demolition site and closest to the front entrance of the hospital, so it was actually quite convenient and comfortable. The demolition work, however, proved too difficult for the nurses to work around effectively, so Steve was moved to room 228 in St. Clare's ward again after the second day.

He knew the routine and all the drugs that were to be administered, and he made sure to ask questions to clarify when things weren't quite as he expected. This had proved invaluable in the previous cycle and again for this cycle when he questioned the nurse about the rate of infusion for his Mabthera. She said it would be infused over three hours instead of the twelve hours that we knew worked best for him and was in fact requested by the specialist. I'm sure the nurse would have discovered the error in time, but Steve was onto it—he didn't want a repeat of the last cycle mishap.

Steve felt much more prepared for the impact of the chemotherapy throughout this cycle. We encouraged visitors for the first few days before the effects set in on Thursday. People were happy to see him on those good days. It seemed their own spirits were lifted when they saw how well he was coping and how jovial he was. The messages kept coming, and the available opponents in Words with Friends—the game on his phone—increased. This kept him entertained and filled the lonely times.

More than just good fun, playing Words with Friends during Steve's treatment week was a valuable source of information on his sleeping and waking cycles as well as the state of his mind and body. Long periods without a Words with Friends response usually meant he was either asleep or not physically up to it.

In fact, some mornings I wouldn't call the hospital until his word arrived, because it was only then that I knew it was safe to do so. While there were so many things I disliked about technology, I really appreciated and valued our phones for that app. Thank you, Words with Friends.

By Thursday, the fatigue set in and Steve's mood changed. It seemed on day four of the Part A cycle of chemotherapy, Steve felt more solemn and agitated. He had the same response during the first cycle, so I knew what to expect and that it would pass. We just needed to endure the next few days of extreme toughness before he would feel better again.

We left the hospital on Friday armed as usual with everything we needed to help the next few days be as comfortable as possible. Although Steve maintained that Part B was much harsher on his body than Part A, when he sat in the toxic effects during the first couple of days home, it all felt just as bad. The only good part about the latest Part A cycle was that he didn't require a blood transfusion at the end of his treatment, and he didn't get an infection as with Part B.

At his next PICC line dressing, the specialist informed us that Steve would require a CT scan to see how the treatment was going. I think a similar feeling reverberated through both Steve's body and mine as we thought about the meaning of that. We were going to see how his body had responded to the treatment thus far. We were both excited and nervous.

We didn't discuss any *what ifs*. We just went about the physical process that was involved. We made the booking, travelled to Dr. Jones and Partners, had the test, and then picked the films up just in time for his next PICC line dressing appointment.

I held the information in my hands about Steve's progress, and yet neither one of us made any attempt to peek. I sat in the waiting area while Steve's bloods were taken, and the specialist casually whisked the films away to view them. We didn't have a formal appointment, but after he viewed the report he happily confirmed great news. With his declaration that "It has virtually gone," I nearly fell off my chair. He went on to give some more technical information about Steve's excellent response to treatment, but I was still lingering in his initial statement. He went on to tell Steve the good news, and in that moment there was a sense of it all being worth it. It felt like a big win.

I was so happy there was good news to report to everyone. The blog post titled "Good News" inspired lots of people to contact Steve.

Needless to say, we felt elated during our next few days at the beach. On Saturday, Steve had a visit from some mates, and they all went out for a meal and time together. It was the first time for a long time that he felt "normal." On every level, he was feeling well and positive, and this was so good to see.

It was so important to have his spirit lifted through this tough process, because the better he was at the beginning of each cycle, the stronger he was to cope with the side effects. But the treatment wasn't over yet, so we needed to stay vigilant and not take anything for granted. There was a long way to go, and I'd seen before how in a moment things could change. But for this particular moment, it was a great relief.

It was the first time in a very long time that I could breathe freely. I'd noticed that I had my own struggles physically some days. I was the carer, but I was also in need of some care. I had experienced palpitations when I watched Dad in intensive care for four weeks, and they were lingering. They didn't seem serious, but they were around, so I knew I needed to follow that up at some time. And my back was feeling the stress and strain from the many nights sleeping on the lounge.

How easy it was to hold these concerns off until another time. But that was what I chose. I saw Steve's needs as more urgent than my own at that time, and I was prepared for the consequences. Sometimes I would either forget or I was just too tired to do things that could have made me feel better. All it would have taken was a small action like a massage, stretch, walk, bath, or heat bag—but sometimes even the smallest things seemed too big.

Luckily, I could find an instant "feel good" that didn't take any effort: the thought of my first grandchild! He seemed to take any pain away. My spirits lifted at the thought. How important it was to have something special to look forward to. It somehow seemed to balance the other challenges.

It's hard to describe how life felt at that time. It was as though I was trying to balance on a wobbly ball. Nothing felt familiar. Every day presented something new and different: the emotions I felt, the challenges I faced, the things I did, the people I met. I began to recognize we were not only going through the physical challenge of the treatment but a whole life change.

I needed to get things off my chest, so I began journaling once more. That became the beginning of this writing. It was a great outlet. I needed help to go the distance with what was ahead. I was away from my work and usual life, so writing became my release and break from the other things. On the days when Steve slept, I had a project—to express in words this turbulent time of our lives.

CHAPTER 10

CYCLE FOUR—
PART B AGAIN

When you bring light to a dark journey, you have another focus. You can't avoid the pain, but you can have something more uplifting sit beside you along the way.

When we left Maslins Beach and returned to Highbury to prepare for the next hospital cycle, I was excitedly nervous about the big project that would secretly take place while Steve underwent his treatment.

At the beginning of the year, before the start of Steve's treatment, Harold and Josie visited us at Maslins Beach on their way home from a family holiday. From the moment they heard about Steve's illness, they wanted to do something to lift his spirits. They mentioned to me in private that afternoon that they were keen to organize a working bee for our garden. They could see Steve wasn't in a physical state to do the work, so they thought it would be worthwhile and fun.

In time, that loose "want" became a well-crafted surprise that had many colleagues, friends, and family involved. The idea grew when many hair-industry people informed Harold that they wanted to give Steve a gift. Harold suggested donating a plant for the garden instead. Before long, this invitation was extended to family and friends, and in time a landscape designer and constructor were assigned the job.

I even played a role in this massive secret. My job was to communicate with the landscaper and come up with a design that Steve and I would be happy with. That wasn't going to be easy! How on earth was I going to do it while looking after Steve? The great thing about Harold is that there was no such thing as impossible. I had to find a way to make it happen, and I did.

It wasn't easy to explain to Steve why I was contacting a landscape gardener. I convinced him it was to find out which plants would be suitable when we eventually decided to do the garden. I'm sure he thought it was an unusual thing to do, but he didn't have the energy to question it. There were many emails to confirm plants and designs, and when each was sent, I got the feeling Steve intuitively sensed something was up.

He commenced cycle-four treatment on Tuesday instead of the usual Monday. The specialist had informed us the week before that after the completion of this cycle, Steve would be have to go to the Queen Elizabeth Hospital (QEH) for a stem-cell collection. The timing for this treatment would be better if his chemotherapy was held back a day.

In my head, I calculated what it meant in terms of the garden surprise. Staying back to do this other procedure meant that instead of going to Maslins Beach on the usual Wednesday after his week of treatment, we would have to wait until the following weekend. This actually turned out quite well, because we then had a reason for holding off going to the beach. That was just what Harold wanted—he had envisioned the garden being unveiled in front of all Steve's friends and family at a weekend event. It would be a wonderful moment of surprise and love for everyone.

We set Sunday, April 1, as the official unveiling of the Garden of Well-Being, which meant there was plenty of time to complete the garden and all the extra bits. I decided that while the landscaper was there, I'd finish off other things at the same time—paving, vegetable patch, irrigation. The emails and planning were underway to prepare for the great surprise.

The event had gained momentum, and it seemed it was fast becoming a major event. So many people wanted to be involved—another testament of the love and respect for Steve. I did, however, start to have concerns about how he would respond and cope with the enormity of the surprise. I think Josie had some of the same concerns.

We had an awful memory of Part B. It seemed as though it took a much greater toll on Steve's body than Part A. As with Part A, he generally felt OK for the first few days, but by Thursday fatigue set in. The worst part of this cycle was the constant toilet stops from the diuretic that was used to maintain his weight and pH levels. He felt worn out.

This time, he was in room 227 in St. Clare's ward upstairs. This room overlooked the southern side of the hospital, which wasn't nearly as pleasant as the northern side, where windows opened to a vista of trees and open sky. Steve had only a tin roof and external stairs to look out to, but on the plus side, the toilet was closer to the bed. That was a good thing!

Saturday was his last day of treatment, and he looked and felt very flat. He was happy to go home. As usual, we left with all his medication. This time, rather than the one injection of Neulasta, I was to inject Neupogen twice a day for as many days as required before his stem-cell collection. He was to have a meeting at the QEH on the following Friday to get prepared for the procedure that was likely to take place the Monday after that.

On the Tuesday after he arrived home, he had his usual PICC line dressing appointment. Because he went in the hospital a day later, his appointment was one day sooner than it should have been. This meant he had one less day to recover from the initial impact of the chemotherapy. So the trip to hospital was even more of a struggle. He wasn't really up to it. His energy levels were very low. The nurses took one look at him and knew he would need a blood transfusion.

About six p.m. that night, I had finished preparing the meatballs— Steve's favourite meal for just out of the hospital—and we were excited to watch the finale of *My Kitchen Rules*, on which his cousin's son was a grand finalist.

Just before we sat down to eat, I noticed Steve had a rigor—a cold shiver that usually presented with a temperature. His temperature, however, was only 36.8. I wasn't convinced. He wouldn't have a rigor for nothing. Within the next half-hour, his temperature jumped to 37.8, and then 38. I knew immediately what that meant. The night we had planned was not going to be. We went straight to the hospital instead, and he was put on intravenous antibiotics.

Once again, he was not a well boy. He not only had an infection, his blood levels were very low. This was a concern not only because an infection was difficult for his body to cope with, but also because he was to have his stem-cell appointment on Friday and collection the following Monday.

It was during one of our first appointments with the specialist at the beginning of the year that he mentioned the stem-cell process. We didn't know too much about when, where, how, or why—just that it would be done at some time.

We later learned how important stem-cell treatment was for those with non-Hodgkin's lymphoma (NHL). It was a complex process with amazing implications. From our discussions with nurses and doctors, we discovered that deep within our bodies are stem cells that have the potential to produce all that is needed to assist and maintain good health, heal, and fight disease. There was a machine that could extract the stem cells from the blood; they were then frozen and stored and later inserted back into the body and cultivated as needed. Given the long-term implications for those with mantle cell NHL—which they said could be treated but not cured—this was a procedure that could certainly help in the future.

Over the next couple of days, we discovered Steve definitely had a bug (it would take a few days to cultivate to know the exact type), and on top of that his haemoglobin, platelets, and white cells were all very low, so antibiotics, blood, and platelets were given. His temperature indicated each day that his infection was slow to clear. To us, this seemed a concern.

I've described what took place, but I haven't told you how Steve was feeling. He was not happy! He knew he had to be in the hospital, but he was disappointed and, just like me, wondering why his body wasn't responding as quickly to the antibiotics and the blood they were giving him. It was an anxious wait to determine the specific nature of the bug and its sensitivity to the antibiotics.

I suppose it was the memory of Dad's experience with infection just six months earlier that had me on tenterhooks. It wasn't until it was confirmed that his particular bug was sensitive to the antibiotics— which meant it would respond to the drugs and not resist them—that I felt more at ease. I had to remind myself that what looked like a serious problem might not be. The doctors seemed confident that it would settle quite quickly and Steve would still have the stem-cell collection. In fact, the more depleted his system, the more his stem cells would kick in, and the better that would be for the collection. His temperature and white blood cell levels, however, needed to be appropriate before it could be done. We watched this closely day to day.

Within a couple of days, the doctors confirmed that the bug was in his gut and was caused by the toxic effect of the methotrexate chemotherapy. Luckily, it was sensitive to the antibiotics he had been given. I can't describe how relieved I was.

In the meantime, I made the decision that the planned garden unveiling on April 1 had to be cancelled. It was Thursday, March 22, and I knew even if he was out of hospital in time, it would have all been too much. Not good for Steve. Although everyone was disappointed, they understood that Steve's health came first.

Friday came, and there was no way he was up to the appointment at the QEH to have his vein quality assessed. It would have to take place on the Monday before the actual collection. Not the ideal, but it had to be.

We watched all the statistics closely over the weekend: blood pressure, oxygen, temperature, haemoglobin, white cells, and platelets. We were beginning to understand the implications of each delay, but we didn't want to take our minds there. These stem cells had to be collected!

We stayed as positive as possible, but it was getting hard for both of us. Steve had had enough. Basically, this was his second week of hospitalization with no fresh air and feeling like crap, and I was getting more tired from the daily routine of hospital, lunch, shopping, cooking, hospital, home, worry, and little sleep or rest after that. It's amazing, when you're tired, your usual clarity and mood seems to change. It became work to keep the right mental attitude. Doubts, questions, and concerns worked their way into my mind. I needed a break and some help with things.

Fortunately, Danielle and Jordan were renovating the bathroom at their home, so they decided to stay with me for a week. This worked well, because Danielle was such a help with cooking and cleaning. I took up the offer from friends and family to have some meals cooked for Steve and myself. It's amazing how a little reprieve really helped me feel better.

I realized the better I was, the better it was for Steve, and that was comforting. It meant he didn't have to worry about me. He had enough to do just focusing on getting himself well. This was something I reminded myself constantly. When people helped me, they were helping him.

On Monday morning, he still wasn't up to the QEH trip. He needed more blood and platelets, and his temperature wasn't yet stable. Apparently his white cells had crept off the mark and increased slightly, so the doctors were confident his stem cells had started to kick in, but they were still not quite up to the required level. The nurses would take blood in the morning and hopefully the QEH visit would happen that afternoon.

When I arrived on Tuesday morning, the doctor was waiting for confirmation on the blood results. By lunch, it was evident that the levels were not sufficient, although they had climbed considerably higher than the day before. This was a good sign, and the specialist confirmed the visit would definitely go ahead the next day, Wednesday.

We started to really believe it would take place, and we got excited. I could see Steve was better, because he started to get impatient and wanted to get out. His nurse, Laura, suggested we take some time out and perhaps even go home until that night for a break. We were both elated at the thought of dinner at home together on a beautiful sunny and mild day. I asked what he felt like eating, and it was fish curry—yum.

Just before we left, Laura gave Steve his last bag of platelets and checked the vein on his right arm to determine its suitability for the stem-cell extraction. She wasn't 100 per cent sure, but the specialist confirmed after a quick look that it wasn't. A Vas Cath would be required.

The doctor briefly explained how a line would be inserted around the collar-bone area, and this would be used for the blood extraction and stem-cell collection. A specialist would have to insert it—they just needed to arrange one from the Royal Adelaide Hospital. It all sounded so simple. A Vas Cath—no worries, we were both cool with that.

Of course, this meant that Steve's day trip that we'd gotten so excited about wasn't going to happen. We'd learned that things could change very quickly, and we had to be prepared for that. And we were. We had discovered much earlier in the process the need to be fluid and flexible to change. There was no point getting involved with any unnecessary battles.

The specialist wanted what was best for the stem-cell collection, and although we were disappointed about not going home, we were happy knowing the best "plumbing" would be connected and ready for the extraction. We couldn't afford any hold-ups. I headed off to shop, cook, and get back to the hospital with fish curry. I entered his room just as he returned from the procedure. As I walked in, I couldn't help but fixate on the gadget in Steve's neck. It wasn't a pretty sight.

Steve told me that the specialist had given him a brief on the procedure and the risks. He was shocked at what was involved. They would insert a four-millimetre tube into his jugular vein, taking great care not to touch an artery—if they did, he'd bleed to death! Not what Steve wanted to hear. The doctor reassured him, however, that because they used the CT scan and ultrasound as guides, there was no chance of that. Steve stayed amazingly still as they performed the procedure on his neck with a plastic sheet covering his face.

At one point, the nurse asked if he was OK, because he wasn't talking. He informed them that he was meditating to keep focused and still. When he told me this, I felt relieved. In the past, he had rejected the concept of meditation, but I found on many occasions throughout his illness that he used his own personal approach to get him through pain, discomfort, or anxious times. It was much more powerful for him to discover meditation in his own way.

So the procedure for the Vas Cath (short for vascular catheter, words we'd previously just heard thrown around loosely by Nurse Laura and the specialist) ended up being a most frightening and stressful experience for Steve. I could sense the level of fear he felt when he was told of the risks of the procedure. The experience seemed to open a floodgate of emotions. Everything that had been bottled up since his diagnosis gushed out. We cried in each other's arms once more—no need for words.

It didn't take long, however, before we were laughing again and taking photos of his new Frankenstein-like appearance. It was nice to have the kids visit. They too helped lighten the situation.

When I returned the following morning bright and early, just after seven a.m., I could once again feel the enormity of his anxiety. There was so much uncertainty: Would there be enough stem cells? How long would the Vas Cath be required (the doctor had said it could stay in a maximum of three days because of the high risk of infection)? How would the procedure feel, and how would the tube in his neck be taken out?

We ventured off to the QEH very early that morning. The procedure itself, to our relief, was quite simple and painless. Steve sat in a chair with two leads attached to his Vas Cath, one extracting blood and one returning blood. He didn't feel any discomfort, or any other sensation. His job was to patiently wait for the slow extraction of stem cells.

The machine and the process used were amazing. We were told the components of blood would separate into various levels in the collection: water, plasma, stem cells, red blood. We waited with curiosity for the precious stem cells to be found. Within about an hour of spinning the blood, we began to see the layer of pink creamy stem cells present in the bag.

I was so excited. I knew they would be there, but I just wanted to see them with my own eyes. The nurse decided to extend the process up to five hours to maximise the chance of getting enough in the one hit. If there weren't enough, we would have to return the next day, and that meant another night's sleep with the Vas Cath and another night in the hospital. After an extra eight days there, it was not what he wanted.

Before we left the QEH, the nurses asked when Steve would be having the cells harvested (that is, put back in his body). He told them the cells were being saved for a rainy day, but that's not what the nurses thought. They suggested that for his stage of illness, the cells would be given immediately after his chemo cycles. That was not what Steve wanted to hear. He was totally deflated, frustrated, and confused. It was the first time I felt a deep dark place in Steve. We left the QEH, returned to Calvary, and waited to speak to the specialist himself. Steve needed the specialist to be upfront about this. It was so important to trust and have faith in his doctor.

A little later that afternoon, the specialist arrived and confirmed his original plans that the stem cells would be stored for a rainy day, provided Steve was in full remission at the end of the cycles of chemotherapy. He stressed that we should not get too carried away with what people said, as they didn't have the full history. He reinforced the importance of asking him questions directly before listening to all that was out there. The specialist was right. We needed to put our trust in him and not get carried away with other people's stories. Everyone's cancer experience was different and individual, and we needed to remember that. We learned a big lesson that day.

We were both elated when the specialist gave Steve the OK to go home. The QEH had confirmed that enough stem cells had been collected. Great news! There was just one more hurdle: taking out the Vas Cath. I decided not to watch. Nurse Margaret asked if I was driving home, and I interpreted that to mean I might not be in a good state to do so if I watched. According to Steve, the removal was quite painless. Within a few minutes, a pressure patch was applied to the hole in his neck, and we were on our way home.

We wound down the windows and let the warm air ruffle our hair . . . well, my hair. Steve felt a sense of freedom again. For that moment, this was all there was—a beautiful drive home.

Chapter 11

Give and Receive

You are in a loop of life. In one instance you are in "give," and then the next you are in "receive." Be gracious and unconditional with both.

If I ever thought I could control things in my life, I had to remind myself it was an illusion. Things were just happening. It seemed our work was to go with the best option and then watch how things turned out. There wasn't much point wasting energy on complaints or getting too upset—we just did what we needed to get through each hurdle.

Steve's last infection and extra hospital time before Easter were just more of those hurdles we got through as best we knew how. Because of that ordeal, the specialist decided Steve's next cycle of chemotherapy would be delayed for a week. That was great news, as it gave him the opportunity to go to the beach and recover more before the next cycle.

Steve decided he wanted to stay at Highbury for Easter, so we could be with the family, and then go to Maslins Beach on Easter Monday. Once he made that decision, I sneakily spread the word to family and a few friends that we would be at the house at around eleven a.m. That would be the day he would receive his garden surprise. For those who could make it, we organized a small gathering to greet Steve as he arrived at the house.

The few days before Easter, we spent with family. It was amazing how much we appreciated the most simple life events. They seemed to feel the most special. A simple meal with the kids felt glorious. We loved being all together, because in that moment life was just perfect.

On Easter Monday morning, I gathered our things and we headed to Maslins Beach for an eleven a.m. arrival. Until then, I really hadn't thought too much about what was ahead for Steve. As we neared the house, however, my heart started pumping hard in my chest, and my emotions over this most beautiful act of kindness from our friends and family became difficult to suppress.

Steve sat innocently in the passenger seat, oblivious to what was ahead, while I was a blubbering mess knowing what he would be walking into. I had never before been involved in planning such a surprise, and my part in the secret mission had been a great diversion over the past weeks. This surprise had uplifted my own spirits, and I was hoping it would do the same for Steve.

The way Josie and Harold went about this surprise for Steve told me a lot about them as friends. Nothing was too difficult—they were just determined to boost Steve's spirit throughout his challenge. They just wanted to give him the surprise and feel the joy from it. His job was to receive.

Steve didn't like fuss. While he appreciated thoughtful actions and communication, he felt uncomfortable about people doing things for him. It was something I had to work on too. It helped when I remembered how great I felt when others received with gratitude and allowed it. I started to see the importance of receiving from the heart.

So there they were, about twenty special people standing in our garden as Steve arrived for what he expected to be a routine visit to Maslins Beach. It was hard to know how he really felt. I had never received such a surprise, so I couldn't imagine what his brain did in that moment.

There was a look of confusion combined with comfort. What was this garden about, and wasn't it nice that everyone was there? There was plenty of uncertainty about everything. So many questions—who, when, why, what, where—all of which were answered slowly that afternoon during a lovely brunch that was organized by all the visitors.

The most heartfelt moment was when Steve ventured upstairs and saw the banner that listed the names of everyone involved in the surprise. I'm sure he felt a range of emotions. He slowly began to realize the extent of the project. Needless to say, he was totally overwhelmed.

I realized how hard it must have been to receive on such a large scale, but it was so deserved for someone who had played a big part in people's lives. I could see he needed some time to let go of that uncomfortable feeling that came with receiving. I'd often heard about unconditional giving, but I was beginning to understand the other side—unconditional receiving.

All in all, we enjoyed a magical day. The sun was out, the garden glowed, and everyone was grateful to witness such a precious moment. I was relieved that I no longer needed to hide anything from him. It wasn't a nice feeling telling white lies, even if it was for a great purpose. The guests left early—they knew the gathering was to be short and sweet, and that it was.

Over the next few days, Steve showed the motivation we were hoping for. He bought a new lawnmower and mowed the two small strips of lawn that had grown significantly since first planted. Although he needed a long rest (a few hours!) after each strip was mowed, he loved every minute of it.

We spent much more time outside viewing the plants and admiring the magical design. I could sense a relief in Steve that everything was finished and all that was needed was maintenance, something he could see himself doing when he felt well. So after his fourth cycle, he had a beautiful gesture of love and kindness to warm his heart and keep him positive.

How important it is to be surrounded by people who love you! Having people around who shared and engaged in magic moments made such a difference to how life felt. I thought about how difficult it would have been if we didn't have a network. Thankfully, there were so many associations and volunteers who offered care and support. I was only beginning to realize the true value and importance of strong networks.

It confirmed to me that the most important thing to give in life was love—and when it was received in times of need, there was nothing better. It was irreplaceable.

CHAPTER 12

GRATITUDE

No matter how difficult your challenge, there is always so much to be grateful for when you take the time to look.

I took on the job of carer with all of my heart. I took on the house and business tasks so that Steve didn't have to worry and could focus on getting better. I took great care to prepare good food, ensure good hygiene, and provide emotional support. I ensured all food was fresh, well prepared, nutritious, and most importantly, tasty and desirable. This meant daily shopping and quite a regular spot in the kitchen. I kept the house clean and tidy to minimize any unnecessary risk of infection, and I was always around to chat when he needed emotional support.

There were many times, however, when Steve just wasn't up to much communication or interaction. His fatigue and nausea meant he spent a lot of time in bed, especially in the first week after treatment. That meant I had a lot of time for my jobs, but there was a lot of spare time.

Spare time required me to use my brain differently. I was not juggling work and life as I had done in the past. I was no longer doing the fast-forward projection to plan and organize ten things at once. There was no need. Even the evening meals were last-minute decisions based on what Steve felt like that day. I never wanted to go too far forward with the *what ifs* or the construction of future stories, so my brain didn't go there. This, in turn, affected the pace with which correspondence travelled down the neural pathways of my brain. In other words, my brain slowed down!

My brain seemed much more relaxed and present as opposed to flitting and on guard. It wasn't geared up for a workplace, that's for sure. I attempted to do one work-related thing and made a fundamental error as I sent out an email. I couldn't believe my brain didn't go there to pick it up. It was certainly asleep on that level.

I had read about neuro-plasticity of the brain, in which the brain pathways altered over time, leading to changes in the way the brain processed. I didn't expect that in a few months such changes would be so significant, but it certainly felt that way. But it was in the newfound slowness that I had the opportunity for other things. I often would retreat into the smallness of what surrounded me until it felt and looked amazingly big. I could see so much more detail and clarity, and life felt different. It felt as though I was living life on a different wavelength.

One morning, when Steve slept in, I was blessed with a treasured moment. I woke quite early to the most perfect autumn morning. The sun rose from the east with a golden glow that penetrated through a spray of low-lying clouds to bring a multitude of colours across the sky and form the most amazing picture. My reality for that moment was a perfect sky, and it had my undivided attention. I expressed thanks for what my eyes had witnessed.

I was grateful.

I was grateful that I knew how to appreciate it—and that the house had a peep window that opened to the east, providing a clear view.

I was grateful that I happened to wake early, fresh, and without resistance that morning.

I was grateful that I caught the light of the sun at that point in the sky.

I was grateful that my body and mind were still enough to appreciate its beauty.

As I took in that moment, I felt I had swallowed the most powerful vitamin that ever existed. I felt the immediate effects on my body—my breathing slowed, my mind cleared, my muscles melted, and my spirit lightened. That moment was perfect. I felt totally alone yet at one with nature, stripped of all the manmade created games, identities, and temptations I had come to know as me and my life.

It was an aloneness where I felt completely comfortable and absolutely free and energized . . .

an aloneness that was not attached to anything yet connected to everything . . .

an aloneness that was not lonely but rather totally fulfilled and satisfied . . .

an aloneness that could easily be lost if I took my mind back to words, thinking, or analysing . . .

an aloneness that held no fear, only comfort . . .

an aloneness that I would treasure as often as possible.

That's just how I felt in that particular moment. I was physically isolated on many days from family, friends, work, and the hustle and bustle, however there were definitely rich experiences like this early morning sky that crept into my days. But such moments didn't last long. It's amazing how quickly I moved on from this. A thought, action, or emotion would bring me back to a different reality like a slap in the face. But that was life—moving into and out of quite rapidly.

There was always stuff that would happen—some I perceived as good and some as bad, when in fact they were neither. Everything that happened was to help me grow, respond, learn, discover, wish, dream, pray, ask, change, and expand. It all was just meant to be. But even though my intellectual mind knew this, I was human with human vulnerabilities. I had fear, tears, sadness, madness—that's just what happens when you're human.

I still felt the pain of Dad's death. I'd cry and cry as I just wanted to hug him, talk with him, and have him back. I felt how much I loved the people in my life, and I'd cry some more. I knew crying wasn't the way to live life, but in that moment it felt like the thing to do. I sometimes felt I even had tears for everyone and everything. It was overwhelming, but at the same time it felt like a deep love and appreciation for all of life.

But my mind would quite rapidly settle me back to earth. My day-to-day actions were my way of contributing in this life. I was developing a positive and healthy way to ride out this time. I felt Steve helped me do this, and I helped him do the same.

Many people had said to both of us, "You've got to be positive." While they had great intentions, positive didn't just arrive from words. Positive arrived from something more. To us, it was a connection to something bigger than the situation we were in. We found an appreciation for the beauty of God—my word for the pure love that existed for the natural world of nature, animals, the stars and universe, and the warmth and love of beautiful spirited people.

I kept a list of things to be thankful and grateful for:

- We were alive on this wonderful earth.
- Steve had an illness that could be treated.
- Modern medicine and science were amazing.
- We had access to an abundance of other natural support remedies.
- Steve was a strong man with a great attitude.
- We had beautiful friends and family.
- We were to become first-time grandparents.
- We had a beautiful and amazing daughter.
- We had a beautiful and amazing son who really stepped up to run Steve's business.
- We were not alone—we were doing this thing together.
- We both had an appreciation for nature.
- We had some beautiful vistas from our beach house.
- We had a western sea view that dimmed to the most incredible sunsets and became the backdrop to our living room each night.
- We had regular visits from the moon as it peered through the upstairs peep windows.
- We had a single tree that sat on the horizon of a paddock we overlooked from our northern facing balcony.

It all felt magical. And on top of that, we had two beautiful dogs that gave us love and laughs every day; we enjoyed many common interests, including music and singing; we enjoyed each other's company; and we loved each other. So overall, I had many reasons why positive was possible.

I knew how to access positive. I knew how to feel positive. I knew how to bring positive to sadness or difficulty. And I knew that positive was real and authentic. It needed to be.

Lying about being positive wasn't positive, so it had no value. A facade of positive would only delay finding true positive. It had to be real and authentic to be effective. And for us, it was. It was a soft and humble positive with lots of power and strength. We acknowledged the ups and downs and saw them as the curve balls in our life. We acknowledged the pain of these.

There were days when I was frustrated that I couldn't take away Steve's pain and even tormented by the uncertainty of each day, but I had an underlying positive that hovered near. I came to realize that true positive could only be found in the most difficult of life situations. I realized it was easy to be positive when all was going well in my life. A true test was being positive when gut-wrenching and critical life events were present.

That was my inner positive test. Steve's, too, and he had it. How did I know? I imagined what it was like for him when on any given day he felt all, a few, but rarely none of the side effects of the treatment he was having—a cough, runny nose, reflux, constipation, diarrhoea, coated tongue, watery eyes, mouth ulcers, numb fingers, aching legs, weak muscles, nausea, vomiting, awful taste and smell, hair loss (body, that is, because the hair on his head was already gone), weight loss, paleness of body and gums, husky voice. And yet during all this, he could place his attention on the good things in his life and show a resolve to get on with the task of getting well again.

Steve sincerely felt joy and fun among the horrid physical things he endured. He enjoyed his food, got engrossed in movies and football, engaged in conversation and laughter, felt for others for their own challenges, and took in the world around him. His mind allowed him to do that, and this I saw as true authentic positive. He wasn't *trying* to be positive—it was a natural response that had roots far beyond the word *positive*. My role as a carer would have been a lot more difficult if he didn't have this quality.

I suppose we had both been through some recent life challenges—my cancer and death of my father—that somehow prepared us. Those times were hard, but we faced up to them and learned. We talked over things and shared our deepest of feelings and thoughts, which at the time felt confronting but paved the way for more honesty and change. It was new territory for us. We had been far too busy and preoccupied in the past for such closeness and honesty. We began to speak more from our hearts. We began to trust and understand each other more, and our relationship flourished.

It was good that we had grown in a way that had us a little stronger for what was ahead. We were once again in the midst of a challenge, but I knew that was the world today—and that there were some in the world doing far worse. I was inspired by a book based on a true story, *The Long Walk* by Slavomir Rawicz (later made into a movie as *The Way Back*). It was an example of extreme challenge. It told of the life of a Polish prisoner of war captured by the Russians and held in a Siberian prisoner camp, who later escaped and trekked thousands of miles through the most torturous terrains to freedom. If someone in that position could be positive, surely we could too.

And we could.

Steve's stem-cell collection was a success. His infection cleared relatively quickly, his body picked up well for the next cycle of treatment, and he had a beautiful garden to immerse himself in. For the fact that he was in good health for his next cycle, we were especially grateful.

CHAPTER 13

CYCLE FIVE—
PART A AGAIN

When situations change, be ready to change up any old routines. What once served you well can in fact become a thorn, so watch carefully.

Going into the next cycle, we somehow felt confident things would be OK. Part A in the past had been good to Steve, and he knew what to expect.

This confidence gave me the opportunity to give other things some much-needed attention. I decided I would go to the hospital later in the morning, just in time to prepare Steve's lunch, and then use the afternoon for dentist and doctor appointments, personal grooming, and house management. I coordinated some help for a couple of evening dinners, which freed me to catch up with friends and enjoy some downtime. I began to feel I needed more time for my own personal health.

I had always been conscious of looking after myself and felt I had done that in many ways. There were, however, some areas I had neglected because I was consumed with other stuff, such as getting my head around what was needed for Steve during this time. This week brought a lot of busy activity, which helped the week pass quickly, and I felt good about doing other things.

In fact, the week passed quickly for both of us. Steve once again enjoyed visitors up until Wednesday, as by Thursday the fatigue had settled in. Surprisingly, he didn't feel as bad as he had in the past, and when I took him home on Friday just after lunch, he seemed quite good.

Then he received a text from his client who had gone through treatment and stem-cell transplant for NHL. The doctors had now found another cancer, which meant more treatment. I could see how disheartened Steve was at the news, especially as he looked to this client as a survivor of the disease.

We both knew it didn't really matter what happened to someone else—it was an individual outcome. Nonetheless, I felt Steve's disappointment, for his client and for himself. News like that took us to places we didn't need to go. It was important to gain perspective as soon as possible. Once we had felt the pain of the news, we brought ourselves back to our lives and what was needed in that moment. Fortunately, Steve felt quite good physically, so his attention was easily diverted. We had learned to really appreciate times when he felt good.

Interestingly, during that week we had a visit from a social worker who popped in to see how we were holding up. She mentioned a government carers' allowance that we might be eligible for. She explained it wasn't a large amount of money, but it could be enough to help out with some of expenses, such as car-park payments or medicines.

I thought I'd check it out, even though we were nearing the end of his treatment, but to tell you the truth, the forms and processes were so complicated it didn't seem worth it. I didn't have the patience to persist, and I realized so many carers would also have walked past opportunities because of the system. So many of our systems were not set up to make it easy for people who really needed it to be during such times. I was thankful that Steve had taken out insurance for illness as a business owner. It was something he recommended to other hairdressers. He felt passionate about making them aware of the importance.

We also had a couple of visits from representatives of the Leukaemia Foundation, who shared information about their services and groups. It was great to know what they offered. Steve felt it wasn't for him, though.

Friday night, he slept well and still felt well enough on Saturday to watch his beloved Crows play. It was wonderful he was passionate about football, because when he watched the game he was totally away from everything else. His energy level even seemed to pick up—there was a fire in his belly and roars of emotion. It was as though he was well again.

I was actually very relieved, because this was the day I was to go to Danielle's baby shower. We had previously organized it to be held at our Highbury home, thinking Steve would be at Maslins Beach and well and truly feeling better. However, because of the delay in his treatment, everything was a week out, so he was home and on the very unwell part of his cycle.

Danielle decided to change the venue to her home, which we hadn't chosen at first for the lack of space. It turned out to be fine, though, and we all enjoyed a magical afternoon of baby games and refreshments. I had moments of sadness for what I had missed out on in the preparation for the day, but I was also happy that Danielle had wonderful friends and a cousin who helped make the day just perfect.

I didn't talk about Steve or our situation with guests at the baby shower. It was really great to just be there and enjoy the day. I yearned for times to feel *normal*. My emotions had been arriving unexpectedly in the past weeks, but I was fortunate they didn't on that day. It was a day to treasure.

By the time I arrived home from the baby shower, I could see a change in Steve's general health. I had started to read the signs well. It was hard to describe, but subtle things about his mood, walk, talk, voice, tone, colour, vitality, and posture seemed to give me information. He ate quite well that night, but we were both exhausted and went to bed early. It was about two a.m. when the side effects of the chemo really set in.

He had taken all his anti-nausea and reflux medication, but somehow they weren't strong enough this time. It took five or six vomits until things settled. I spent the night by his side, cleaning out bowls. He would say, "Go to bed, I'll be all right. I'll ring the bell if I need you." But I couldn't sleep until I knew he had settled.

It was at that moment I remembered a night a few days after my own cancer operation, when for some reason I got a tachycardia and intense nausea that made me feel so unwell. I remembered feeling quite scared because I didn't know what was happening to my body. That was the only time Steve stayed the night at the hospital, by my side, waiting for my heart to settle. It was his presence that comforted me greatly, and that was the thing I needed most. I knew how good it felt to have someone close by when your body was under such stress. I knew my place was by his side for this challenge.

He was still very ill the next day, and in fact seemed to have less energy than he had before. I noticed his tongue was very white. This was a sign of toxicity, so he increased the dose of Nilstat, and that seemed to help.

To tell you the truth, this period of time seemed so much longer and more difficult than previously. I'm not sure if it was the accumulative impact of everything that had happened, but it didn't feel good. We both felt the same. In the silence of our tears and embrace, we felt each other's struggle. We had been at it for a long time, and suddenly "only three more cycles" felt like a mammoth task. The number three seemed small before that day, but in that moment it felt epic. I felt scared at the thought.

By lunchtime Monday, Steve had slowly crept back and turned a corner. When that happened, the side effects started to lessen. Everything started to improve, physically and emotionally.

On the Tuesday of his usual PICC line dressing change and bloods, he still felt very fatigued, which suggested he might need a blood transfusion the next day. He entered Kimberley House while I quickly signed some papers for our insurance guy. By the time I arrived, he was already seated and ready to go. I noticed Steve looked a little low, and in the next moment I realized his client was sitting next to him having his treatment. It was bittersweet—bitter to have to face his client going through treatment again, and sweet that he had the chance to chat with and support his friend. It took a while for Steve to settle after that meet.

We left Kimberley House with a tip for his white tongue: mix one-half teaspoon salt and one-half teaspoon bicarbonate of soda in a glass of warm water and gargle. That seemed to help him a little, so we added it to the regime until the condition improved.

Steve was doing well with his personal self-care regime. Before starting his treatment, he visited the dentist and was advised on mouth care to support him throughout. Floss, brush, and swish were performed after each meal.

It was important for Steve to take great care of his body to minimize any spin-off problems from the chemotherapy side effects. For the first time, his body and self were a priority. He was getting a sense of what it took to really care for his body, and it took effort.

In the past, it was common to put everything else before that extra personal care. I had learned not to fall in that trap during my own time of illness and thought I'd never do it again, but there I was putting some of my own self-care on the back burner again while I focused on other important things. But I realized no matter how important those other things seemed, my own health was also a priority.

This hit me hard when I started to get sharp back pain that impacted on my movement and mood. This could have happened for many reasons—I hadn't exercised or stretched properly for a long time, I had slept for many nights on our lounge, and I hadn't visited my usual chiropractor for a "tune-up." In addition to the back pain, I felt my body was going through a change. Well, I did just turn fifty last October, so it was likely. Great—I was having mood swings (as Steve pointed out quite brutally), so this was another thing to get on top of.

It was time to bring some focus back to me, otherwise I'd be no good for Steve. Well, that was interesting. I'd formed a pattern and habit around how I cared for Steve. I think I mentioned before how important it was for me to make routines and patterns, but that needed to change. It was a few months on, and I needed to break what I had created. Not that what I created was bad, but it needed modification.

In the beginning, I went into survival mode. It was a rough version of what felt best to do when I knew little. But time had passed; we'd learned how to ride the better days and manage the more difficult ones. We'd discovered there were pockets of time when I wasn't as needed, and that was where the pattern break needed to occur.

I felt I caught myself just in time, before I was swallowed up by a pattern that looked like martyrdom. Not that I wanted that title, but it was hard to move from the helping pattern and the "I'll do it all" pattern. I realized how difficult it could be for full-time carers to gain distance and space from their gruelling role, but how important it was to avoid the co-dependency cycle all around.

Steve knew I needed some space. He encouraged me to take time out, but a part of me felt he still wanted me close. I tried to ignore that feeling. I knew that to go the distance, I had to nurture other aspects of my life. I didn't want to end up worn out, neglected, or unable to cope.

So we found a little space during the third week after cycle five. Steve's health really picked up, as did his energy level, motivation, and need for independence. Until that point, I had been by his side for all appointments and outings—barring the few where mates took him out. He started feeling more confident about doing things on his own, and by the time of his next PICC line dressing appointment, he decided that he would drive himself there.

I must admit, I was nervous to see him venture off to do what he knew he felt up to. We had booked a tradesman to fix our wardrobes that morning, but he was running late, and it went into the appointment time for the PICC dressing change. It was confirmation that Steve was meant to do it alone that day. It was great to see him get out and be independent again. I felt he was getting himself ready to re-enter life healed and well. It felt like we were in another transition with the process. It just started to feel different.

I thought back to my life before my own illness and realized that without the intense events we had experienced over the past five years, I would have found the ups and downs so much more challenging. I had transitioned over and over again from the peaks and troughs, and that helped me see that things did pass and there was life on the other side. I was grateful for all I had been through. It had prepared me well.

So cycle five led us both into new territory. We knew it felt different, but it was hard to define. It seemed the enduring nature of what we were in had taken hold. We struggled a little more, and it seemed we needed to change this up—get some space from each other and do some more normal things. We made some mental and emotional adjustments at this time.

Heading into cycle six, we knew there were many uncertainties. When would he have his next bone-marrow biopsy? Would he need another two cycles? Would he be in remission? How would he respond if he was or wasn't? When would he begin to feel better? This was going too far into the future, though—we just needed to focus and prepare for the next round and go with everything that unfolded from that.

CHAPTER **14**

HEALING THE DEEP WOUNDS

When you address all your woes—physical, emotional, mental, spiritual—you bring a deeper healing to your being. You do not only rid yourself of disease, you rid any hurt, stress, and anger that fed it.

How was Steve going to heal and recover from the deep wounds of this disease? The cancer was at a high level throughout, so an equally high level of attention would be needed to resolve what lay deep within his body. The approach would have to be wide and varied, because the source and foundation of the disease would have been just that. While it might have been a single trigger that broke the chain to commence the disease, it was his body's internal environment that allowed illness to fester and grow.

Medical treatment would certainly play an important role in his recovery, because of its immediate and powerful influence at the root level. We were grateful that the mind of man had found a way to enter into the depth of the cells. That meant there was a good chance for his survival. Many years ago, someone with this disease would have found it very difficult.

But while his disease presented on the outside, its origin was deep within the many years of our evolution. I felt sure we inherited many weaknesses from the past that led to illnesses. Western medicine alone couldn't be all that was needed for full recovery and healing. I felt deeper healing was needed.

Steve's cellular environment was sensitive to life—it had been forever reacting and responding to many things. That's what we do as humans! The key was to find those things he reacted and responded to that caused him stress. Only he could identify and understand the information that arrived as signals and signs. That level of healing for anyone could only be done by the person affected. But that wouldn't be easy, because like most of us today, he was disconnected from many of his feelings, emotions, and physical sensations.

One day, when I was looking at my tongue, he asked what I was doing. I replied, "Checking my tongue." He thought that was really strange, and in the next moment I found him looking at his own. It was then he noticed the thick white coating and a small ulcer. He hadn't realized there was something going on with his tongue.

Slowly he began to recognize the signs and symptoms of his physical body. At first, he didn't know he was so fatigued. He would say, "I'm all right," when in fact he was very low and needed hospitalization. Later, he was able to recognize he wasn't all right, and he was much more tuned in to what was happening.

Slowly he began to recognize the signs and symptoms of his mind. He realized that worrying about bookwork and the salon was a meaningless exercise. It made no difference if he worried or not—he had no control over it, and the work got done anyway.

Slowly he began to recognize the signs and symptoms of his emotions. At one stage, Steve got upset over something Dion had done on the computer. He really overdid the emotion and paid the price later. He soon learned to be selective with where and what he gave his energy to. His energy was limited, and it helped him sort out what was actually important.

It was an ongoing process, learning to discover what generated comfort in his body, mind, and feelings and what didn't. He was learning what to challenge from his own past ways. He worked on his patience and began to let go and trust—all of which he found challenging. He witnessed the staff doing a great job in the salon and in other areas of the business. This was a positive reward that came from trusting and allowing. In a way, he was loosening his grip on control and finding he could do it.

I witnessed ongoing subtle changes in Steve. In time, he learned the what, how, when, who, and why for most things in his life: food, beverages, activity, exercise, remedies, relationships, thoughts, patterns, behaviours, work, health practices, and so on. He made the choices that he saw as worthwhile.

Not everything described as "good for cancer" was good for him. He was on a low-listeria diet, so no raw egg, pre-prepared salad, shellfish, or soft cheeses. He also needed food, especially meat, to be well-cooked. There were also some natural products that would interfere with the drugs.

He made what I felt were sensible yet simple choices throughout his treatment. I supported him with these. It wasn't about what I wanted, although at times I found it hard not to use my power of influence to offer other ideas and ways. He would let me know if I crossed the line. I'm glad he did.

Even though I had access to many of the latest remedies and natural products known to help cancer—I subscribed to the latest research sources and read many books—that didn't make them right for Steve. He only took on what felt best for him. He didn't overcomplicate things. He chose what he would try and not try. He was the director of his own healing process, and that was what was so powerful.

He was intrigued by the latest research, but that didn't mean he would go for it all. He took on things that felt OK to him—for example, coconut water, organic foods, turmeric, transfer factor, probiotics yoghurt, bicarbonate of soda, and active meditation reflection. He established his own way.

There wasn't a silver bullet. Yes, there were many opinions and approaches, but they often contradicted each other. In isolation, each philosophy or health claim had merit, but it seemed that the deeper and more broadly you went, the more confused you'd get. And that sort of stress was not good for healing.

Steve was happy and confident with his own choices, and this was an important feature of his healing process—personal empowerment. He was driving his treatment. It was great to hear him say, "I know my body, and it doesn't feel right." This showed a strength and ownership that reverberated to the depths of his cells. Subconsciously, he was discovering his own personal truth. He had escaped the roller coaster of mindlessness and was on his way back to good health, moving with what he knew within. The patterns and habits that had previously made up his life were beginning to change.

I witnessed a change in Steve's walk, talk, reactions, and tone. He was less the critic and much more accepting of difference. He could also see and feel the changes in himself. From a more mindful state, he made choices that worked better for him. He tackled each day with a healthier and more powerful attitude.

Personal shifts occurred more frequently for both of us. Every day felt better when we improved how we saw things. We were creating a better future.

It seemed Steve was doing a lot of "looking in" for answers rather than "looking out." The changes were in how he dealt with things rather than expecting the outside things to disappear. We were both taking more responsibility for what was happening.

Steve had developed a greater sense of confidence to do this. He was so much more comfortable in his own skin and more relaxed and open with his thoughts and feelings. He tapped into what his heart had always known; he just needed the time and situation to do so.

He accepted consequences for his choices without mindless fear. He was taking action in ways that he wouldn't have done in the past. He expressed his gratitude to his friends and family, and he went out of his way to make sure they were aware. He wasn't scared to tell or show them he loved them. He took more time to understand what was happening with others—me included—and I could feel the change.

So in many ways, he was supporting the medical treatment that was chopping away at the disease. We were both doing life differently. On the outside it may have looked regular, but our mindset and attitude were anything but. The love and appreciation for each aspect of our time together during this gruelling treatment made everything feel different.

Each meal not only nourished Steve's body but warmed his heart and spirit. He never lost his appetite, apart from the days when he was too sick to eat. I enjoyed preparing food that was pleasant and tasty. I loved to watch him eat with gusto and passion.

He had favourites, and often they became the highlight of his day. On the first couple of days after he returned home after treatment, he loved my meatballs served with fresh beans. As each day passed, he requested some of his other favourites, including Kaffir Lime Salmon, Chicken in White Wine, Veal Coated with Fresh Breadcrumbs and Capsicum and Mushroom Sauce, Curry Turkey Rissoles, Vegetable and Cheese Omelette, and Lasagne. You can find these and more of our most loved recipes in the back of this book.

He also enjoyed some healthy lunches and snacks that included banana pineapple smoothies, pureed apple with yoghurt, and banana spelt muffins. I included some known quality ingredients to most meals to ensure that nutritionally, he was well looked after: olive oil, garlic, turmeric, ginger, lemon, chilli, sweet potato, spelt flour, pineapple, bananas, coconut water, and coconut oil. I used leafy green vegetables like kale, spinach, endive, and green beans, and lean protein like lamb, salmon, and turkey. Occasionally we ate hot chips, because that's just what he felt like. That was good too!

I had fun exploring new recipes and using different preparation techniques. It was a time of adventure and learning in the kitchen. I made my own home-made spelt pasta—first time ever!

But it wasn't only in the kitchen that I explored new territory. I washed windows using the "professional" gadget that Steve had been given by the window cleaner at the salon. Steve gave me instructions on how to get that squeaky clean look, but I had to admit they never looked that great.

I mowed the lawn using the new lawnmower Steve purchased after his Garden of Well-Being surprise. Steve didn't want me to do it, but the grass was getting very long and he still wasn't up to it physically. One day he tried to start the lawnmower, and after three attempts he needed a rest for a few hours. That's how bad his fatigue was. He taught me well, and before long the lawn was trimmed nicely.

I spent time in the garden and enjoyed menial tasks like weeding. I weeded with focused attention, and it felt meditative. I crouched down low with my bucket and tools and became engrossed in the ease with which the winter weeds slid out from their roots, much like a pimple squeezed from its pore.

I discovered quick and efficient housecleaning techniques and found those jobs to be more rewarding than arduous. I enjoyed using more natural products and approaches to maintaining the house. I had planned to do that for a long time, but now they had finally been put in place. I lived a simple and yet fulfilling and active life that felt very healthy. There was no need to go to the gym to get fit.

I had always wanted to sew a quilt for my grandson, but I realized a knitted one was the perfect alternative because of our long hospital stays. I'd do rows to forms squares in the spare moments throughout the day and found this to be another very meditative pastime.

We had a focus, and that was to do this time the best we could. Along the way, we discovered another way to live life, and this helped us shape how we saw out future life together—a future of unknowns that we were somehow OK with. The reality was that life was full of unknowns. This experience certainly expanded and deepened a trust that lay deep within. It was a true test.

I never knew how I would truly be under such a challenge. It was only as it unfolded that I recognized where I was at with my own personal inner self.

I never knew how Steve would truly be under such a challenge. It was only as it unfolded that I recognized where he was at with his own personal inner self.

That's an opportunity these situations offered.

CHAPTER 15

CYCLE SIX—PART B AND ANOTHER INFECTION

Life is a fine line, so never be complacent. Watch the signs and respond. Sometimes seconds count, not minutes; minutes, not hours; hours, not days; and days, not weeks.

A few days before Steve's sixth cycle, we were told that the test results on the blood samples taken the week before were clear of infection. There was a suspicion he may have had one because his temperature was elevated at the last dressing appointment, but all was clear, which meant he was in a better state of health to tackle the Part B cycle that was always hard on his body.

There was something different about this drive to the hospital. Neither of us spoke, yet we felt we were saying plenty. We knew the ropes. There was no need for words, explanations, or anything else. It was a matter of getting in and hoping for the best.

It was a crazy time. Danielle was nearing the end of her pregnancy. She was off work, getting bigger and more uncomfortable. I balanced my time between the hospital and helping Danielle as best I could. It was nice that I could be around a little at that special time.

Steve went in on Tuesday for the cycle of treatment, which meant he wouldn't finish until Saturday. All went well on the first day, and then on the Wednesday morning there was fun and games with Steve's PICC line. The nurse attempted to access the usual morning blood from the line, but it was slightly blocked, which caused a spray of blood to go everywhere. Unfortunately, the PICC line split and couldn't be saved, so that morning he had another procedure to insert a line into his other arm. All went well with that procedure, and by later that morning he was back on track with his chemotherapy treatment.

We discovered something new in relation to the required number of treatments. The specialist informed us that if he got another infection after the cycle, it would be unlikely for Steve to have the eight cycles of the protocol. The specialist's view was that six cycles would be effective anyway, but CT and PET scans following the treatment would confirm the situation. That was different from our initial understanding, so it was good to know a little more.

It was a weird contradiction. Part of us hoped he didn't get an infection so he could have the next two cycles, and another part didn't want him to have the next two cycles because of the risks involved. What was really better or worse? How could we ever know?

In the end, it was great that the natural unfolding of the situation would determine the next steps. No need to try to wish for anything—just allow things to unfold and trust the universe on the outcome. The way it went was going to be the best way.

As usual, Steve felt quite OK during the administration of the chemo that week. By the end of the week, however, he felt very flat and low. This usually meant his blood levels were low, and this turned out to be the case. Instead of going home on Saturday, he received blood to pick up his levels, and it was decided it was best if he waited until Sunday morning to be discharged.

That was Mother's Day. How nice to bring him home on that day! He was my present, and it felt great. He didn't actually feel too bad, so it seemed the blood had done the trick and helped him out.

It was the first time we didn't celebrate the day with our own mothers. I felt sad for Mum, as this would be a hard day for her—the first Mother's Day without Dad. She had a nice day with my sister. There was a part of me that cried inside, but not too hard; I didn't feel strong enough to let go of my emotions too much.

Some days were like that. I just didn't feel up to the release. I felt that if I went to the depth of the emotions, I'd find it impossible to break free from them. So on days like that, I avoided taking my mind to the thoughts and stories that would leave me a blubbering mess. It wouldn't help me or anyone else. Mother's Day was one of those days.

The next couple of days, Steve was very fatigued but did not vomit. He was so pleased about that, but he was very emotional. It was good that he released what was welling up inside. Amazingly, the base of his emotional release was gratitude for everyone's efforts throughout the six months. But I'm sure there was more behind the tears.

By Wednesday, while at Kimberley House for the usual PICC line dressing and bloods, he began to feel even more extreme lethargy and fatigue and looked very pale. His temperature was good, which was a positive sign in relation to infection, but the nurses felt sure he would need a blood transfusion given his colour. This was confirmed within a couple of hours.

Throughout the afternoon, I got a sense that he was very unwell. He looked more pale than normal and slept more than usual. By the evening, I'd hoped the usual meatballs and pasta would pick him up, but it wasn't the case. I took his temperature immediately after tea, and it read 38 degrees. We both said nothing but knew exactly what it meant.

Steve tried to convince me that eating his dinner could have temporarily raised his temperature. I'm sure he knew that wasn't the case, but we waited for about ten minutes and tested it again. Confirmed: 38 degrees, so straight to the hospital.

When we checked in, his temperature had dropped below 37 degrees, but that wasn't indicative of what was happening. He was very sick once again, and he looked it. Even the administrator at the hospital was concerned about Steve's appearance. It was the first time I was really scared that the intensity of the treatment was greater than his body could take.

The next day he seemed better, and there wasn't much sign of infection. By Friday, however, it was clear his body was trying to fight something. He was extremely unwell. With no immune system—it was totally depleted in the second week after chemo—he required antibiotics to fight what his body couldn't. This time, they had him on three different intravenous antibiotics as well as the usual five or six pints of blood plus platelets. This indicated the intensity of help that was needed to get him over the line with each treatment, and it seemed he was in need of more and more support each time.

It was great he had started on the antibiotics early and didn't allow his body to deplete further, because his body was already finding it very tough to get on top of the infection. His blood levels were once again dangerously low, and as the nurse kindly reminded me, times like this could be critical. Not what I wanted to hear. Steve and I had no intention of anything other than full recovery from this challenge. We knew it would take time to get on top of things because we had been in a similar situation before, so we remained calm and positive that things would be good.

During this hospital stay, Steve was in a room next door to the client I mentioned previously who was also back being treated for his NHL that had returned. It seemed he had another lymphoma growing near his kidney, which had affected its function. His specialist, who was also Steve's specialist, joined forces with other specialists to plan a strategy for his condition.

I spent a bit of time talking with his wife, which helped us both unload some of the angst involved in caring for someone with this disease. Her husband was to remain hospitalized until the following week to begin the treatment protocol the doctors thought was necessary. We met up with them regularly throughout the remainder of the days that Steve was in the hospital.

I could sense Steve's sadness for this client. The man had been in remission after having many types of treatment. He and his wife were both looking forward to a holiday, but were forced to cancel because of the setback. It brought back memories of when our trip was cancelled five years earlier because of my own cancer diagnosis.

It was important to not let the disappointment of his client's situation affect Steve's focus on getting better. It didn't take long before we refocused our attention on our own business once again. On Monday, we saw a minimal climb in Steve's blood levels, and we were positive that in the next day or so he would have a rapid climb in levels. The doctor agreed this would be likely based on his past patterns.

We didn't want to put the specialist under any pressure, but our grandson was due on Wednesday, and we really wanted Steve out and well by then. Danielle had started having some regular contractions on Monday, and it seemed possible that the baby could arrive on Tuesday. This would mean a birthday on the 22nd. I had always thought the number 22 would play a significant role. My dad's birthday was the 22nd of October, and the number 22 was significant in many situations around the time of Dad's passing. I felt this number would reinforce Dad's energy around the birth of his great grandson. It was a master number, and somehow that felt comforting.

On Tuesday, however, Danielle's contractions became less regular, and it was evident it wasn't going to happen that day. I went in as usual to the hospital and prepared Steve's lunch before planning to go to Danielle's to help her with shopping and cleaning and preparing Steve's dinner for the evening. Steve walked me out to the lifts, and as we passed the nurse's station, I joked that I was taking him home with me. The nurse looked a bit horrified, because she thought she had read a report that indicated his blood results had declined.

I couldn't believe it—it didn't seem possible. But in the next breath, she said she may have confused his results with someone else, so to disregard that comment. I left the hospital crying at the thought that he wasn't recovering as expected. The tears forced me to pull up at the side of the road, and it was there that another emotional release made its way through my body.

I was tired. I was starting to feel the effects of our time through the treatment. Once I regained my composure, I phoned Steve for an update on the situation. He asked where I was, which I thought was a bit strange because he knew where I was going. I was elated when he told me to turn around and come back to the hospital, because he had been given the all-clear to go.

The nurse had confused his results with someone else's, and in fact Steve's bloods were good enough to go home. It felt like another win. He would be home in time for our grandson's arrival.

Despite the ongoing contractions, the baby was biding his time to allow Steve to really pick up before he was born. Well, that's how we saw it, anyway. The extra few days were perfect because each day Steve got stronger and more energized. The longer it took, the more likely he would be able to meet his newborn grandson at the hospital.

We knew this was going to be a delicate balance of timing, and we were living it out with suspense.

CHAPTER 16

22:44—
A WHOLE NEW LIFE

When things are tough, often you can't imagine that a special gift could arrive. When it does, it's another reminder of the *give* and *receive* of life. There are no mistakes.

Given the events of the past year, I excused myself for the angst I felt in the lead-up to my grandson's birth. I just wanted to hear that everything was OK.

When it was finally confirmed that Danielle was in labour, I anxiously waited for the phone call saying they were on their way to hospital. When another twelve hours passed, with the process very slow, I shuddered at the memory of my own labour with Danielle.

Danielle had been in a posterior position, and these births were known to be long and painful—but until now, Danielle's baby had been nestled in the anterior position, which was supposedly best for childbirth. It didn't take long, however, to realize that he had changed position during the labour and was now heading sideways and backward. I tried to stay at home and wait for the news, but when she went into the next afternoon with little progress, the anxiety got too great.

Jordan's mother and I did what any mother would do given the situation. We went to the hospital to be around for support. I was so fortunate to share that time with her in the corridor waiting for updates. It somehow felt better to be close by. In fact, it turned out we were of some use, buying coffees and whatever was needed for Jordan, who had already endured so much.

At about nine thirty p.m., we decided to head out and have a quick bite and get a meal for Jordan. We arrived back at around ten fifteen. While Jordan sat outside and ate his dinner with his mum, I sat in with Danielle. By that stage, it seemed she was heading for a caesarean section. At eleven p.m., the obstetrician was to return to check the situation—so whichever way the baby would be born, it would happen before midnight.

Although Danielle had always wanted a natural birth, she ultimately wanted what was best for the baby, and of course her own safety. She was amazing—calm, clear, and strong.

I'm not sure what happened next, but I suddenly felt very faint and needed to sit down. I thought it best to leave the room at that point. I didn't want to embarrass myself. I sat for a while in the kitchen with Jordan and his mum before heading off to the bathroom. When I returned to the kitchen, his mum briefed me on a change in Danielle's status. Her heart rate was raised and the baby's was dropping, and she had felt pain in her back again. Jordan's mum felt excited by the prospect that the birth could in fact be natural, but somehow I felt more apprehensive.

In the next breath, people were running from everywhere to an area near Danielle's room. I couldn't look. I felt crippled by anxiety. Jordan's mum at first reassured me that the commotion was for room 15, until she put her glasses on and realized it was room 16—Danielle's room!

One thing's for sure, we knew the baby was coming. It was like the world stopped turning for I'm not sure how long. It was really only a few minutes, however, before a nurse came and told us that our grandson was born. It had been an unexpected and tricky entry, but he did well. He was born at 10:44 p.m. We managed to catch a glimpse of him before he was taken away for observation, and in that moment I felt a great relief and amazing joy.

Danielle was OK, apart from the shock of a rather quick and dramatic birth. It was wonderful that Steve had the energy and felt good enough to travel to the hospital to meet his grandson that night. At close to midnight, both families met their new addition—Sidney Hugo, a beautiful and healthy baby boy. We were so fortunate that we had the chance to be there at such a special moment.

It ended up that Wednesday, May 30, brought new beginnings. Even our front lawn that the landscaper had promised to replant for three years was completed that morning. Was this a significant turning point? All we had to hope for now was a new beginning for Steve.

Steve was due to have CT and PET scans on the Friday, June 1, so in time we would learn the status of his disease and his destiny for future chemotherapy or other treatments. I felt so strongly that his treatment was over. My body had started to go into wind-down mode, as if it had already lost the energy for the ongoing hospital routine. Steve had a similar feeling.

After having the scans, Steve was unable to see the baby for twenty-four hours because of the radiation levels. He was disappointed, but he knew it was best. There was nothing stopping me, though. I picked up Mum and my sister the next day so they could meet Sidney. It was so nice to be heading to the hospital together for a joyous occasion rather than what we had endured when Dad was critically ill.

Dad would have been so proud and excited over the baby. He was an extremely emotional man and would have cried tears of joy. I felt strongly that he was around.

When we arrived at the hospital, Sidney was nestled in his crib, and it was the first time I viewed the details of his birth. I stopped and stared at the time he was born: 22:44 p.m. There it was—the significant number, 22. I knew it would be around somewhere!

It didn't matter what anyone else thought, 22:44 gave me comfort and reassurance. Life felt perfect. Sidney was doing well, as were his mum and dad. They were in love with their new little man, and it was joyous to watch.

Now for the scan results for Steve.

CHAPTER 17

SCAN RESULTS

When you eliminate the anxiety associated with waiting, the time between events—even receiving test results—can be lived and not wasted.

I mentioned before about the waiting concept. It did weird things to the body and mind. Steve was anxious, and for a day or so after his PET scan, he really struggled.

His mood was difficult, and I thought how hard it would have been if he had been in that state throughout his whole treatment. Caring for someone who felt ongoing sadness and anxiety would have been so much more of a challenge. Fortunately, he snapped out of it quite quickly and accepted that nothing would speed up the time.

He realized anxiety wouldn't help anything, and it was best to enjoy what he had—and that was his grandson. He visited Sidney again in the hospital, and it brought him lots of happiness.

It was that day I began to feel my own body struggling. A deep tiredness nestled into my muscles, and before long soreness made its way to my throat. All I wanted was to enjoy some time with my grandson and be with my daughter, and guess what? Too sick to visit! So I spent the next day trying to stay clear of Steve and doing whatever I could to get well as fast as possible.

On Tuesday morning, I was concerned about how I was going to get Steve to his doctor's appointment. Breathing sickness into the car would nearly guarantee a spread of germs, but there was no way I would not be there for him. So off we went that morning, both wearing face masks that were given to us by our good friend and dentist to use if or when needed.

The masks meant I could get him to the hospital safely. He would then have his bloods and PICC line dressed, and I would only pop in quickly to the specialist's room for the appointment that was scheduled forty-five minutes later. I thought that would best, because the last thing I wanted to do was to spread any germs to other cancer patients getting treatment or blood.

We decided that while Steve had his bloods taken, I would kill some time and visit the salon for a small job that needed to be done. We felt we had a good plan. Needless to say, we looked a sight in the car—especially Steve with his beanie and mask! The endless amount of roadworks along the way meant lots of council workers had a good laugh, and I must admit, we did too.

The mood changed quite rapidly, however, when just before we reached the hospital, Steve received a text message from the wife of his client with NHL with whom we had shared time just a few weeks earlier. Sadly, he had passed away on Sunday.

We were both in shock, and emotion overcame us both. I felt heartbroken as I dropped Steve off. My sickness didn't even allow me to give him the hug and kiss I so wanted to. He walked off into the distance in sadness and uncertainty, and it felt awful. I drove off to the salon through a cloud of tears.

When I arrived at the salon, the staff also felt the sadness of the loss, as they had also just seen the client a few weeks prior. I fell into my son's arms, and it was such a beautiful comfort. He knew just what to say to help me settle down a bit. He had grown so much over the past months.

I once again felt I was in a whirlpool of emotion. I just wanted it all to be good for Steve, but in that moment nothing felt good. I headed straight back to the hospital because I wanted to be close by.

Travelling back to Kimberley House, I received a call from Steve telling me to get there straight away. His voice sounded OK. I felt uplifted. What was happening? He wasn't due to see the doctor for another half hour, so what was the urgency?

Steve proceeded to inform me that the doctor had already told him the news: he was in remission! He could have his PICC line taken out, not cleaned up, because he wouldn't be having any more treatment. My emotion shifted to the other end of the scale—elation!

When I arrived at Kimberley House, the specialist spoke to us and explained the scan results and his intention for the next few months. Steve had negative status on the PET scan and CT scan, and given those results, the doctor didn't feel another two cycles of the chemotherapy would have been in Steve's favour. Given the severity of the infection and response to the Part B, he wouldn't even attempt it. He felt there was no need anyway.

Steve would have a blood test in four weeks, another CT scan in three months, and from then on every six months he would have a monthly dose of Mabthera—the monoclonal therapy he had been having prior to his treatments. Mabthera was known to help keep mantle cell NHL in remission, so it was great that he was able to tolerate that therapy.

Basically, the specialist instructed us to keep up with the special food requirements and immune protection for a few more weeks, but other than that, get back to as normal a life as possible. We knew what was ahead, and it sounded very manageable. What a weird feeling!

It took a while to actually register. After our earlier news and the fact that I felt really bad with a cold, it didn't feel real. I drove home with the mask on while Steve started making phone calls to the kids and family informing them of the good news.

By the time we arrived home, it was like my body had surrendered to sickness. It seemed it was my time to be nurtured. It didn't matter how much I wanted to be well to see my grandson—it wasn't going to happen. My place was in bed. I wasn't going to help or care for anyone or anything but myself.

Ironic, I thought. On the day of Steve's remission, he was caring for me, with lemon drinks and hot soup. The timing couldn't have been better. He felt good. He hadn't had chemo for a few weeks, so his energy was up and mentally was on a high.

He decided he would visit his grandchild, so he did it without me. The tide had turned, and there I was in bed while he was out. How beautiful. He loved every minute of it.

After a few days recovering at Maslins Beach, I felt much better.

CHAPTER 18

MOVING ON

When the challenge is over, it is over. When you take the learning from it and get on with life, life becomes so much richer.

We hadn't thought too much about what would happen after chemotherapy because we didn't really know what was ahead. We had spoken about the celebrations we would have with the many special people in our lives who supported us throughout. Steve talked about a return to work on a part-time basis and perhaps in a different capacity—salon coordinator/receptionist.

But when the time arrived, I think we both weren't really prepared to get back to life. There had always been that looming cloud of stem-cell transplant and talk that mantle cell NHL was difficult to treat. So it was now about how life would look given what we had been through.

Steve was eager to get back to work and life as usual, but the doctor had fortunately recommended part-time only. I just wanted to keep the lessons I learned close. I remembered when I returned to work after time away for my own healing. I needed a self-check every now and again for the old patterns that somehow crept back in. I wondered how this would be for Steve. I hoped it wasn't going back but rather going *to*, which was a new look and feel.

That applied to me too. What was I going *to*, rather than going back to? What did my future look like? Once again, this time brought me the chance to create something new, something that when I was too busy I rarely had the time or ability for.

I started to shape my life to include all the pleasure and joy of being a grandmother. I started to address all of the ailments that arrived during the past ten months, with visits to the physio, doctor, and acupuncturist along with gardening and exercise. I didn't do what I would have done in my younger years—push through and get straight back to a busy work schedule and life—because there was a part of me that knew better. I felt I'd been kinder to myself.

I stopped working at TAFE (I felt that chapter of my life was over, for the time being anyway) and transitioned slowly back to working with people. And who knows where to from there? But change and dealing with the unknown was something I was slowly getting used to—and would continue to, because there would always be the chance of others things flying in from any direction.

I felt that with what we experienced, we learned how to better enjoy and embrace what fear would normally have destroyed. It was time to enjoy the fact that we came through it alive. It was time for family, celebrations, a well husband, and many opportunities.

I started a short online writing course, grew my own veggies and herbs, learned better Italian, and volunteered in a caring role. Steve took an online photography course (to capture our beautiful sunsets) and started playing in a band and engaging with what he loved.

For the future, our plans are to find the hidden gifts in each day and not get swallowed up by nonsense.

CHAPTER 19

A QUICK SUMMARY OF THINGS THAT HAD MEANING IN OUR LIVES

1. When something doesn't feel right, pay attention and take note of what that could mean.
2. Don't make excuses for an ongoing unwell feeling or health symptom. Get checked.
3. When unusual events occur over and again, a message might be intended.
4. Being there for a loved one during an illness is a great gift.
5. Allow your emotions to flow freely and unconditionally when they arrive.
6. Give love to your loved ones until the very end.
7. Do what you can while you can.
8. In a blink, everything changes.
9. No matter how you got through a challenge—you did it!
10. Take note of the coincidences—they often offer something intriguing.
11. Sad and happy can coexist in your life.
12. Find something to be grateful for in any situation.
13. The sooner you adjust to your new situation, the sooner you can make the best out of it.

14. Let go of what you don't need when you are faced with a new challenge.
15. When things get complex, find a simple approach.
16. Being fit and in good health does not exclude you from illness, so watch with vigilance.
17. However you decide to manage your health condition, do it with positivity and certainty.
18. To see more clearly, sometimes you have to step outside of yourself and watch.
19. Rather than find the outer blame for something *they* did, *they* were, find the inner vulnerability—*I* did, *I* was—and resolve that because you can.
20. Everyone deals with adversity differently, and that's OK.
21. You can change the momentum of negativity when you stop feeding it.
22. Inspiration from the stories of others is powerful.
23. Whatever your decision, respect and value it, because that was the winner at the time.
24. When you're open to see magic, you'll see magic.
25. You are never on your own. Others are around and play a role, even if you can't see it.
26. You can choose to have positive and helpful people around you.
27. When you're still enough, you can find other points of view.
28. Don't wait for perfect to arrive. Perfect is already there.
29. Be ready to catch opportunities before you walk past them.
30. It is up to you to go for things in your life.
31. Be ready to change things up until you find what you seek.
32. It's not others you have to worry about letting down, it's yourself.
33. When you've learned some lessons, you can bring so much to others.
34. When something no longer feels right, change it.
35. When you're in the fast lane, it just keeps getting faster.
36. When someone gives you feedback about what they see in you, check it out. It might be useful.

37. No matter how busy you are, make the time for your personal well-being.

38. You can create space in your life when you choose not to be in business that doesn't belong to you.

39. No matter how much you think you've got it, there's always more to it.

40. Stress in any aspect—physical, mind, or spirit—produces deep cellular disharmony in the body.

41. Even when you think things can't get worse, they can.

42. Even when you think things can't get better, they can.

43. When you're not waiting, you're just in what you're in.

44. Animals are a wonderful comfort during times of illness.

45. Sometimes it's better to know what you're in for rather than be in an unknown.

46. Sometimes it's better not to know.

47. Fighting battles that have no real relevance in the big picture may not be worth the energy.

48. Make it your business to know what is being done to your body. Have a say.

49. No one knows your body better than you.

50. The body can heal itself.

51. Don't wait for things to get worse—take action and get on top of things.

52. Know what you love to do and bring a bit of that to every day.

53. Friends and family feel our pain. We are connected, even if just by thought.

54. No matter how hard it might be to make contact with those who are struggling, it's so worth it.

55. If you can do just one act of kindness for someone who is in need, it can make their day.

56. It's OK to accept help—anything to make the process easier.

57. It's OK to ask for help—it's a sign of strength.

58. There are people in your network who would love to help. Allow them to do what fuels their heart.

59. It's OK to throw away some of your old beliefs that don't work for you anymore.

60. You can contribute to your own healing when you find balance and harmony in your body.

61. When you feel bad, do what you need to feel better.

62. When you feel good, just appreciate it.

63. Ups and downs will always be.

64. No matter what your age or stage, taking care of you is most important.

65. Let things out rather than burying them where they'll fester and grow.

66. Whether you give or receive, do it unconditionally.

67. No matter how much you try to force things to be, there is usually a bigger force driving it.

68. Watch out for words and actions that scare and worry you. Don't give them power.

69. No matter what your job, paid or voluntary, approach it with your love and heart.

70. Good food can be a great comfort.

71. Allow the beauty of nature to be with you.

72. Talk and walk what's in your heart.

73. When you share a challenging experience with someone you love, your relationship can be strengthened.

74. When you give your time with love, it feels amazing.

75. Focus on what you can do, not what you can't.

76. It's useful to make and break routines as quickly as needed.

77. The sooner you can gain independence and take responsibility, go for it.

78. Let go of nonsense—the stuff that is more like gossip and unnecessary.

79. Know when you're all right and when you're not.

80. Take ownership of your choices. You have personal power.

81. Enjoy the challenge of learning new life skills.

82. The only thing for sure is that nothing is for sure.

83. Have trust that things unfold just as they are meant to.

84. Wish or pray for what is best, and have faith that the outcome is just that.

85. Have gratitude for the smallest of things. It feels good.

86. What appears small and insignificant can in fact be life-changing.

87. Just around the corner lies something to lighten your heart. Hang in there.

88. When things change, take the opportunity to also change.

89. Celebrate life with those who are important to you.

90. When something ends, something else begins.

PART

FIND THE WAY

In 2006, I found a different way through the maze of life's complexities. The experience pushed me to ask questions, look at the hard days from new eyes, and discover some key things about me and life. It really helped me face Steve's cancer with love, hope, and strength. It helped me cope with that and so much more. I'd like to share what I discovered, and I hope that it will bring a ray of light to whatever challenges you have had or are currently facing. It starts with the trail of thought that led me to explore. It follows with some key findings that surfaced along the way.

CHAPTER **20**

THE START OF
MY SEARCH

On the night I was diagnosed with cancer, as I lay alone before I drifted into sleep, I felt a rush of knowing, of connection, of amazement, of hope, of appreciation for life. A familiarity—something so powerful. It happened in a flash of a moment. I wanted to explore more.

This feeling was the start of a search into something that took me to where I had never ventured before. I became excited by this sense of approaching life with curiosity and vigour. In time, I slowed down to observe, take in detail, remove previous patterns, and seek new ways. A new world seemed to open.

During my recovery from cancer surgery, these realizations transformed *how* I went about my life, and slowly I could identify *what* I wanted for my life.

On my quest to find and embrace the health and comfort I was seeking, it became increasingly clear that there was no silver bullet. In the past, I looked for the answer—the something to fix. I discovered there was no one treatment, one food, one natural approach, one therapist, or one cure out there.

I realized my body was constantly under threat from a broad range of stress: emotional, relationship, personal, environmental, physical, and nutritional. All of these were potentially moving me against what I was seeking.

I came to see it was me—the only one constant in among it all—who held the key to how stress or any illness played out in me. I took the time to observe what seemed to be responsible for any discomfort and unrest. It wasn't easy at first. Slowly, as I peeled away the hidden traps that menaced my days, I realized I had some powerful influence to change things.

I gained more confidence to choose and act from my improved ability to know what my body, mind, and spirit needed. This helped lessen the confusion and uncertainty I faced from many external opinions, challenges, and "information abundance" that previously engulfed me.

Along the way, I discovered so much more. I found gifts in moments that I had never seen before. Part 2 of this book highlights my findings.

I didn't have to climb a mountain or swim an ocean to discover them. I used day-to-day events to discover the things that changed my life.

You can do the same. You are the key. You are the best person to refer to along the path. Listen to your body, mind, and spirit. They will let you know loud and clear if there is something to look at or change up, Enjoy being your best guide.

In the pages that follow, I'll take you down the trail of thought that got me started, and share the key findings from my personal observations. You'll also enjoy a splash of quick tips and inspirational words from others along the way.

CHAPTER 21

MY TRAIL OF THOUGHT

We are on the universal timeline.

After the powerful moment I glimpsed the night of my cancer diagnosis, I was open and willing to seek new perspectives. I entered a world of reading and exploring, and before long I became excitedly passionate about what I discovered.

Presence on Earth

> **We are living this time on earth—it is ours to influence and offer. We are alive, and while we are, we have the chance to embrace it fully. What are we waiting for?**

In the past, I had lived with great opportunities in a wonderful world, but my life and personal struggles limited my potential to fully appreciate them. During my recovery from cancer, I came to see things differently.

Somehow, the concept that we were living at this time seemed absolutely miraculous. When I considered all that had been in the past, it was an amazing concept that this time on earth was now for me. I saw that everyone in history had had their time to affect the future and now it was mine to influence.

I began to think of my time on earth differently. My time was important and significant. I had a responsibility for my own actions to help ensure there was a future. I had an overwhelming urge to live. I had an overwhelming urge to protect humans and the earth.

I felt quite desperate to do something, but I had no idea what. How could I really help? What was I meant to be doing?

I explored many types of books, some of which were about quantum physics and microbiology. The books I read included *The Body Quantum: The New Physics of Body, Mind, and Health* by Fred Alan Wolf and *Quantum Healing: Exploring the Frontiers of Mind/Body Medicine* by Deepak Chopra, MD.

They had me thinking more about the concept of creation. Reading them made me realize it was people who had the power to create both problems and magnificence. And that was how I found my answer.

I wanted to help by being constructive rather than destructive, healthy rather than unhealthy, contributing rather than inhibiting. It led me to become more conscious of the many ways to do this— including saving water, recycling, composting, and nurturing and caring for people (including myself)—but I found it was actually very challenging.

So what got in the way?

*Twenty years from now, you will be more disappointed by the things you didn't do than by the ones you did do.—**Mark Twain***

> **What is something you won't want to leave earth without having experienced?**

Quality Human Form

Well-being, good health, and quality choices are something we focus on, but they are often short-lived and hard to sustain. When we discover the greater relevance—that is, the survival of the human race—our purpose becomes bigger than our own needs and a much greater motivation.

I began to see the value and significance of growing as a person. This growth was very different from the constructed strategies used in the "personal development" I had tried in the past. Back then, I saw development as something to do for the sake of having a good life, improving my position at work, and achieving personal goals.

But now, I knew there was something much more meaningful at stake. I was working for something bigger, creating a future life for myself and for the generations ahead, to ensure a capacity for quality decisions, relationships, and actions that would nurture and respect the human race and earth.

I began to feel the importance of lifting the lid on my closed-minded approaches. I began to see the value of what I was about to embark on.

It would be through much personal work that this vision for my future would be unleashed.

I noticed how I had fallen victim to my patterns. I would have to face them if I had any chance of living with more purpose. It wasn't going to be easy!

It took me back to the area of health and fitness, where I had spent most of my working life. There was so much scientific evidence and information about what was good for our bodies, but despite people wanting to live longer and feel and look better, they were still struggling to maintain quality practices. Ironically, our bodies were all we had to take us through our life, but even knowing that, we often found it hard to do what was best for them.

Wanting and knowing something did not necessarily mean it would happen. When I wanted to cut out sugar, knowing I felt better when I did, I still didn't do it. Why was that so? I became more and more curious about what happened in the gap between good intentions and action.

The gap appeared regularly in my life. I knew what was best for me—I did have a choice—but my will and good intentions were often threatened. One of those threats I became very familiar with was the mindless way I'd come to live my life. Often I acted without even realising or knowing why I chose to do the very things that were against what I really wanted.

I yelled when I wanted to love. I binned instead of composting. I ignored messages about destructive and dangerous chemicals. I ate food that disagreed with my body. I wasted water when I knew of the shortage. I chose fried over grilled. I avoided the stretches that helped the pain in my body. The list goes on. Why was I doing these things?

What was so hard about living out what I wanted? How did I move so easily off course? What didn't I get?

If you want to make your dreams come true,
the first thing you have to do is wake up.—**J. M. Power**

> **Admit to what within**
> **may be stopping you.**

Pain Avoidance

When we accept that pain and discomfort have a purpose, we no longer need to fear them. Without fear and avoidance of pain, we can embrace what arrives. We can grow and become what our heart desires.

I realized that in my world, there was a range of obvious and not-so-obvious distractions and difficulties that steered me off track. I wanted to find a way to maintain actions of good intention in the face of the very things I used, either consciously or unconsciously, as excuses: difficulties, hardship, unfairness, pain, ignorance, sadness, negative emotions, confusion. *I'd rather be elsewhere, doing something different. It was easier not to. It took too much effort. I didn't know how. I couldn't be bothered. I liked my way.*

I began to identify the essence of my lifetime: avoiding discomfort! I generally equated discomfort and difficulty with failure, problems, or personal deficiency. Somehow, it was as though I'd come to expect life to be smooth, easy, and just right for me. And with that mindset, I didn't expect tough things to happen to me.

To me?

When things that felt uncomfortable arrived, they felt personal. When I got cancer, it felt so personal. It happened to me! It wasn't meant to happen to me! But when I looked outside of myself, I could see that cancer was happening in other people's lives as well. It wasn't just me.

I had a breakthrough. Things weren't happening *to me*, they were just happening as a natural evolution of all that was possible in today's world. I was living in times in which cancer existed, relationships were breaking down, financial struggles were common, people struggled to care for others, and computers were leading the way. It was all possible, and it was inevitable that these things would happen—the feel-good and the not-so-feel-good.

If we loved, we also felt pain. If we won, we also lost. If we prospered, we also suffered. Pain couldn't be avoided if we chose to live life and feel the joys that it brought. I came to see it was more about what to do with and how to be with pain—to make the most of things and not let pain destroy the good it opened the door for.

> *Clouds come floating into my life, no longer to*
> *carry rain or usher storm, but to add colour to*
> *my sunset sky.*—**Rabindranath Tagore**

Leave "to me" out of it!

Inherited and Universal Influence

We can't take all the credit and we can't take all the responsibility for things that happen. The incidentals that arrive by virtue of evolution play a role in what happens. We are, however, part of the incidental, so in that we have some say. When we discover the part we do have a say in, we are best positioned to influence.

My here-and-now situation was a culmination of factors that had their own influence—many of them far beyond my mortal control or ability to have any say over. I was beginning to see how history and the great universe played its part in how things had evolved in my own life.

- **My ancestors** had a role and influence in my existence. Their features were inherent in my own physical body; their choices in partners, vocation, and lifestyle all contributed to a slice of the inevitable in me. They left a legacy of some things in credit and some in debt—nice teeth and an inherited genetic weakness for cancer.
- **Inbuilt ideologies** of institutions, governments, religions, organizations, communities, policies, rules, customs, and laws also had impact.
- **Physical and natural laws** played a role in some of the most valuable and amazing creations, inventions, and technologies. They also explained the how and why of disasters and tragedies.

When I began to appreciate the magnitude of these external influences, I was more able to see it wasn't all personal. It began to change what I was in battle over. Rather than fight the things that arrived, I fought the way I dealt with them. That was my road ahead—to learn how to influence, cope, grow, and thrive in the face of what came my way.

The pessimist sees difficulty in every opportunity. The optimist sees the opportunity in every difficulty.—**Winston Churchill**

> **Acknowledge any of
> your challenges that
> have led to success.**

Breaking Free

When we break free from the mindless state of doing what we've always done, we create other choices and possibilities. With choice, we are no longer trapped.

Somehow, while alone in my body and mind, I didn't feel so alone. The past was entwined in me and I was entwined with others in the creation of my day and the future. I felt I was a live character on an unfolding live stage with a definite purpose, and the rest of the world was on that stage with me.

I got excited when I felt I had power within to influence rather than feel it was hopeless. I began to see how that was already being played out on the world's big stage in things like election results with Barack Obama, health choices and natural alternatives, work practices and flexible arrangements, and the list goes on. People were breaking free from the ingrained models they had come to see as "just the way it is."

There was definitely a change happening, and I wanted to be part of it. My biggest battle, and one I felt was significant for others too, was the gap that kept arising in my day-to-day between what I believed I wanted and what I actually did. I came to see that the gap was the unknown in me—the unknown of what I needed from myself to be and do what my heart and spirit were beginning to discover.

> *There are two primary choices in life: to accept*
> *conditions as they exist, or accept the responsibility*
> *for changing them.*—**Dr. Denis Waitley**

> **Discover, create, and live**
> **your own life script.**

Face the Enemy

Often, the biggest enemy is hidden in ourselves. When we face the enemy that has been holding us back from what we desire and hope for, we have the opportunity to influence.

It was time to face the unknown in me. As I unveiled many of the approaches and patterns I lived by to achieve a pain-free life, I soon came to see the characteristics of my behaviours and thoughts. Although they weren't visible or obvious at first glimpse, I recognized the subtle traces of manipulation, control, blame, guilt, resentment, intimidation, hedonism, punishment, fear, judgement, and evaluation.

Oooh! It sounds harsh, but that's how it was for me—and probably for most of us.

When I became more aware, I could find the things I disliked in others and in myself. I heard others state their dislikes, but I could see those very things in them. I could see it in them, but they couldn't. They could see it in me, but I couldn't.

I'd assured myself that my reality was the one I told myself and saw in myself, not the others things that I didn't like or want to see. When I discovered I was responsible for many of those things, I was horrified! In the past, I would have vehemently denied it, but I was beginning to see how traces of those undesirable traits played out in me. They had helped me survive—to communicate and achieve things—just as they had for others. It was not, however, what I wanted for my life anymore, so I had a lot of work to do.

I began to change the game of hide to seek. I wasn't going to let fear, denial, or unawareness get in my way anymore. I was on the lookout for them. I was determined to catch myself out—not to punish myself for what I found, but to break the patterns I had unconsciously developed. I was entering the gap.

I felt the relief and lightness of allowing myself to bring these findings to the surface. I trusted I would be OK because it was my true intention and purpose to make a difference with how I lived my life.

But in reality, it was still painful on many levels. The old saying "the truth hurts"—that's what I found as I walked this path. What I saw in myself hurt. What I saw in others hurt. I was often disappointed, shocked, and frustrated. There was still pain on this journey, albeit for different reasons.

As with any pain, this one had a natural cycle to move through. It felt much like the grief cycle. At first there was denial; then came the pain of guilt, anger, and sadness, even depression and loneliness. But then there was a turnaround. And in that turnaround, I found acceptance and gratitude. I was grateful that I had started a process to explore the hidden in me, expand my conscious awareness, and grow in my ability to live better and to the best of my potential.

I've missed more than 9,000 shots in my career.
I've lost almost 300 games. Twenty-six times, I've been

trusted to take the game winning shot and missed. I've failed over and over and over again in my life. I can accept failure, everyone fails at something. But I can't accept not trying. And that is why I succeed.—**Michael Jordan**

Admit a silent enemy in you.

Find Within

To find what we want "out there" is to firstly find it in ourselves.

I realized the face of the enemy was my own inability to live out conscious quality choices in an ever-changing world. The world was in need of some tender love and care. If I was to contribute to that, I wanted to know how.

I came to see that if peace, love, justice, and nurture were what I wanted from situations, people, and the world, then I had to find them in myself. I was a person existing in that world. I was one of the ones I was looking to find it from. Unless we each found those things in ourselves, we would never be able to find them. It strengthened my quest to continue. "Out there" was an illusion that had kept me off track from looking within.

You must be the change you want to see in the world.—**Mahatma Ghandi**

Find what you seek in you.

A Turning Point

We have the ability to change the energy flow of what we are involved in. We are intelligent enough at this point in our evolution to challenge some of our mind's limited creations.

I began to realize that in this time in our history, we had the potential—because of our intellectual capacity—to view things outside of the square and outside of ourselves. It was evident in many of the stories I read about people's personal journeys. The places they ventured and the things they endured took them into their hearts and minds to discover what they couldn't see before.

Some had faced great trials, either from adventures in the wild, feats on the sporting field, inconceivable tragedies or circumstances, or chronic pain and illness (Bear Grylls, Lance Armstrong, Anita Moorjani, and Eben Alexander, to name a few), and thankfully, they told their stories. I realized despite the difference in their circumstances, their message was basically the same. It was the challenges that had them look at themselves and discover what lay within. And within, they arrived at a common finding.

That finding was simple, yet it hit me like a sledgehammer: we were all in times of challenge! Those challenges might not be like the ones described in the books—a trek in the wild, an incident with cancer, a debilitating accident, a tragic event—but they were challenges nonetheless. I was facing them, and many others were facing them too. I had a strong feeling we were all meant to discover the same truth.

I felt that we were in a significant time in our history. We had an important job, and that was to discover ourselves. The importance of the quote "Know thyself" by Socrates made more sense to me than ever.

It may help you to read, as I did, *Dying to Be Me: My Journey from Cancer, to Near Death, to True Healing* by Anita Moorjani, *Proof of Heaven: A Neurosurgeon's Journey into the Afterlife* by Dr. Eben Alexander, *It's Not About the Bike: My Journey Back to Life* by Lance Armstrong, or *The Kid Who Climbed Everest: The Incredible Story of a 23-Year-Old's Summit of Mt. Everest* by Bear Grylls.

The most difficult thing in life is to know yourself.—**Thales**

> **Take the challenge to
> get to know you.**

Truth

**When in our truth, we need to do nothing more than
live from it. We will talk less and listen more.**

Ultimately, the only person harmed or fooled by not facing my truth was me. I was bemused by the tricks I used to avoid facing stuff. It was so easy to tell a story about what I did to convince myself and others. I began to feel the difference between words and the truth. Words tried to explain, construct, defend, and prove, whereas the truth just *was*.

I somehow didn't need to do or prove or show anything about that. It was purely the beginning of a deeper awareness of myself, and I was grateful for that. The truth felt silent and releasing. And in that truth, I could love and respect others more deeply in spite of everything. I could be more open to listen to the perspectives of others, and that helped shape something new in me.

I became more equipped to change things up when I heard my own noise (proving and convincing). I'd step off my platform and silence myself. From that place, I could find what I couldn't see before. And that was all I needed to do.

The pure and simple truth is rarely pure and never simple.—**Oscar Wilde**

> **Admit one thing to yourself about yourself that you've never let on.**

A New Relationship with Yourself

When we lighten up about how we see others, we can lighten up about what we find in ourselves. From that space, we can admit things more openly, and that is our gateway to growth.

I began to have a different relationship with myself. I began to have fun with what I discovered and not feel compelled to convince myself of all the bad things about me and all the problems with the world.

I also felt I was getting stronger at accepting feedback from others. Criticisms and judgement became opportunities to look at myself again. They didn't feel so threatening.

It became OK to look at what at first seemed to be differences between me and others. In time, I saw they were in fact similarities. I became more grateful and appreciative of others in my world. Everyone offered me something to observe and question about myself.

This helped me stop being so hard on myself. I was prepared for what I might find. For the first time, I felt non-judgemental and could love and accept myself for who I was. I didn't need to uphold self-imposed standards to try to be perfect and do things perfectly.

I was beginning to feel different about myself; a confidence to just be me was emerging. For the first time, I had found a way to do that. It changed how I sat in relation to everything else, and life felt different. It helped me be not so hard on others, too. Being non-judgemental and accepting was a pathway to better relationships and a better way of life.

Men occasionally stumble over the truth, but most of them pick themselves up and hurry off as if nothing happened.—**Winston Churchill**

> **Laugh about something quirky in you.**

Self, Others, Earth

When we honour ourselves first, we are in a position to give our best to others.

To know myself was to face the facade of patterns and ways that had accompanied me throughout my life. Truth was my destination—I wanted to get there, not avoid it or become damaged or hurt along the way. It was very important to nurture and be kind to myself. Being kind, however, did not mean falling into the traps or tricks of pleasure-seeking and pain-avoidance—those would only lead me back to my old cycle. That went against all I was striving for.

To stay true, I used a simple framework called SOE, which stands for Self Others Earth. SOE helped guide my choices and actions. When in doubt or just for a check, I would ask myself: *Is this nurturing and enhancing my quality self (my body, mind, and spirit)? Will this in some way bring something positive or useful and nurturing to the overall well-being and survival of others and the earth?*

It was important to always honour myself in the equation.

> *Love yourself first and everything else falls into line. You really have to love yourself to get anything done in this world.*—**Lucille Ball**

Feel how good it is to love yourself. Notice how that helps others.

Love

When we feel love, we can love others.

I began to understand what had happened on the night of my diagnosis. I had glimpsed love. It was a love so powerful, it catapulted me into this trail of thought where I felt very strong compassion, love, and empathy. I had glimpsed it before. It somehow felt vaguely familiar. I remembered it from a long time ago, back when I was a very young girl.

I felt grateful to have experienced that moment of love, but perplexed at how and why I had travelled so far from it in my life. I realized I had learned many ways to meet my needs and wants that had taken me away from my most powerful guide—the truth of love. No matter what I or anyone else needed or wanted, it was only love that provided the way.

If I wanted peace, it was love that led to an acceptance that brought peace.

If I wanted health, it was love that strengthened my determination and willpower for better choices.

If I wanted life, it was love that brought me the courage to live it.

If I wanted security, it was love that brought comfort that felt secure.

If I wanted adventure, it was love that helped build my confidence to attempt things.

If I wanted to love, I had to allow love that brought it.

When I injected love into my life, love brought the truth to my needs, and that truth lit the path for my actions. I came to see that if I used anything other than love—logic, *shoulds*, nonsense stories, ego, memories—it eventually led to worry, confusion, win/lose thinking, disappointment, fear, and more.

I came to see that love, the only constant truth, had been there since the beginning of time. It had been documented over and again. I felt that it was in getting to know myself that I would find my heart and live by that truth. To find my heart, I had to discover what was blocking it.

True love begins when nothing is looked for in
return. —**Antoine de Saint-Exupery**

> **Look into the eyes of
> someone or something you
> truly love and feel love.**

 Before moving on, you may want to:

- Allow the essence of this message to resonate within you.
- Feel gratitude and wonder for your life.
- Close your eyes and look down the path of all that existed in the past and all that will be in the future.
- Enjoy what your presence means to you right now.
- Hold any magic feelings close to you.

CHAPTER 22

KEY FINDING 1– KNOW YOUR TRAPS

I began to nab the root cause of the traps that unsettled my body, mind, and spirit. I sought ways to lessen the disruptive impact they had on me.

"Busy Do" Way of Life

When we are too busy to notice what we are actually doing, we are too busy!

At the beginning of my recovery, in my initial trail of thought, I did a lot of pondering on how amazing life was. That alone kept me going. It was as though the usual things that upset or worried me had lost their power.

As time went on, however, and I re-entered the maze of life, life itself seemed to pull me away from that. What was happening? Where did it go? What changed? I began to take a closer look to understand what was going on.

I found that the complexities of life had a bigger influence than I realized. I recognized how they had affected me before my illness and were steering me off course again. I was determined not to fall into the same traps.

Before my illness in 2006, I had become very consumed by a "busy do" way of life, constantly thinking, worrying, stressing, planning, learning, creating, body-working, playing, fixing, building, and purchasing. I realized the impact and cost of accomplishing the many things that needed doing was my connection to all the other things in between.

While I was busy doing all the things I thought I needed to do for my family, I neglected the most important thing, and that was giving my time and undivided attention. I wondered what I modelled to my family in terms of appreciation of the simple things. I wondered if they were yearning for me to slow down and enjoy more of their music, movies, friends, and conversation.

Fortunately, I had other family members and good friends who filled those spaces. My children received quality guidance and support from a loving external network. I thought how challenging busy lives were for those bringing up children in today's world when such external networks weren't always available. Too often, social media and technology filled those gaps.

In an overly busy world, it was easy to miss the signs: less communication, greater distance, greater and more complex and intense problems. When busyness crept back into my life, my challenge was stop, reduce, connect, and communicate. It was in the simplest of situations that I lived that out. Rather than cooking and listening and conversing, I stopped and listened and conversed. I left the cleaning until morning. I spent more time getting to the bottom of issues and took more time to explore what was happening for others. It's amazing how different listening felt when I wasn't busy doing other things.

Beware the barrenness of a busy life.—**Socrates**

> **Remove one "busy"**
> **thing from your day.**

The *Should* Story

When we live by *should* we are contained by the boundaries we set.

Conditioning over the years on how things *should* be had influenced my life experience. I *should* get a good job, become a professional, do more, get married, work harder, learn more, achieve better results, buy a new home, get a better car, start a family, give my children the best, save for the future. My husband *should* . . . my son *should* . . . my daughter *should* . . . . The *shoulds* I had in my life were the subtle expectations, rules, and habits that I felt compelled to strive for and uphold. The roller-coaster ride had me very busy, quite often hardly knowing how it really sat with my values or wants.

Many of the *shoulds* I followed had stifled the natural flow of life. I saw this with the *should* story we had with our son. He *should* go to university. He was smart, so he *should* be doing something more with his life. He was good at music, so he *should* be doing something with his music.

When he dropped out of university, I'm sure he sensed our disappointment—it was certainly no secret. As we began to let go of the *shoulds*, we watched him work in cafes and saw his charismatic character unfold. We realized studying in a formal institution was not him. His spirit needed something different to feel alive.

It was in his own time that he found his way to the more creative work of hairdressing. This path was powerful for him and for Steve during his time of sickness. I learned a great lesson to allow and watch magic unfold. That's what it felt like when my son was in place to take on the load for Steve during his long recovery. My son taught me about having courage and confidence to defy the imposed *shoulds* and follow your own internal guide.

I came to see how easily I formed *shoulds* in my life. When Dad died, I established a ritual of lighting a candle every day out of respect. I even termed it a ritual to convince myself it was a very important thing to do. It was only a few weeks after Dad's death that we discovered Steve's cancer, and the ritual fell by the wayside.

At first I felt bad that I'd abandoned the ritual so quickly. I fortunately woke up to the fact that I had tried to associate the ritual with the magnitude of my respect and love for my dad. When I came to my senses, I realized I had created a *should* ritual—and that didn't indicate my love for him. My love was in my heart, and I could connect with him at any time, on any day. I didn't need the ritual.

The sooner I became aware of a *should*, the sooner I could declare an equal and opposite *shouldn't* and vice versa. I began to look for an opposite reason to any of those statements that arrived in my talk. This helped me to break free from the guilt feelings that underlined the *should*.

For example, one day when I caught myself thinking *I should walk the dogs* even though I didn't feel like going out, I used the reverse approach, and it became *I shouldn't walk the dogs*. I found a reason why—it was quite warm and might have been uncomfortable for their paws. With that reasoning, the guilt and bad feelings attached to not walking them left me. I felt much lighter and less burdened. That night after dinner, Steve and I walked the dogs together, and it felt good for all of us.

The *should* ritual gave me the space to ask myself what I really wanted, given the current climate of things. Somehow when I approached it this way—without guilt attached—I was able to move toward what I wanted. What's more, I did it in a far more nurturing way. It seemed to give me the permission to choose.

I found that *shoulds* were not an effective guide for me. My guide was within me, and that's where I began to turn. It saved me when I was overdoing things, doing things for the wrong reasons, doing things to my own detriment, doing things at inappropriate times, and doing things without knowing why. Challenging those *shoulds* gave me permission to break free and work with things around me in a more effective way.

> *A man should look for what is, and not for what he thinks should be.*—**Albert Einstein**

If there were no rules, *shoulds*, shouldn'ts, or *have tos* right now, what would you be doing?

Before moving on, you may want to:

- Think about the *shoulds* in your own life.
- Where have they come from?
- What would you choose if there were no *shoulds*?

Hidden Intentions

When we are open to look at ourselves and the intentions behind what we do, say, and think, we are more likely to catch a glimpse of the truth.

Taking an honest look at my intentions was another path to discovering my truth. Only when I was fully aware of the intent behind my talk and walk could I have any influence on it. I came to see how easy it was to make a statement about my motives and then believe those words without question.

- "I'm doing this for my family."
- "I'm doing this to get us ahead."
- "I'm doing this because it's important to me."
- "I'm doing this because I care about you."

Powerful statements like these made me believe the message. My perceived intentions kept me out of touch during the very busy times in my life.

I decided to question and look more closely at the reasons behind my actions. Was I doing it for the family, or for my own personal gain, or because I really loved the buzz from work, or because I was scared if I didn't, or because I wanted something better for myself? This challenge helped me glimpse a more subtle ulterior motive. It was the beginning of admitting something in myself that didn't feel comfortable or nice.

I listened in my everyday situations to my talk—the reasons I gave for my actions and thoughts. I challenged myself, asking *Could it be something else like . . .*? In so doing, I found more and more hidden things that made me feel I'd been living a deluded life.

When I said I couldn't do something for someone because I had other things to do, I found a hidden element of *can't be bothered.*

When I got upset over not being heard or respected, I found a hidden element of wanting my own way.

When I stood up for what was best, I found a hidden element of proving myself right.

When I had an opinion to share, I found a hidden element of wanting to win.

The point to facing up to things in this way was to see the side of me I couldn't see before. I had always found these subtleties and undertones of inconsistent intention easy to feel and see in others but nearly impossible to see in myself. When I finally did see those subtleties in my own behaviour, I began to hear feedback and perspectives that I once would have denied.

When my intention was for the good but it wasn't received that way, I had something to explore. What went wrong in the translation? It helped me once again identify some of my communication patterns and approaches that were inhibiting things. Not to say others didn't have a role in it all. But others were not *me*, and I couldn't make others change or do whatever. That was for them to decide. My mission was just to do my part in being constructive, not destructive.

I realized my personal work had begun to shake up lots of stuff, and it was very challenging. Humour was a useful approach to some scary things I discovered. It kept things light, and that helped me face the new realizations. With a light approach, I could admit to more, and that enabled a more honest version of me to emerge.

Intentions count in your actions.—**Abu Bakr**

**Are you seeing from
murky water?**

Abundance, Technology, and Information

We can receive the benefit of expansion and abundance when we know how to live with them.

In addition to "busy do," *shoulds*, and intention traps, I began to recognize the abundance trap. There was an abundance of everything: information, products, services, and anything else in between. On the one hand, abundance was a great thing in my life—I had lots of options to choose from and they were readily available. On the other hand, abundance often left me confused. Too many choices! And that made it time-consuming to decide.

With all the technology of the computer age, information was now available at the touch of a finger. But it wasn't actually that easy. Hidden in what was meant to be simple were so many complexities. What was valid and what was a scam? What should I listen to? How do I deal with the contradictions? How do I fix my computer?

The speed with which technology was changing didn't help. Before I knew it, the next version of a computer program was the thing to use, just as I got to understand the two versions before. Change was occurring at an exponential rate, and it seemed in many instances that my right hand didn't know what my left hand was up to. Everything was moving so quickly, I hardly had time to grasp one concept before the next was introduced. The problem was, I felt I needed to keep connected with it all to have any chance of working with it. I didn't want to lose my grip, so I kept it all close. It felt overwhelming.

I subscribed to sites of interest, and before I knew it, I was inundated with hundreds of very interesting emails. If I read them all, I would need another day in the week. There came a day when I accidentally cleared out my inbox, and rather than feel upset, I felt relieved. I knew if it was something really important, it would arrive again. I realized I could actually delete things and nothing bad would happen.

And so I did. I deleted things that came along unless something really extraordinary jumped out at me. I found a way to live with email abundance that was previously causing me grief. I unsubscribed to those newsletters I hadn't used or didn't need, and that also lessened the load and time wasted.

When I removed that from my life, I realized I could still function. If I needed to find out information, I knew how and where, and that's all I needed to know. I realized I had actually been in an information, technology, and abundance trap. It was a combination of all three, which felt even more treacherous. I was consumed by this monster.

Then I realized abundance had been a monster in other aspects of my life. As I looked around my house, in my cupboards, wardrobe, drawers, fridge, and office. I asked myself, *What do you actually need? What is its use? What is its value? What does it bring to your life, work, family, and relationships?*

Abundance bred a form of greed, a mindless determination to get more without truly knowing the value of that action or thing. It became the thought that spurred a great clean-out in my life—junk, clothes, technology, anything non-essential, non-useful, non-helpful. It felt liberating. With less clutter and congestion, there was more space. More space brought a clarity that allowed me to breathe more freely.

I thought about some of my friends and the devastating effects of similar traps in their lives and relationships. One friend had left her husband because of the World Wide Web trap. He was on the computer every spare moment, and it did in fact become an addiction that took him away from his family life.

The "over" trap was everywhere—overspending, overdrinking, overworking, overplaying. It didn't matter what it was, the fact that it was overdone led to clutter.

When I found myself getting too attached to anything in my life, I remembered my exercise in clearing. It helped me to let go again. And by letting go, I moved back to a space where my vision was clearer.

Growth for the sake of growth is the ideology of the cancer cell.—***Edward Abbey***

Reduce now to gain more.

Wobbliness

When we allow ourselves quiet and idle moments, things become clearer.

I discovered much of my wobbliness was from having a very busy and noisy mind. My mind was everywhere and in everything, and sometimes it felt as if I did all of that at once. I stayed constantly attached and connected to all that was going on around me. In the blink of an eye, I could emotionally connect with every problem and situation that was in my world at the time—and with the amount of exposure to everything via real-time TV and Internet, there was a lot of world I was attached to!

In quiet times at home, my mind was not quiet. My mind was on the job. What job? It seemed like every job! I would go over details and planning steps in a mental dialogue that kept things alive and blooming. I was in a permanent state of buzz. Maybe I thought I'd lose my power or influence if I stopped thinking about something.

The noise around me also kept me switched on. I would turn things on to fill the space with noise. The television, the computer, the radio, the phone conversations—they all ensured my brainwave frequency was turned up and tuned in.

When I decided to connect more with the family, I declared mealtime a no-TV zone. With that, I noticed our time around the table increased and our conversation improved. I have since brought a quieter environment to the day with soft background music. The car trip is a no-radio zone. My computer is on for work times only. These changes have made a marked impact on my wobbliness.

It may help you to read, as I did, *The Attention Revolution: Unlocking the Power of the Focused Mind* by B. Alan Wallace, PhD.

Silence is more musical than any song.—***Christina Rossetti***

Ssshhh . . .

Minding Our Own Business

When we mind our own business, we have lots more space and energy for more useful and healthy endeavours.

I began to realize the disproportionate amount of time and energy I spent in my mind thinking about things I had no influence over. I began to feel how this affected my mood, focus, and situation. My time was often consumed by talking or thinking about the lives or actions of others.

The impact of this came to light when Steve and I went through the crazy busy time in our lives. The few moments we had together, we spent with our heads in the problems of others: the children, the staff, the family, the friends. In time, these problems felt like our own. Many of our arguments were fuelled by overwhelming feelings related to others. I recognized that we spent little time nurturing our own relationship, and it suffered.

When things got really tough, we arranged a date to talk about what we were going to do to get our lives back on track and rebuild our relationship. I began to see how important it was that we stopped trying to own what didn't belong to us. We had our own business to attend to without taking on the problems of others. What did that do anyway? In time, I got better at steering conversations back to us and our relationship, often with either a hug or a "Let's go for a walk" or a "How are you doing?" or a change of topic.

I began to see how easily I went where I needn't and that I stayed for far too long. In everyday things, I found myself in the lives of others rather than my own—with people I knew (family and friends), people I didn't know (those on the same road, at the same shop, the same street), and people in the spotlight (in newspapers, magazines, television).

I was often emotionally affected by things outside of my own concern. Sometimes it was frustration over someone's driving that had nothing to do with me, or the impatient or rude person at the checkout. Sometimes it was sadness and discomfort for the lives of those affected by tragedy or disaster. Sometimes it was angst and confusion over the disillusioning lives of many superstars in Hollywood—at one point, I wanted to reach out and offer my humble home as an escape for Britney Spears when the news headlines showed her in trouble.

It was healthy to listen, feel, and notice others and their life situations, but to keep them alive as my own emotional stories in my talk and walk became unhealthy. I became more conscious of the line between healthy communication and gossip, judgement and nosiness. I shifted to something more constructive.

It is the mark of an educated mind to be able to entertain
a thought without accepting it.—**Aristotle**

> **If it's not yours,**
> **don't wear it.**

Before moving on, you may want to:

- Separate from the things happening in your environment right here and now.
- Commit to not giving those external factors any thought, focus, or attention.
- Sit in that space for a moment. Feel what it brings. For that moment, you have saved yourself energy by not paying attention to non-purposeful business.
- The more skilled you become in guiding where and how you place your attention and focus, the more energy and time you have for more purposeful actions.

Worry Mind

When we bring action to the things we have concern over, we can experience influence rather than helplessness.

I began to notice my trails of thought that led to worry. The worry was over an endless amount of possibilities. Worry was the pattern. I could feel worry transfer to any topic. The worry seemed to have mostly to do with the *what ifs*. The *what ifs* felt ominous and scary. They became more like a pattern of feeling. I began to recognize when the *what ifs* were controlling me, and I began to recognize it in others.

I had a friend who worried about money. The thing is, she had a lot of money, a beautiful home, a good job, and savings in the bank. Yet her worry about money came through in every conversation and in many of her actions. She was scared to spend it and to lose it. This in turn affected her quality of life, for she lacked generosity and the spirit of giving.

The sad thing was that during the global financial crisis, she lost a lot of money through her investments. And guess what? She was still worried about money. Nothing changed. It didn't matter if she had money or not, she worried about it just the same.

I recognized how I had used worry. Saying "I am worried about you" made me sound like a caring, sensitive, and thoughtful person. I challenged that and wondered how I was actually caring about the person. Worry kept me in my mind and not in my body or spirit. When I placed the care and concern in my heart, I got into my body and spirit. I took the time to actually help with an action of some sort and brought thoughts and wishes of love, strength, and courage. It felt very different from a worrying mind.

This is how I found the courage to sit beside a friend's mother in her last days on earth after a long experience with cancer. It was how I cooked weekly meals for those going through hardship, helped out when people were struggling, and had tough conversations with friends who were in the midst of their own tragedies.

We applied this to our business situation just recently. Everything was getting harder; expenses were rising, demands were changing, legislation was more constricting, and there were so many unknowns. Life as we knew it was in jeopardy. It was easy to wallow in worry over it. Instead, we began to focus on ways to make a difference. That led to some creative alternatives with operational procedures, working hours, and marketing strategies that have all proved promising.

The turmoil erupting around the world also helped change my concept of worry. When I saw people who lost everything during the 2011 floods in North Queensland and the Victorian fires band together and work as a community to not only survive but climb back, I felt there was always a way to exist with tragedy, no matter how devastating. No matter how bad something seemed in my thoughts, it was possible to survive and prosper. That knowledge helped me get on with business and find some joy during our own tough or uncomfortable times.

> *Worry does not empty tomorrow of its sorrow. It empties today of its strength.*—**Corrie Ten Boom**

Worried? Help instead.

Nonsense Stories

When we track our trail of thoughts, we are more likely to discover where the nonsense stories were formed. We can see how assumptions, distortions, and generalizations clouded things.

Our brains have enabled us to learn and create meaning. That's been instrumental for our survival as humans. They have enabled us to function in life, learn language, communicate in relationships, follow instructions, create new technology, and grow in knowledge.

What I'd come to see in my busy life, with so much happening at once, was how quickly my brain created meaning. It took only a couple of bits of evidence to generate thoughts that led to meaning. And it was the meaning that I retained. No matter how thin, sketchy, or untrue the evidence, the meaning had been given and that felt like the truth.

In my busyness, there was little time to challenge or sort out what was happening in the confines of my mind. When my life slowed, however, I started to capture my own thoughts, meanings, and stories, and I began to see their influence in my relationships and how I went about things.

I recall a time well after my surgery when Steve made a mess in the kitchen and didn't clean up. Not long after, I went to our bedroom to see his clothes scattered everywhere. I thought it was unfair that he didn't consider me; after all, it was only a few weeks since I'd had major surgery. I thought he should know better and be more helpful. I could feel the meaning creep up inside of me. It arrived with a surge of emotion: *he didn't really care about me!* I felt so hurt. It was painful. I was living with someone who didn't care about me. I could feel my hurt turn to anger, and that impacted on my mood for the rest of the afternoon.

Steve sensed something was wrong, although he had no idea what. Eventually, in the argument that followed, my false truth came out. "You don't care about me!" I shouted. And then he had to spend time proving why that wasn't true.

My personal work helped me realize how my trail of thought led to unhelpful conclusions. These became my reality, my version of the world. I started talking to my thoughts differently and interjecting sense before a nonsense assumption arrived. Bringing in other perspectives had the power to change my perception of things. And my perception was my reality. So in time, my reality changed, and that's how things began to feel different. I had something else to do with my reality rather than believe it as my truth.

Steve and I have since developed a line to help us snap back from nonsense when we heard it in each other: "So, that's your story?" Funnily enough, we have continued to discover more of them each day.

I came to recognize many of my entrenched stories and themes that tended to arrive regularly:

- The "Poor me" story (focusing only on what's happening to me)
- The pain story (focusing only on my own pain)
- The "I'll never have money" story (focusing on what I didn't have)
- The "I'm not good enough" story (focusing on my flaws)
- The "They're not good enough" story (focusing on the flaws of others).

How easy it was to build and uphold these stories! When I was in one of my stories, I could easily pull evidence from everywhere to support it. I began to use the power of a good old chat with myself the moment I realized what I was up to. My words and language were creating nonsense before my very eyes, and the only way to stop it was to *stop it!*

> *Every theory is a self-fulfilling prophecy that orders experience into the framework it provides.*—**Ruth Hubbard**

Talk less, listen more.

Blame and Hurt

**When we become open to new perspectives, there is
no need for blame. Without blame, we can move on.**

When I took blame out of the equation, I became empowered. It
changed the tone of my voice, the energy field around my body, the
expression on my face, and the nature of my relationships. I realized
how I had blamed others and others had blamed me. It was a blame
game, vying to be right. As if there could be a *right*.

It brought me back to the circles we travelled in our arguments. No
one was prepared to budge. And it wasn't just us. It happened in other
families, in workplaces, in religions, in politics, in relationships. But to
be *right* insinuated there was a *wrong*, and that felt like blame. There was
a cost, and that was generally the relationship. To blame or accept blame
for others was not the way to build long-term quality relationships or
support networks or better outcomes.

I could see the cost of blame in marriages. So many of my friends had
separated because they were to blame for falling out of love, unruly
children, financial woes, being horrible . . . or even seemingly lesser
"crimes" like never putting the rubbish out, not buying gifts, not
talking nicely, or putting on weight.

Staying in the blame mode inhibited the desire and power to influence
a change before the crisis set in or when sitting in one. Getting off the
blame cycle—*he did, she did, they did*—let me look at situations differently.
From that point of difference, solutions actually arrived. Relinquishing
blame helped me to live more wisely and safely. My eyes were more open
to my own contributions, and that it wasn't just what I saw in others.

I remember one day, when I was leaving our local shopping centre, a
mad driver sped up as I was entering the gateway and nearly smashed

my car. I heard my version of events loud and clear. I was so angry at him. When I stopped and thought about it, he was probably calling me the mad driver for entering into the gateway unsafely. Whichever was the most accurate version of reality, the point was it alerted me to how I could do it differently next time. Instead of blaming the other driver, I gained something worthwhile: a safer practise.

I began to take more responsibility for myself. I became aware when I was acting as a victim and found my way free from that.

When there was a mix-up with Steve's medication in hospital during his treatment, rather than go down the blame trail, we looked at how we could keep it from happening in the future. That was our power—the power to change things for next time based on what we learned. We had the power to do something and not feel helpless. Our response helped us maintain a respectful communication with the hospital staff, and that was important during Steve's hospitalization.

When I stopped blaming Steve for making me feel upset, I started to look for what caused what. When I found that it was a tone in his voice, not anything he did, that triggered anger in me, there were lots of options on how to deal with that. I could let him know how I felt, or I could admit my sensitivity and find a way to live with it.

When I stopped blaming myself for my weaknesses and admitted them instead, I started to find ways to support myself with them. Removing blame enabled me to tackle things that created angst, not expand them in my life.

I was on the lookout for things "out there" that I blamed for my woes. I found a part of myself that influenced the situation instead. This approach had a positive impact on many aspects of my life, including my health.

Instead of blaming indigestion on certain foods, I changed those foods in my diet.

Instead of blaming my age for my weight gain, I lessened my calorie intake and exercised more.

Instead of blaming my back for not exercising, I found stretches and exercises that helped.

Instead of blaming a sensitive gut for feeling bloating, I got a health check.

> *When you blame others, you give up your*
> *power to change.*—**Robert Anthony**

Make it better next time.

Beliefs and Habits

Beliefs and habits change when we change.

Knowing that all of my lifelong beliefs and attitudes had developed from perspectives, of which there were many, I was more able to observe and be intrigued by them. Situations in which I believed one thing and others believed another no longer drew me into wrong or right, win or lose, but rather to an appreciation for the difference and possibilities. I was more open to exploring new views.

When I was stuck in a belief or thought that caused me pain in the form of anger, sadness, hurt, frustration, resentment, or jealousy, I'd isolate the reason I'd given for that feeling. Then I'd flip that belief—knowing my reality may not have been the whole picture—by stating the opposite as a reality.

For example, "They're trying to upset me on purpose" became "They're not trying to upset me on purpose." "They don't care" became "They do care." "I'm no good at business" became "I'm good at business." Then I'd find at least one (or more if I could) reason why that could in fact be a possibility. There were always things I could find to support the opposite view.

And that started me moving differently. It helped my confidence with business, writing, coaching, building our beach house, approaching the unknown, talking with different people, learning new things, and living with two dogs. If I hadn't moved, I would have remained in my past ways and solidified that version even more.

Whether I believed the alternative version initially or not, it helped to diffuse the intensity of my emotional state, and that in itself made things feel more comfortable. It was amazing how that alone had an effect. Things seemed lighter quicker.

My biggest challenge was to catch the talk and walk of my beliefs and then give the new eyes (perspectives) the opportunity to reshape things. The beliefs often appeared as labels and assumptions, and they became habits of expression and approach. *That culture is . . . young people are . . . that business is . . . that system is . . . I am . . . there is no way . . . lazy, selfish, uncaring, archaic, impossible . . .*

The exercise of finding inconsistencies and other perspectives seemed to always shed new light. I could usually find a time, a place, or a situation when a particular thing happened, and that was a good starting point. Somehow it broke the cycle and changed the energy that once surrounded it. It was a powerful catalyst for change. It helped me move from judgement and opinion into openness and compassion. It helped in my relationships, work, and life in general.

I realized how sticking to beliefs and habits made life easy. There was no need to think or challenge. It was a "full stop" to opening, learning, or expanding. It was as though I had placed a box around myself and that's where I stayed. It gave credence to the old "Ignorance is bliss" point of view.

But that state of ignorance was fraught with danger. It left a trail of clashes with the outside world—people, generations, systems, lifestyles. It seemed the clashes were arriving more often, and I realized they always would, given the rapid pace of change in our world. And that was something I didn't want. I had a new grandson, and I wanted to speak his language and be in his life, so it was important for me to keep my mind expanding.

I thought about structured learning situations. All learning started with basic training, and then through practise, challenge, feedback, trials, and tests, a more evolved ability and understanding came about. For example, when we learned to drive a car, we were taught the basics, but in time, through experience and challenges, we developed new ways to tackle the more difficult roads and terrains.

When I trained fitness instructors, I used the same approach. I provided students with some basic skills for taking a fitness class. In time, however, they brought their learning to life and challenged themselves with new steps, listened to feedback, readjusted, trialled, and tested again. That enabled them to design, develop, and create an ongoing style of classes that brought more success with a broader range of clients.

I saw that I too grew in my learning experiences, but many of my early established beliefs and habits were contained in a box and resistant to change. For years into my adult life, I didn't eat dinner later than six p.m., I didn't talk about achievements or celebrate milestones, I didn't spend more than I earned, I didn't rely on others, I didn't use my quality plates and cutlery, and I didn't have my dogs inside. I overdid trying to have things right and please others. Now, I chose to lift the lid!

It may help you to read, as I did, *Prisoner of Belief: Exposing and Changing Beliefs That Control Your Life* by Matthew McKay, PhD, and Patrick Fanning.

> *It is my firm belief that the strength of the soul grows in proportion as you subdue the flesh.*—**Mahatma Gandhi**

> **Ask yourself:**
> **Is that really true?**

 Before moving on, you may want to:

- Identify a belief you have about yourself or your life that seems to be holding you back in some way.
- Spend a moment in your mind imagining what life might be like if your reality of that changed right now.
- Feel your life from this altered view, because who knows? It could well be possible.

Fear

When we acknowledge the purpose of fear in our lives, we may find the courage to face it and act differently.

I realized how our primal-fear instinct for the purpose of survival had made its way into our twenty-first-century lives. It was no longer a fear that brought out the wild beast in me in a life-or-death situation. It felt like fear of the many day-to-day threats that potentially jeopardized my way of life.

The more I acted from this fear, the more I entered into a cycle of games. I was trying to make things right for myself. I tried, manipulated, avoided, controlled, withdrew. The more I lived that way, the more I found myself in an adrenalin-induced state of stress (a common illness of today) and the further I moved from living in harmony with myself.

Fear camouflaged itself and was often difficult to trace. But when I looked at how I approached my life, I found its influence.

When I feared loss, I'd hold tighter.
If I held tighter, I'd worry more and
become more excessive.

When I feared going for things in
life, I'd sabotage myself.
If I sabotaged myself, I'd lose faith in my ability.

When I feared getting sick or cancer
returning, I'd worry about it.
If I worried about it, I'd feel stress in my body.

When I feared death, I'd avoid facing it.
If I avoided facing death, I'd fear it more.

When I feared not being perfect, I'd avoid trying things.
If I avoided trying things, I'd miss out on life.

When I feared being alone, I'd seek out others.
If I sought others, I'd dislike being on my own.

When I feared failing, I'd stop my attempts.
If I stopped attempts, succeeding
felt even more impossible.

When I feared losing love, I'd try to do more.
If I tried to do more, it would require more.

When I feared being judged, I'd stop my natural flow.
If I stopped my natural flow, I wasn't being me.

When I feared upsetting someone,
I'd be cautious with my steps.
When I was cautious, I wasn't free.

Fear impacted how I went about my life. I noticed the very things I moved away from often fed the fear. The more I avoided, the harder it became, and the more vulnerable I felt. The more vulnerable I felt, the more I avoided or hid from it.

When I became open about my vulnerabilities and stopped hiding, I somehow felt more supported in my quest to break the hold of some of my underpinning fears. I began to admit to Steve the things I discovered about myself that were holding me back or harming me to some degree. I tended to procrastinate, sit on the fence, put others first, jump to conclusions, and avoid challenges—to name a few. I felt that if he knew, he could better understand how to support me.

I discovered that, when I wasn't hiding, fear lost some of its power to scare me. When its power lessened, I seemed to have more influence and become more relaxed with life. I realized that I could live *with* the fear (it was part of being human) rather than *from* the fear. Fear was there to protect me in life, not inhibit me in life. When I kept fear in the background rather than the foreground, I allowed my love for what I wanted to win out.

Facing the fear of cancer enabled me to talk freely about what I wanted and needed in case of certain scenarios. It gave me the chance to influence how I wanted things to be. I wrote down which special things I wanted left to whom, some special messages I wanted to share, and most importantly, how I wanted my funeral to be if that was how it turned out.

Once I was done with the fear and said what I wanted, it was as though I was free to get on with other things—and one of those things was getting better. Facing a fear, no matter how big or small, decreased its crippling effects. I decided if there was something I wanted for my life, I wasn't going to let fear be the factor that stopped me. I wanted to discover for myself whether it could be or not be. I wanted to speak from my truth and be free.

As I began to learn more about how I wanted to live and what I wanted to achieve, I found a natural urge to give different things a try. I began to talk and live more from my heart. I was on my way to a breakthrough. The fear of failing or of not being successful or whatever it was that stopped me was no longer going to inhibit me in the same way.

It felt more empowering to say, "I am working on it." It felt more empowering to face the possibilities with openness despite the fear that still sat close. Letting my family and friends know I was writing a book was a sign I had come a long way. Yes, me! A book! I wasn't hiding the fact.

> *I learned that courage was not the absence of fear, but the triumph over it. The brave man is not he who does not feel afraid, but he who conquers that fear.*—**Nelson Mandela**

Fear it? Do it anyway.

The Construct of Time

When we worry less about time passing, we can be in the time we have more fully. We may be in less of a hurry, and from that state, things are more likely to arrive sooner.

I was so busy chasing all the things I had marked as important that they became my focus. I had constructed time frames and markers of success, and my life was the timeline to achieving them. I was in such a hurry to get them done that this approach brought a sense of life passing by very quickly without me.

Yes, there were many things I had crossed off the list, but I realized that those accomplishments didn't make life joyous or give me a sense of living. I had worked hard to achieve some great things in my work, sports, and family life, and I had undertaken overseas trips and adventures, but somehow they came and went so swiftly. I realized it was how I had come to live—on the timeline that held the next thing to strive for.

When my life slowed down and I began to really appreciate more of each day, I felt the difference in the quality of the experience. When Steve and I went overseas the year after my cancer operation, it was as though I had just woken up to the beauty and magnificence of the world around me. I saw and felt the detail of the experience I was in rather than just passing through it.

When I reduced my workload to spend more time as a grandmother, wife, and friend, I realized I was finally *in* my life, living it in a way I had always dreamed of. When I stopped the chase, I received so much more. The chase stifled my ability to be in the experience, where so much more could be found.

Hurrying to get somewhere more quickly, or fuming in the queue while waiting to be served when running late, did nothing to remedy the situation. I came to look at it differently. I saw it as possibly the very thing that saved me from a further hold-up or incident. I learned to be more grateful for whatever arrived.

Moving away from the timeline changed how I experienced time. It felt more textured with opportunities. It was much more enjoyable and adventurous than a clock or a calendar.

> *Let him who would enjoy a good future waste*
> *none of his present.*—**Roger Babson**

> **When you let go of the**
> **hurry feeling inside—you**
> **can enjoy and prosper.**

The Grass Is Greener on the Other Side

When we see there are shades of green and every colour on both sides, we'll be more likely to accept and appreciate the array we are in.

I often wished to be in another space, for reasons I set for myself—*It will be better, this was not good, right, or how it should be* or whatever it was. I was often oblivious to the opportunities right in front of me.

There would always be something happening in each moment in each place, and I could never know in which one I had more or less to gain. Sometimes I'd expect something great to happen when in fact nothing did. Sometimes I didn't expect anything great to happen, but it did.

When I kept the perspective that each moment was the universe's best possible outcome, with everything happening at once, I began to accept that where I sat was in fact my best possible position. I accepted the bigger picture—things were just as they were meant to be.

I began to observe in awe the actual unfolding of each moment. I appreciated when things went smoothly and accepted it when they didn't. Sometimes they would, sometimes they wouldn't. The odds of the universe were that each of these would happen at some point. No two moments could ever be the same. My influence in the outcome could only be in the way I approached my moments, days, weeks, and life. It felt empowering to take responsibility and be gracious no matter what happened, through ups or downs.

When I was feeling low, I'd take myself back to this knowing and remember that it would pass. All things did. I had been through troughs and peaks over and over again, so I knew that was the case. This helped me greatly when I was faced with the news about Steve's cancer. We had been through tough times before, and I knew there was light on the other side.

The more I accepted this relationship with difficult events, the more it changed what I had previously felt very uncomfortable with: waiting. I passed the time between the troughs and peaks differently. I no longer sat in the hope of time passing more quickly. I was able to live in the moments in between with more purpose and influence. It was instrumental to enjoying so many precious moments during the tough days of Steve's chemotherapy.

I began to replace *waiting* as a concept with *experiencing* and *being*. I spent time experiencing things like the queue in the supermarket. I have had many great and rewarding conversations with people in my local area. Many were older folk who really appreciated the chat.

I found myself more able to get on with life rather than wait for a result; enjoy work rather than wait to go home; enjoy the cinema rather than wait for the movie to start. This made moments between points feel much fuller. It had a big impact on my anxiety and my hurrying state, and that was a great relief.

> *All I have seen teaches me to trust the creator for all*
> *I have not seen.*—**Ralph Waldo Emerson**

> **Enjoy with faith that it is
> just as it's meant to be**

Ego

Knowing our ego helps us recognize when it takes over. When we keep things light, we can shift from it. It is not our true self.

Like all of us, I have lived my life in established habits and patterns that emerged over time. It's just what we did, how we thought, how we lived the life game. That was the ego, as it was often called. I saw it as my image, and that was created from the internalization of all my life circumstances.

All our life, we have lived with our ego, and that was what we presented to the world through our actions, talk, beliefs, and attitudes. Our ego represented our time on earth. It was a significant part of us. It deserved respect, for it did its best to make sense of our existence. It helped shape us and project our strengths and weaknesses as a means of survival.

But probably like many, I had come to see and believe it to be *me*. I slowly realized I was more than this interpretation of myself. I was far more than my own attempt to describe. I was the potential within, which I was just beginning to explore.

Ego distortions had impacted my life in many ways. Sometimes I'd minimize and sometimes I'd exaggerate qualities and strengths. I lived and identified these as *me* without question. I thought it, talked it, and walked it. *I'm no good at . . . I am good at . . . I am . . . I'm not . . .* there was a whole long list of things I could insert into these headings.

It wasn't wrong, it was just how my ego did it. It was just how it walked with me through my life. But my relationship with it was beginning to change.

I began to get to know my ego better and respect it for its development, history, tendencies, patterns, limitations, and strengths. It felt as though the compassion I gave my ego promoted a healthy relationship with it. It felt comfortable and willing to open up and accept challenges and the new perspectives I explored.

An example of this was a story I told myself about my ability to write. Somehow, when a high-school teacher told me I couldn't write, that was what my ego told me about myself. Writing was something I avoided. My new relationship with my ego, however, allowed me to challenge that story. Not long after my recovery from surgery, I decided to write blog posts on the website I had established for my coaching service. I noticed my talk was beginning to change.

It didn't matter whether others perceived that I could or couldn't write—it was my message, and I wanted to share it. I felt confident to stand up to it. My ego had been protecting me from the humiliation of writing because that had been its story about me. I began to understand my reasons for avoiding formal writing situations. It was hiding this about me! Standing up to it not only taught me a lot about myself but freed me to do something I wanted, and that was express myself.

It allowed me to be honest and have respect for myself just as I was. I didn't have to prove anything to anyone.

There were other instances when I caught my ego exaggerating my qualities. I'd often say things like, "I am a healthy eater." Saying "I am . . ." anything was another way my ego defined and boxed me. It must also have felt that fitness instructors were meant to be healthy in all things. But in my heart, I knew that wasn't the full story. In time, I gained the confidence and ability to say it as it was—on most days, like many people, I had an unbalanced diet! I began to describe myself differently.

But then, there were many instances when I wasn't aware that my ego existed, and I just went about things as I had always done. My ego was so familiar to me that everything sounded true. It could be very convincing. It could give the reason not to challenge. It could prove why it was right, why it deserved to have its way, or why it would try to control things. It could battle with the things "out there" that didn't fit in with what should be. It could battle with itself when there were two opposing views. The words of others often meant nothing if they didn't align with my ego identification.

I had a friend who saw herself as unattractive. Her ego-identified self could prove how and why that was so. It didn't matter how much anyone told her otherwise or how attractive she looked in photos—she could only see herself as unattractive. It could only be in her own time in her own way that she could challenge the stranglehold of her ego.

It was a few years after her decision to embark on personal work that the breakthrough arrived where she could see and feel her beauty. She was happy in her own skin—she could even go out without the mask (make-up, that is) and feel comfortable doing so. How she saw herself changed, and how others saw her changed too. She was free from that inhibiting identity that had stopped her from interacting and engaging in a way that was true to her. Her relationships began to change.

I watched her flourish and enjoy her life so much more. I came to see that it didn't really matter what others said, good or bad. It was her ability to love and accept herself as she was that mattered.

 Before moving on, you may want to:

- Close your eyes and create a space that allows you to glimpse your ego-identified life.
- Observe, feel, and remember events, people, places, achievements, and collections that have become the story of your life. Honour this for whatever it has brought you. It is the life that your circumstances led you to.
- Now, take a slow and conscious breath. Still the images and quieten the sensations in your mind and body, and pause again.
- Connect with what presents. Feel the distinction between the ego (the voice that sits close by at all times) and you (the silence beyond). No need to explain or describe, just feel it. Become familiar with this dimension.
- Remain in this space until a strong awareness of its presence arises. You can access it again at any time in the future.

As I continued to learn and appreciate the dynamics of my ego, I began to consciously integrate some new practices into my days. It was a rough integration at first. I usually realized my ego's antics after an event, dialogue, thought, or action.

Retrospection and reflection were powerful. As I looked back, I could see what ego story I had operated from. I began to see the humour in how it played out in situations. As I got better at recognizing it, I got better with my relationship to it.

On days when I told people that I *couldn't, could, was, wasn't,* I acknowledged to myself in my own mind that it was my ego. I knew what it was up to. Some days I laughed about it and sometimes I stopped and admitted my vices. It didn't matter what I chose—the fact I was onto it was the important thing. Having an influence over my ego was powerful. It was not as likely to sweep me away to feeling inferior or superior, to pass up opportunities, to hide, or to disengage from others.

I had a friend who worked with her ego beautifully when she took on a challenge to go overseas to sort out some staff issues for her husband's business. While on the plane, the part of her ego that identified her as "just the wife" took hold. She felt anxious, and self-doubt shot through her. She questioned her ability to undertake such a task and felt like running away.

She was, however, determined to be successful in her quest, and she explained to me how she called on another aspect of her ego, one she called "Snow White," to save the day. Snow White represented the unassuming girl with much power that she knew herself to be. Snow White managed to stay with her during her trip and help her do just what she set out to do.

> *Whenever I climb, I am followed by a dog*
> *called "Ego."*—**Friedrich Nietzsche**

Be friends with your ego.

The Brain

Our brain is an organ that will operate based on how it is treated. When we understand how the brain works, we have the chance to treat it differently.

I wondered why some days were just harder than others. Some days I could do certain things, and some days I couldn't. I came to realize that the way my brain was wired had a big influence. The more I read about the brain, its structure and evolution, the more I was able to understand.

Our brain consists of three distinct parts, each with various functions that enable us to be the most amazing species on earth:

1. The part known as the *first brain* (more commonly termed *reptilian brain*) is more involved in movement, coordination, automatic reflexes, and the maintenance of our basic life functions.
2. The part known as the *second brain* (more commonly termed *midbrain, mammalian,* or *limbic brain*) is more noted for the emotional and internal states and responses to external environments.
3. The *third brain* (more commonly termed *neocortex*) is responsible for the thinking, reasoning, analysing, and learning that allows us to operate at high levels of functioning—the brain that differentiates us as humans.

The continuous adaptation of the neocortex brings the ability and potential to rewire itself, which means to change. That is how it is possible for us to adapt, learn, invent, and imagine undiscovered possibilities. However, while there is potential for new awareness and growth, there is also a potential for that to be sabotaged by the traps and vulnerabilities of other aspects of the brain.

In our way of life, we have come to respect and give credence to those well developed "left brains" that are behind many advanced functions of learning. They are thought to be more important for professions that rely on the linear logical, structural, and analytical approach.

The challenge with the left brain is that once it is switched on, the more switched on it gets, and the more difficult it is to switch off. That means it is more difficult to take in information from the "right brain," which is also very useful and important.

The right brain brings the more heartfelt emotional and intuitive capacity to our experiences. In more recent times, less value has been granted to it. An overemotional right side is seen as problematic, and as a consequence, our intuitive gut feelings are often disregarded. The more scientific left brain is usually looking for concrete scientific proof to validate concepts. The right brain isn't about that.

This information about the brain felt liberating to me. I was starting to understand more about myself and the emergence of my patterns. I recognized the bias toward my left brain. My left brain had been given encouragement during my school years and urged me to revel in science and maths in preparation for a more academic life. That brain was working hard in me. Meanwhile, my right brain was yearning for input. I valued all aspects of my brain and saw the key was to bring that to balance.

It may help you to read, as I did, *Evolve Your Brain: The Science of Changing Your Mind* by Joe Dispenza, DC.

> *I like nonsense, it wakes up the brain cells. Fantasy is a*
> *necessary ingredient in living; it's a way of looking at life*

through the wrong end of a telescope. Which is what I do,
and that enables you to laugh at life's realities.—**Dr. Seuss**

> **Give your thinking brain**
> **a rest—it has a big job!**

Painful Emotions

When we engage our emotions, we are responding
to life. When we engage them rather than react to
them, they are not as painful.

I began to look at emotions differently. They weren't bad. They were essential and natural to experience.

I had in the past identified negative emotions as bad mainly because of the pain I felt when experiencing them. There goes that pain avoidance again! I also felt there was an element of it not being right to have what I considered to be negative emotions—anger, resentment, frustration, sadness, and regret.

I had plenty of experience with anger and frustration. My dad had the characteristic Italian volatile temper, and it was something that always made me feel uncomfortable. Anything that made me feel uncomfortable, I worked to steer away from. So logically, the idea was to get rid of any of those "bad" feelings as quickly as possible. Not that it was bad to move on from them, but there was a difference between moving on by suppressing the emotion and moving on after dealing with it.

I began to notice that rather than feel the pain of the emotion, I somehow went into business mode and intellectualized strategies and actions. From the outside, I looked like a cool, capable cucumber. When I started to be true to myself and think less and feel more, though, I realized I had a lot of emotion that just wasn't expressed or shared. How could anyone ever know how I was feeling when I never gave that part of me away?

When I began to change my attitude and respect my emotions, I discovered they were powerful for many reasons. I began to understand how they played out in me, and in turn they gave me more information about myself. I felt I was really onto something. I was getting to know myself better. I was beginning to articulate more about what I wanted and liked with confidence and certainty.

I began to notice more about the nature of my emotions. Sometimes it was things on the outside that caused an emotional reaction in me (words, tones, people, situations). It was from those things that I discovered more about my likes, dislikes, values, sensitivities, and interests. When the emotions came from within, I took time to discover my thoughts and body cycles that impacted on them. Was I tired, hungry, overworked, bored, unsure, hormonal?

In the past, when an emotion arrived, I tended to blame the "outside" or blame parts of myself. Hormones especially made my whole world view change. Everyone and everything would set me off. As I got better at knowing what my emotions were about, I could move through my body without as much of the fight, flight, or freeze that took over in the past.

I got better at naming each emotion and noticing how and when the emotion crept up on me. I got better at letting it pass without the added extras to worsen the situation. When I added distortions, stories, nonsense, and assumptions, the emotion lasted longer and felt much worse. I was more likely to act from my emotions—arguing, blaming, worrying, fearing.

When I woke up to the fact that I'd moved on from the emotion and into behavioural traps that didn't serve me well, I realized it was time to take a break and settle down. In the past, I'd never really understood how to be with my emotions, and I was grateful to be learning to feel more comfortable and honest in expressing them but not acting from them.

When I expressed the purity of an emotion, it felt liberating. Crying with sadness or love, shouting with anger, expressing my frustration, gasping with fear, squealing with joy—each felt like a release. Allowing my emotions to be expressed proved so valuable the night Steve was diagnosed with cancer. Oceans of emotion entered my heart, gut, and whole body. At the end of it, I somehow felt clear and confident in how to support Steve on his journey back to health.

After that emotional release, I realized how much I had suppressed the fullness of my emotions in the past. My emotions had never been truly released. It made sense that an illness had formed in my own body. Holding on, being strong, and moving on too quickly kept my emotions residing in my body, waiting to resurface in some way.

Engaging and allowing my emotions made me feel like I was living. I was responding and riding the wave of life. I wasn't denying love or all the other emotions that arrived because of it. It was OK to be an emotional being, as that was an honest part of my whole self.

I wondered more about illness. Whether it was cancer, depression, chronic pain, or migraines, I felt that emotions that remained as a stress in the body played a huge role.

It may help you to read, as I did, *You Can Heal Your Life* by Louise L. Hay and *Emotional Intelligence: Why It Can Matter More Than IQ* by Daniel Goleman.

*Any emotion, if it is sincere, is involuntary.—**Mark Twain***

> **Love your emotions, and
> then set them free.**

A Change in the Circuit

When we break the cycle, we can move in a different direction

No matter what I learned about the brain, my emotions, and the traps of the left brain, there were times when I couldn't rationalize with myself or get a thought or belief out of my head. Some things felt so solid they seemed unchangeable.

I remember during a large period of my life when I was stuck in the busy work cycle, I was often tired and frustrated. It felt like it was a fixture in my life—something I couldn't escape. I distinctly remember that I often had the urge to sleep through the day. Steve would laugh at me and my need to just nod off. In fact, it was a family trait. We all had an uncanny ability to switch off with a quick nap, even on a rock!

That has changed since my illness, and it made me think about why. I came to recognize that I used sleep as my break, my pause from what felt uncomfortable in my life. I used sleep as an escape. Sleep broke the cycle for that moment and took me away from the intensity I was in. Since my illness, I had discovered others ways to create a break from the busyness in my life and mind, bring well-being back, and shake myself free from discomfort.

Breathing created a powerful break. I learned the technique on my road to recovery and it became my best friend. I used breathing to regularly break the solidity of my state—especially when I felt anxious or troubled. It acted as a circuit breaker, bringing me back to a settled, calm, and balanced state. It was something that my brain usually couldn't do through thought alone. Bringing focused attention to the mechanism of my breath immediately stopped the sound of any chatter. That helped when my head was in a spin or when thoughts kept me from sleeping. Breathing changed my focus and attention and veered me away from constricting habits or feelings of being stuck.

I went on to discover the power of other types of breaks: walk breaks, talk breaks, appreciation breaks, exercise breaks, food breaks, play breaks. The more I tuned in and admitted any discomfort that arrived in the form of thoughts, emotions, moods, attitudes, and interpretations, the more I recognized when I needed a break. Breaks had the power to take me to a more centred and silent space where clearer views and solutions seemed to arrive effortlessly, seemingly from nowhere.

I came to see how useful the simple approach of breaks could be for anyone experiencing depression, anxiety, or any other debilitating state or situation. Whatever the state, it *was* a state—it was not a permanent situation or solid condition. But a shift was required.

I began to have empathy for those who resisted change or shifts. Like me, they may have felt it was easier to be in the pain of something familiar. Shifting may have seemed a harder alternative. But I found it wasn't as difficult as I had once thought.

I started with simple breaks, as I have described, but they led me to something much more. I began to more easily approach things differently. I could say no to what I normally said yes to, and yes to what I said no to. I'd find the opposites. I'd experience rather than think. I'd change the way I drove to work, the hand I used to brush my teeth, the order in which I prepared breakfast, the books I read, the recipes I cooked. These became differences in how I experienced life.

Breaks took me outside of my usual routines, where I could tune in to seeing more freely. I found the inconsistencies, the patterns, the *whys*, the *why nots*, the contradictions, the ironies. I got better at word puzzles and picture puzzles, seeing patterns and ironies. I found humour, and that brought lightness.

On the day I was penning this concept, I took time out to shop and found myself driving behind a car that had a message boldly plastered on the back window: "What if every day was a celebration of life?" It caught my attention, but it was when the driver neglected to use his indicator at the next turn and drove blindly through a pedestrian crossing, nearly bowling over an innocent walker, that I found the irony.

I felt that when I changed up my experiences, I shook up my brain, and somehow that confused it out of its usual way. I held close to my mantra of "Shake it up!" to remind me.

Sleep is the best meditation.—**Dalai Lama**

Change things up now!

CHAPTER 23

KEY FINDING 2—
BE YOURSELF AND
CREATE YOUR LIFE

Reducing the impact of the traps opened the way to discover more about what I actually wanted. I found the confidence and desire to work with my strengths, needs, priorities, and circumstances— and for the first time, I felt I was the director of my life. I was creating a positive and purposeful way.

Different Priorities

When we live from a place of love and care for ourselves, others, and earth, we find time for what is most important.

After my illness, I was more concerned with how I wanted to live my life and feel in my life. I realized I had confused what was important to me and what I really wanted. It wasn't all about the material things, getting ahead, getting my own way, or feeling good about myself and making things right. It was more about the quality and nature of my engagements in my day-to-day experiences. My energy and focus were no longer on working toward all those things that were once so important. I was doing different things for different reasons.

My priorities changed, and that meant the things I put first changed. I valued spending time to really listen and see. I was doing better with following what aligned with my important things. The usual fears and stories from my headspace about how and why I couldn't changed to how and why I *could*. I felt like I was growing up!

It was not about trying to please others but rather honouring myself for the good of others and the earth—adopting the Self-Others-Earth framework (SOE). Everyone was honoured in that equation. Doing to please others was fraught with danger. It was one of those things that when I stopped, it felt to others like a punishment or like I was no longer pleasing. An intention for pleasing others for the sake of pleasing others often meant I lost my power. It was win-lose. Putting anything before myself to the detriment of myself was not the way. If I put something before myself, it would have to be because it brought nurture and honour to me at the same time.

I had a friend who enjoyed wonderful experiences with her partner until, out of the blue, he left her for another woman. My friend was obviously hurt and confused by it all. In time, through the personal work she embarked on, she discovered a deeper understanding about her patterns and also about her needs and ways to honour and love herself first. When her partner decided to re-enter her life, she found herself in a dilemma. She knew her values revolved around relationship and family, and a key driver in her life was companionship, so it would have been easy to swim around in confusion for a long time over what path to take. When she brought her values to the SOE framework, however, her decision was clear. Having him back in her life would not be nurturing or honouring to her; in fact, she felt pain in her gut about that prospect.

She decided not to take up his offer to reunite, and she could identify how it was in fact the healthier option for him, too.

Using the SOE framework, I was able to do more that was aligned with me, without that uncomfortable feeling of confusion or guilt. I could help a loved one in a moment of need, give time to my family, provide a quality service to my clients, cook for friends and family who needed support, drop unimportant things for an emergency, be reliable and trustworthy in my friendships, take time for rest and self care, and nurture my body, mind, and spirit.

Usually, on any given day, I was able to balance these important things. It seemed that one thing often made way for the next. When Dad passed away, Mum needed support. When Steve needed care, Mum was a bit stronger. When my grandson was born, Steve finished his chemo. When Sid was a bit older, I supported our friends with meals during their difficult times.

There were days I needed to say no to some things or put them on the back burner—the lunch arrangements, the cleaning, the shopping, even meeting friends. Those things could wait. My priorities came first, and no one ever challenged that. It was as though people respected that I was honouring my priorities.

If I felt confused over what to do, my heart would let me know. I would ask it. I'd connect with the deep feeling of love that resided in my heart. It wasn't love for anyone or anything, it was just love.

When I brought a challenging issue to my heart space—I did this by focusing attention around my heart with an image or symbol of love (of late, I have used my grandson's face, because he brings me to the level of mush needed for my heart to be true!)—my heart answer appeared. The answer was usually one that I knew deep down but had often overanalysed my way against. It made sense of the expression "in my heart, I knew."

I thought about how many times it was the image of loved ones that got people through difficult situations during tragedy, sadness, illness, or war. Loved ones spurred courage, hope, and strength. That was the power of love. It brought vigour to our lives. True stories like the one I read during Steve's illness, *The Long Walk: The True Story of a Trek to Freedom* by Slavomir Rawicz, showed evidence of that power.

> *Things which matter most must never be at the mercy of things which matter least.*—**Johann Wolfgang von Goethe**

> **Feel love in your heart and your answers will arrive.**

No Expectations

When we do and give to others without expectation, we can focus on how good that feels—and that is big enough.

I came to see how expectation played a big role in my life. I expected things to happen—my son to clean his room, my husband to know that I was upset, my boss to care for me, everyone to enjoy what I had cooked, plans to work out. The thing with expectation was that I relied on someone or something to make it happen. The fact that these were all factors outside of my control set me up for the roller-coaster ride of disappointment or happiness. My state was dependent on the outcome. It was always an up-and-down ride.

During my really busy days, I recognized how I needed and wanted even more from others, probably to balance the imbalance, so I had many expectations. As a result, disappointment arrived more often. The dishes weren't done, the TV wasn't turned on, everyone didn't get along, people weren't ready on time, someone rocked the boat, and nobody but me noticed when the plants needed watering.

Expectation was not a powerful place from which to live life. It meant I always wanted something in return. When I decided to drive my own life and not rely on others or situations to bring me what I wanted, I needed to find that within myself.

I allowed expectation to provide the clues to what I wanted. I then found ways to bring that to my life. I wanted my son to take responsibility, and so I spent time teaching him how to organize, and I communicated the relevance and importance of responsibility in his life. I wanted open communication with my husband, so I shared my feelings and expressed my truth to him, no matter how weird that may have sounded. I wanted people in my workplace to be more nurturing, so I took time to chat with people and offered support more quickly. I wanted a nice food experience with my family, so I took the time to learn new recipes and approached it with love and enthusiasm. I wanted a holiday at Christmas, so I talked and walked it and took responsibility to plan it.

Whether things turned out well or not, I had somewhere to go with it. I looked within myself and the approach I used. I found I engaged in more adult conversation with my son, husband, colleagues, and family, looking for feedback and deeper understanding. I began to shape the things I wanted under my own influence. I'd be more inclined to ask things like, "What didn't you like?" or "What got in the way?"

My family sensed I was curiously seeking rather than complaining. I heard the difference in my tone and felt my questions sounded more sincere and open. I felt our communication had more truth and depth, and the feedback was more valuable. When I wasn't so sensitive and didn't take things so personally, I found they spoke from their hearts.

I felt the shift in our relationships. We were far more honest with each other, and I realized we were forming a great relationship base for something long-lasting. I was grateful for that. I had so often witnessed families who could never give feedback for fear of hurting someone's feelings. Many families drifted apart.

I had been at the other end of the guilt trip, and I most likely created the guilt trip with the expectations I had once lived by. But I felt true relationships broke down under those conditions and became acts of duty rather than love. In removing expectations, I became more aware of another inhibitor: letting people know what I had done for them—"I've just cooked you a nice meal, washed your clothes, worked so hard, and been so nice!" I discovered I was giving *to* them, not doing it *for* them.

Giving was my way of attaining what I wanted in my life—giving my ideas, the truth about my feelings, my time, my food, my creativity. Yes, they received, and that was important to me. It also expanded and enriched me and my life.

The irony was that I felt I received more from others, albeit in a different way, than I ever had in the past—things like gratitude, a deeper connection, trust, and better understanding. This in turn brought something far more powerful without having to force or expect things back in return.

I began to recognize how relationships suffered from expectations. I had a friend who gave so much to her partner, especially in the early stages of their relationship. She would put him first, leaving herself without money or time, and she moved away from the other things in her life that were important—friends, family, and her own well-being. It wasn't conscious, but there was a part of her that thought, *If I do all that for him, I'll get love and a lasting relationship in return.*

This approach may have worked in the beginning, but as time went on, they were both expecting something very different from each other, and that led to ongoing disappointment. They each relied on the other person to bring what they wanted, and when that didn't arrive, they went into the blame cycle. It was a pattern; it had happened before and was likely to happen again unless her approach to the relationship changed. For that to happen, she had to trust that she could do it differently. If she allowed herself the time, she could break that cycle—a cycle that is prevalent in our society today.

I was learning about myself through the lives of others. It was through the people and circumstances of my life that I achieved my greatest learning, growing, and meaningful living. I didn't need to venture anywhere or find a different medium. My life experience was embedded in my circumstances, and it was up to me to create what I envisioned from that.

Expectation is the root of all heartache.—
William Shakespeare

> **Do something just
> for the joy of it.**

Circumstances: the Vehicle

When we value the fact that our life circumstances are the things that provide our unique experience, discovery, and growth, we will walk and talk it with pride, humility, confidence, and love.

That's what each of us had: our circumstances. Our circumstances were the vehicle for each of our physical journeys through life. Job, home, friends, finances, health, state of mind, physical state, community, country—whatever the vehicle, it provided the ups and down, the likes and dislikes, the differences the similarities.

When I realized that about my life, how I viewed it in relation to everything around me changed. My thoughts about the vehicles changed as well. They were in my life for a reason, and I was beginning to see that. Seeing them as my way to the life I envisioned helped me to respect and nurture them all. It was up to me—not something outside of me—to be willing to make the choices that led to my quality life.

That was what I was working on: finding the courage to stand up to those thoughts and patterns of expectation and judgement that I had in the past employed to take the easy way out or follow some elusive option. I knew running away from a situation to find a better circumstance was not the answer. It helped me settle into where I found myself rather than search for a way out.

I can remember times when I didn't want to be somewhere, and I could whip up an excuse for why I had to leave. I could find ways to avoid being with something or with someone I didn't want to face. I was on the lookout for a different route when the one I was on was jammed. In time, however, I didn't feel the need to escape in that way. Rather than excuses I exercised choice. I became curious and interested no matter where I was and that changed how I coped.

I wasn't so afraid of being with things I'd once avoided. I had something else to do with them. This opened the door to instances of magic that I had ignored in the past. I became more curious about my culture and family overseas. I felt part of their lives and they a part of mine. It propelled me to explore more; I came to understand more about my history, learn a language, cook different food, visit amazing places, meet interesting people, and discover more about the people in my circle.

I felt I didn't have to hide or avoid anything in my life. I had no need to explain or justify or change or be different for anyone. Whoever and whatever was in my life was just how it was. It didn't matter if I had a different family structure, a quirky family member, a colourful history, a lively dog, a sick or disabled person, bad weather, or ill health—that's what I had. I was not making excuses for anything.

Circumstances weren't my life, they were where I practiced life. And it was a practice *for* life.

*Everything can be taken from man but one thing: the last of human freedoms—to choose one's attitude in any given set of circumstances, to choose one's own way.—**Viktor E. Frankl***

> **Express sincere thanks for that someone or something in your life.**

Appreciate the Small Steps

The more we focus on what we did do and the things we achieved, the less we'll focus on what we didn't do.

I began to recognize the subtle nature of change. It arrived in the day to day in what seemed like the smallest and most insignificant motions. As I discovered, though, it was anything but small and insignificant. Being small was what made it so powerful and transformative. It kept things alive. Doing it big was fraught with danger, as it often disregarded other important aspects of me and my life.

In the past, if it wasn't big, and I didn't notice or receive the rewards, it didn't seem worthwhile or effective. Whether it was related to saving, weight, work, attitude, caring, listening, helping, or learning, I wanted the prize!

Small steps of difference in my approaches were actually signs that something big had happened. They were evidence of a long path travelled from my unconscious desire to my conscious thoughts, attitudes, and behaviours. I began to acknowledge and appreciate that in myself. It's amazing what appreciation brought. Rather than look at what I didn't do, I focused on what I *did*.

After I stopped exercising for a long period of time after Steve's illness, I slowly clawed my way back, starting with one repetition out of the recommended twenty-one in the sets. Instead of the usual undervaluing of my efforts, I exclaimed, "I'm on my way!" It was the kindness that motivated me to take that first step and slowly build. Within two months, I had reached the twenty-one.

I focused more on what it actually took to achieve, and that brought evidence that it was no small thing. Minimizing worth with talk like "It was just . . ." or "It was nothing . . ." was what I challenged. To shift any thought, pattern, or belief was no small feat—sometimes it required a pull so strong that it felt as tough as breaking through a solid brick wall. So any movement was big!

This approach also helped me shift from another pattern I recognized from my past, and that was focusing and dwelling on mistakes or failures—what I didn't do, could've done, should've done, what that all meant, and how bad that was. It reminded me of when I worked with students and asked them to give feedback to each other on their performance in role-plays. They could each find the many things others didn't do well but really struggled to name and state what they *did* do well. They found it difficult to acknowledge small actions of worth. No wonder we were all so hard on ourselves.

Finding the "did do" was a practice that encouraged a better balance in the positive versus negative focus—the optimistic versus pessimistic. In reflection, I could acknowledge my successful efforts of simple actions, responses, dialogues, and choices and what it took from me to do so. I could usually find respect, sincerity, courage, love, kindness, integrity, patience, tolerance, physical effort, understanding, or compassion. Whatever it was, I drew it out and let myself know. I appreciated when I did or could do it, and in time this helped me accept positive feedback I once found challenging. In the past, I couldn't see the value of small, so I didn't believe it.

Now I could appreciate the smallest of things from others too, things that I once would have walked past. The spiral effect from the appreciation of small things generated a consequence that felt big. In my fast-paced life before slowing down after cancer, I hardly had the time or inclination to give things the appreciation they deserved. I ate a meal without a thought as to what was responsible for its quality. I listened to songs by artists without empathy for the energy, focus, and passion with which they were created. I was disconnected from appreciation and gratitude.

I came to understand how people who had everything felt unhappy and discontented. They may not have been able to appreciate and feel the many great things in their life—their focus and attention was more on the pain that arrived from the challenges. Their life was more like a wound.

It all helped me be able to enjoy the give and receive of simple things, such as a tender hug, a helping hand, a smile of reassurance, or an acknowledgment of effort or achievement. I knew what to search for— the smallest of things!

*The man who removes a mountain begins by carrying
away small stones.*—**Chinese Proverb**

> **Feel the bigness of
> something very small.**

 Before moving on, you may want to:

- Acknowledge the "did do" in your day, week, month, year, life.
- Acknowledge the magnitude of the smallness.

Unique Drivers

**When we discover what makes us happy, we can
choose to bring that into our lives.**

I realized some common characteristics that were significant in creating an experience that vitalized me. I called them *drivers*. They motivated me and added value and quality to the way I felt about life. My key drivers (the ones I found most powerful) were creativity, freedom, balance, and peace. I somehow always knew they were important, but I began to understand their true value. My life felt different when I lived by them and with them.

Recognizing my drivers helped me know what to bring to an experience, to my day, and to the choices I made at all levels of my life. They gave me the direction for my global and universal interests (freedom of speech, saving animals, innovative designs) as well as for my major vehicles of work, recreation, sport, hobbies, travel, food, and relationships.

Within each of these, I found ways to continually infuse subtle aspects of freedom, peace, balance, and creativity. In my day-to-day decisions, actions, and approaches, I chose freedom over structure, peace over unrest, balance over obsession, and creativity over the mundane. I would find ways to loosen the structure, settle the unrest, change things up, or add a little spice.

I found my drivers in the simplest of things: a short break, a hug with my dog, a short stretch, a heart-to-heart, a quick read, the sorting out of an issue, a quick write, a doodle, a thrown-together meal, a change in the room set-up, or a candle infusion of scent and ambience. There were multitudes of ways to bring the internal nature of my drivers to life. Big or small, my job was to bring them into my day and feel the joy they brought.

The drivers that were external in nature—money, a house, a new car, a job promotion—were very limited. I had to have that specific thing to feel better. This had once been the predominant nature of my drivers. It was when I accessed the internal feelings triggered by the external things that I began to have the influence I was looking for. It was a factor that helped me opt for more time over more money, work satisfaction over title, self-discovery over more degrees, creative renovations over a new house, and relationships over things.

When I became confused over decisions, it was often due to a contradiction among my key drivers. For example, to gain freedom in my relationship, I needed to stand up for myself, and that didn't feel peaceful. Just knowing the reason for my discomfort lessened it and gave me the courage to face things I'd once walked away from. I found compromise rather than the all-or-nothing choices of the past.

I looked for the things that seemed to be drivers for others. For some, it was adventure and independence; for others, fun, discipline, fairness, security, organization, passion, purpose, connection, achievement, energy, and many more.

I thought about a friend I'd known since high school. She regularly coordinated our school-reunion gatherings. When we were all together, she remembered everyone's name and could tell stories from the past that had us all in fits of laughter. She would be in touch regularly and kept us all posted on who was doing what. She loved to have people around.

From the outside, it appeared her drivers were connection, friendship, fun, and loyalty. They seemed to enliven her spirit, but only she could truly define them. For many years, while she endured the challenges that came with multiple sclerosis, she continued to bring that happiness into her life. Despite being wheelchair-bound and limited with her speech, she recently organized another school reunion. She was an inspiration. She helped me see that our life circumstances didn't really matter, and we could all find something to drive our spirit to joy.

It reminded me of the life of Victor Frankl, who in 1932, while imprisoned and waiting to be executed, exercised an extraordinary ability to bring the gift of his insight to the prison guards and others around him. It was a tough circumstance, but he found a way to make the most of his situation. It saved his life.

Drivers aren't wrong or right, better or worse. They just are. I became familiar with how to work with mine. I knew they had the power to change the feel of my day.

What lies behind us and what lies before us are tiny matters compared to what lies within us.—**Ralph Waldo Emerson**

> **Bring a splash of colour
> to your day.**

Before moving on, you may want to:

- Think about the drivers or qualities that enhance or enrich your life experiences.
- Think of times when situations brought you joy, inner harmony, a feel-good sensation. Observe the common thread that links them all. You may find there are a few that enhance any experience immensely.
- Spend a moment testing the power of your drivers by imagining a situation that causes you dissatisfaction. Then in your mind create modifications that integrate your key drivers into that experience. Note what happens.

The Designer/Creator

When we know what we want from our life, we can use every situation to help create that. We can ride the ups and downs differently.

As I grew in my understanding of myself, I found more and more of my underlying potential. I did what I had never thought was possible—I started up a small business. What's more, I did it in a way that was very different from how I had previously gone about things.

As I felt myself growing, so did what I sought for my life. I had more idea of what I wanted and had more confidence and knowledge in how to achieve that. I started to see how I wanted things to be. I was able to envision possibilities in a way I had never done in the past, when I lived with what was handed to me.

When we went to Bali just before I opened my work studio, I went straight to the trinkets I knew would enliven it. When I arrived home, I pulled out bits of furniture from storage, and it came together in a flash. It was perfect. I wasted no time on uncertainty, confusion, and procrastination.

I took a similar approach with our beach house. I spent an hour in the selection centre picking colours and fixtures, a day choosing the furniture and finishings, an hour deciding on the garden structure. I had come to realize having a vision for what I liked meant that as soon as it walked in my path, I snatched it.

I noticed the stronger I held the vision or feeling for something and the more I knew my heartfelt reason for it, the more it would eventually come to pass. It was as though everything knew my intention, and it all fell into place.

It reminded me of a visualization study to help players get better at throwing goals in basketball. Visualization, in real time, had a profound positive effect on the goal-throwing outcomes. I remembered back to when I competed as an aerobic athlete. When I saw and felt myself doing the moves that were actually quite challenging, I was somehow able to achieve what my mind usually told me I couldn't.

Competitive aerobics arrived during a busy time in my life, when my children were very young. I had stumbled onto it through my involvement as a fitness instructor at that time. Although I did well at the sport and discovered the rewards of commitment and effort, I never truly realized the power of mind, vision, and intention that lay within. I did, however, watch someone in the sport who had discovered it early in her career. From the beginning of her involvement, she stated her intention to be the best in the world—and that is what she became.

I came to see the value of intention and vision in even the most simple and relatively insignificant things: killing flies, for example. When I merely thought about killing a fly in the house, I had little success. Killing a fly for the sake of killing a fly didn't work for me. Flies were living creatures and had their own purpose in life. When, however, my intention was clear, meaningful, and intense—I wanted to stop its germs from getting to my grandson's touch—I had 100 per cent success every time. Everything within me knew just how to make it happen.

I took the same approach when cancer arrived in my body. I felt so strongly that I'd recover from it. I could see my body cleaning up those radical cells. They weren't going to take over, because I wanted to live. I'm sure my body cells, nervous system, and everything else in between went to work to make it happen.

I thought about the power of purpose and vision for anyone fighting for life. They were important drivers of the will. The will to live often became the deciding factor. When I thought back to a close friend who was crushed by a tree during a violent storm, he wanted to *live!* He mentioned how the sound of his loved ones' voices in intensive care became the pull that drove his intention to not only survive but to walk again. He was determined. He knew what he wanted. How liberating to know.

In the past, I had often found myself in the unknown state, not sure of what to buy, select from the menu, read, and watch on television or at the movies. I was a procrastinator, tossing up all the possibilities, the pros and cons, in a way that eventually left me idle. It certainly inhibited my growth, my adventures, my engagement in activities, and my opportunities. I was waiting to get it right—the right time, the right place, the right person, the right approach. I always felt there was a right, and I was searching for it. Trouble was, I really didn't know what that right was.

When I started to envision more opportunities, I didn't wait for things in the same way. I created them. I knew the lifestyle I wanted and what was important within that. This was powerful in my day-to-day—in getting our beach house happening, in my new work direction, in setting up my studio at home, in the renovations to our bathroom and laundry, in gathering people together for dinner parties, and in the shows we attended.

I had so many more uplifting times. Those times were in the spirit of how I wanted to live and my priorities: peace, lightness, creativity, nurture, balance, and love. It was as though I was saving energy in my "happy tank." Life felt so much fuller.

When a "down" arrived in the form of a problem, issue, event, argument, illness, or death, it didn't feel so all-consuming. It was as though I had changed the balance between the ups and downs. That seemed to bring me more energy to cope with problems. It was as though the energy saved in my "happy tank" supported me during those times. Life wasn't all bad.

On top of that, I had more influence in how to work with it. I saw problems or issues as merely the name I gave to things that didn't fit with my vision and wants. It lessened the stress and discomfort that problems once created. I learned to have more influence and take more responsibility.

I had an issue with Steve when he would arrive home from work. I wanted to chat about his day and share my day with him, but he would usually snap and give little away. I felt frustrated and hurt, because I hadn't seen or spoken with him all day. It was my drivers and yearning for peace that took me to the heart of the problem. I began to envision what I was seeking, and that led me to sit in his shoes and take his side. I realized how tired he must have been from his heavy client schedule and intense personal interactions. He needed some space. I hadn't been listening in that way in the past, and I was in fact feeding the problem. If I gave him about fifteen minutes to unwind from his busy day with time alone and quiet, he was so much more responsive to conversation. That only took me twenty years to discover!

I wanted to feel at peace in my relationship, and this helped me create that. I went on to realize it was best not to ask him questions during a live televised football match, for example, or to do a job when he was in the middle of doing another job. These were small shifts that, in time, contributed to some big changes in our mutual consideration for each other. I had found a way to achieve a more peaceful environment. Despite things that ruffled my world—like Steve's cancer and other challenges—I had some influence in how to lessen their dramatic impact.

It may help you to read, as I did, *The Power of Intention* by Dr. Wayne W. Dyer.

The only thing worse than being blind is having sight with no vision.—**Helen Keller**

> **Feel what you want to create and let that guide you.**

Our Way

When we listen to signals from our body, senses, and feelings, we will find many clues about ourselves.

I began to realize that when I listened to what someone else told me about what would be best for me, it didn't feel right. And it couldn't, because much of what was suggested just didn't fit with my life.

This realization arrived strongly when I decided to change my lifestyle after cancer. There was so much information about what to eat, what not to eat, what to do and what not to do, what to take and what not to take. At first, I felt overwhelmed at the thought. Then fear crept in. What if I didn't do all that I should to keep my body well? One naturopath virtually told me I was doomed if I didn't! Worry, confusion, uncertainty, and fear filled my body and talk.

Then I heard myself. I caught myself out. All the traps had arrived in me again. I was trying to follow someone else's rules and had lost connection with myself. I started to listen without fear and with my heart—with a sense of love for myself and what was best. As I considered my options in food, supplements, and lifestyle practices, I learned to read my initial sense of what felt right and what didn't. Calmness, cooperation, and willingness often indicated *yes*, while agitation, objection, and angst usually meant *no*. I tried things out and felt for myself, and when I really tuned in, I received the information.

This was how I settled on some approaches initially (blood-group diet, herbs, caffeine-free, wheat-free, body scrubs, meditation, EFT, Chinese medicine, chiropractic). I noted the impact each had on my body. I observed, listened, and sensed. I learned for myself about what gave me energy, what disturbed my system, what balanced my body, what fitted with the important things in my life, what I enjoyed, what I valued, and what felt right. When those things no longer agreed with me, for whatever reason, I changed things up again.

Some things came into my life through coincidences that couldn't be ignored. That was how I was introduced to transfer factors, and in time they became another addition to my regime—and went on to help Steve during his illness. I found this also to be the case with the exercise I chose. When I stumbled upon the five Tibetan rites by a similar coincidence, it became a physical routine that had a marked impact on my body and my mind. I noticed it brought sharpness to my recall—of names in particular, which was very useful—and relief from many aches and pains.

I had created my own approach to nutrition and lifestyle that worked and felt good for me. I could explain the reason for all my choices, and I felt positive and comfortable with them all. I began to create habits around the things I chose for my life rather than remain in the habits of the past. I set the environment, changed my talk, and established approaches to support my new way.

I had moved away from the *shoulds* and chose more mindfully what satisfied and worked for me and was achievable and sustainable in my life. I did not need to justify my decisions. This confidence helped me take ownership and accept the consequences of my choices. It took me away from the fear, uncertainty, and worry.

Doing it my way felt empowering and true to me. I didn't rely on the naturopath for my path back to health but rather chose from among the options the naturopath offered. I decided who I would listen to for information and opinions.

I came to see the importance of getting to know myself to read the clues. I discovered they usually arrived in the form of a vitalized shift: an expression, significant metaphor, tone, volume, energy, gesture, relief, or lightness. My subconscious was a powerful tool in finding my inner truth.

I began to notice the subtle shifts that occurred when I was working with people. I remember one man who, for the love of his family and his desire to provide them with security, worked tirelessly from very early in the morning until late at night. His eyes would light up when he spoke of his family and the rare times he spent with them. When he needed to make a decision about a change in work, his subconscious gave him the clues he needed—but he had to listen. I asked him to notice what happened when he spoke about the two options, and he discovered for himself the one that offered a path to what he was actually seeking, and that was more time with his family. He felt good about his decision.

When I lost a dear friend to cancer, the words in her eulogy highlighted that she did it her way. That stood out to me. It was at the moment when Frank Sinatra singing "My Way" started playing that I saw the powerful importance of that—not only for those with cancer but for anyone facing anything big in life.

Be who you are and say what you feel, because those who mind
don't matter and those who matter don't mind.—**Dr. Suess**

> **Listen. What is your**
> **body telling you?**

Balancing It All

When we are more conscious, we have eyes to notice what no longer works for us. We don't settle for, rather we influence a shift.

The difference between my present and my past was that my needs and values were beginning to play a much more significant role in my choices and direction. In knowing myself better, I directed my life more and chose how and what to balance, juggle, and integrate—not only in nutrition, but in physical activity, health practices, relationships, work, home, and all other aspects of importance. Somehow life felt more fluid because I was allowing myself to move and change with it.

I realized that one day things felt OK and the next day things appeared different. As new and different things appeared, the balance got disturbed.

The balance—what was that? The balance of what? Balance wasn't a formula of contributing time to all aspects of life. It wasn't putting more or less of something into my life. Balance was a feeling within me. Balance came when I was moving with ease, choosing with clarity, contributing to what I valued. It meant that I was aligned with my drivers and passions and feeling happy.

I began to see how the old models of work-life balance didn't function well. In the past, I had worked in organizations that focused on models, systems, and processes to get the balance right for workers. But we were humans, not machines, so a set structure and approach wouldn't guarantee anything. Many people still had high levels of stress, felt overworked, and remained unhappy—me included, when I was at the height of my imbalance.

No matter how much talking and training on balance and stress reduction we received, it was easy to take stress and overthinking along to leisure activities, dinners, family outings, and holidays. It was just too difficult to switch off. It wasn't until fatigue or burnout arrived that a complete recharge was sought. And that recharge was often out of balance too. It felt more like a see-saw ride.

The all-or-nothing approach—on a diet or not, getting fit or not—happened so often. I experienced it with my work cycle back in 2003. I went to the edge of my capacity, and it wasn't until I nearly fell off in a bad way that I reached for the other side to balance it out. A dangerous game!

To gain what I felt was balance, I began to really listen. It was a moment-by-moment thing, rather than a formula or rule, that helped me integrate and adapt. The sooner I took charge, the less likely I was to feel overwhelmed. I used the natural responses of my body, mind, and spirit as my guide in assessing the new players on the scene.

229

- When a new player arrived as a pain or discomfort in my body, balance told me to slow down with what was causing it.
- When I felt sluggish and slow, balance told me to get up and move.
- When I was disorganized and all over the place, balance told me to form a strategy and system.
- When it was all about me, balance told me to think of others.
- When it was all about others, balance told me to take care of myself.
- When I was too structured and regimented, balance told me to throw away the structure.
- When I felt tense about meeting a deadline, balance told me to take a break and find clarity.
- When I felt overwhelmed with so many things to do, balance told me to stop and have some personal time and fun.
- When I was experiencing uncertainty or challenging emotions, balance told me to lighten up.
- When I was feeling frustrated with someone, balance told me to take a short break from that person.
- When I was out of proportion with my focus, balance told me to vary it.
- When I felt bloated in my stomach, balance told me to rest from that food.
- When I felt full in my stomach, balance told me to stop eating food.

I made it my business to check in regularly, especially when discomfort hit. I was open to changing things up and found the courage to do so. I allowed myself to take a break, go for a walk, say no to extra work, go away for the weekend, eat out, or change a pattern. I did things others never expected from me because in the past I just endured nicely whatever I was in.

In moments when I felt in balance, I enjoyed the feeling. Sometimes I had a delusional thought that I "had it." But balance was not a static thing, because each day brought something new to the mix that would have me challenged again. It always would. Everything was constantly changing, so the only way to stay in balance was to keep connected, listen, and adjust.

I laughed when I heard people and myself say "I'm getting there!" I always wondered where *there* was. It seemed to be another trap—getting to the elusive *there*—so much so that in the past, I'd set goals to try to get closer to it and then believe it would all be good. In the end, I'd set more and more goals to reach the next *there*, because the other *there* didn't seem to bring the feeling I expected.

In the past, I was striving for more and often doing things mindlessly without really enjoying or appreciating what happened along the way or when I got there. I'm sure I wasn't alone with that. I now saw that *there* wasn't a destination. It was the *how* of embracing life.

Almost every wise saying has an opposite one, no less wise, to balance it.—**George Santayana**

> **Bring the see-saw back
> to balance now.**

 Before moving on, you may want to:

- Take a moment to notice where the see-saw is positioned right now in your life, your year, your month, your day, your moment.
- Think about what you can do to bring it closer to equilibrium.

231

Goals and Challenges

When you set goals, make room for challenges and shifts. Be prepared to change course.

I found setting goals held other dangers. I had a very determined nature, and when I set a goal, I believed I had to achieve it. I'd forget it was a just a construct for that moment in time. Sometimes it wouldn't even feel right or fit in with other parts of my life, but I felt I needed to make it happen because I said I would. It was likely to be part of the reason I struggled when things didn't go according to plan.

My new understanding saw a goal as more a beginning version of a general vision. It was my way of generating a future possibility, and for that it was extremely useful. It was not something, however, that was concrete, or something I was locked into. There were too many external influences that could have had other plans. It was not something to indicate my success or failure, become obsessed over, become sick over, lose life perspective over, neglect other important things over, or become blind over when other more meaningful or useful possibilities arrived.

It was just a post in my life, but it was not my life. It was another mechanism to shape my circumstances and utilize on my journey of personal growth and expression, something I was prepared to alter if, along the way, I discovered something new that challenged its value.

I began to practise this more fluid approach on a small scale in my day-to-day tasks. For example, in the past, I'd plan a course of action for the day's events and methodically and systematically work through the list. As I began to relax and release some of the rigidity, I loosened my grip on the plan. I knew what I wanted to achieve and looked for the best opportunities to do so.

This approach was powerful in writing this book. As I relaxed with structure, I was able to change the shape and content as I grew with it. I came to see how important it was for our fast-changing times. Locking into too rigid a plan would only keep us in the version of old and not moving with the new. This was a whole new world for me—someone who had stayed in one workplace for twenty years!

Moving and working with the flow felt so much more enjoyable. I connected with more of what was available to me, and there was a lot available.

> *When it is obvious that the goals cannot be reached, don't adjust the goals, adjust the action steps.*—**Confucius**

Change up something that no longer works.

The Outcome

When we are compassionate and consider our body and circumstance along the way to achieving our goals, it will be a healthier, more expansive and rewarding outcome.

Sometimes when I just didn't feel up to doing things, I listened to my body and stopped. Amazingly, in what seemed like a short time later, I listened to my body again and it felt more motivated. I'd then find myself able to do those things with ease and energy rather than struggle and pain.

I learned to trust that I would get things done. I slowly developed a confidence to relax and work with myself rather than against myself. Somehow I actually felt I achieved more with fewer struggles. I moved more freely and gave myself the OK to address those things that were top priority. When I listened closely, my body, mind, spirit, and emotions guided me.

Life wasn't feeling as tense and hard. I felt I was living the term "go with the flow," not just saying it. I started to feel how to do it. It felt good when I was flowing on a path in the direction of my dreams and honouring my well-being along the way.

I began to make small yet significant shifts with my choices. I reduced my work to part-time, restructured the number of hours I worked in a day, took time off when needed, and engaged in things that brought me a sense of feeling good.

I felt my decision to not work during the time of Steve's illness was another testament to my growth in this area. My healthier approach to how I maintained my life vision among challenges made me feel I was not only coping better but thriving. I didn't need to sacrifice one for the other.

I have always found that mercy bears richer fruits
than strict justice.—***Abraham Lincoln***

Acknowledge your success
when you nurture yourself.

Inner Resources

Every challenge in life draws out some amazing qualities, strengths, and skills. When we consciously acknowledge these, we show ourselves that they exist—and that's all we need to know.

My life challenges took me in new directions, and among those I discovered capabilities I never knew existed. During my coaching course qualification, for example, I was faced with an activity that required me to use metaphor. When I learned of this task, my immediate reaction was, "I can't write—I can't do that." I didn't think it was possible. I hardly knew what a metaphor was!

Later that evening, before I started the exercise, I settled my mind from all the ego talk, all the chatter about *can't*, and found a still and silent place. I waited for something to arrive. I waited . . . and in the next moment, I turned my head and looked out the window to our outdoor entertaining area. Nestled in the ficus tree I noticed a small bird's-nest. As I looked more closely, I saw a tiny bird peer out to the sky. I became mesmerised by its first attempts to engage the world. I was in a trance, I'm not sure for how long.

When I returned to my task, I tried to create my metaphor. *Nothing.* Blank. Then it hit me. It had arrived in the form of the bird in the nest. Metaphor or not, this is what arrived. It took only a minute to write:

New Life

The birdling peers above the boundaries
of its lovingly constructed nest to view
an expanse so vast . . . so daunting.

He asks,

"What am I meant to do—how can I journey afar?
If I don't try, I may be here forever!"

With an overwhelming sense of courage,
he looks to a destination near . . .

and instinctively knows just the way to get moving . . .

the answers within.

Support and love of those who care . . .

his attempts more able.

With confidence building, small journeys . . .

nest to tree, tree to nest, nest to big tree, big
tree to nest, nest to new neighbourhood, new
neighbourhood to new neighbourhood.

So the wonderful adventure begins.

Journeys . . . not just journeys,

learning, sharing, giving, inspiring . . .

"How this is worth it," he proclaims

as colour, sound, smell, movement
swirls from everywhere.

He ventures deeper with an inner peace and
confidence into an ocean of space along the
flight path with other birds so grand.

There is a sense of belonging.

Share the spirit . . .

be the eagle within.

I sensed how vital it was to value these findings in ourselves. We were all
facing changing times—job losses, redundancy, illness, death, financial
crisis, changing institutions—and it was more and more difficult to find
the elusive motivation "out there" for our personal fulfilment. I began
to find my fulfilment from the motivation within, where my resources,
creativity and ingenuity lived and were available.

It may help you to read, as I did, *A Whole New Mind: Why Right-Brainers
Will Rule the Future* by Daniel H. Pink.

*When I stand before God at the end of my life, I would hope
that I would not have a single bit of talent left and could
say, "I used everything you gave me."*—**Erma Bombeck**

> **Do it different—discover
> something new.**

CHAPTER 24

KEY FINDING 3 —
CONNECT WITH OTHERS

I realized it was never a solo path. It was from
others that I learned most about myself. They were
the path to my own insights. No matter what they
brought—like or dislike—they were important. My
heart slowly opened. My compassion grew. I began
to feel the nature of the unconditional. I began to
feel the power of love.

We Can't Do It Alone

Nothing we do or have achieved has been done on
our own.

I would often stop and ask myself what everyone else in the world was
doing right now. Each and every other person was like you and me,
in an experience of some sort. We all experienced the outcome of the
universal unfolding at each moment.

Each moment contributed purpose, challenge, experience, understanding, legacy, and influence. We were all recipients of some awe-inspiring moments and some tragic or challenging moments. No one was exempt from that inevitability. We were all dealing with the same uncertainties and possibilities, but we weren't experiencing them alone. I affected others, they affected me. I provided for others, they provided for me. We relied on each other in the unfolding of our life experience.

I saw that in the simple activity of purchasing food to prepare a meal, there was a whole team of people involved: farmers, transport drivers, food-preparation operators, vendors, bank-facility operators, gas and electricity suppliers, and more. Every aspect of the service and product relied on a chain of support to reach the final destination—my dinner table.

We each played a role in the functioning of life. While some may have thought one role was more important than another, it was in fact each role that was significant in our ability to achieve our life vision. No one can do it alone. Everything I have achieved has been enabled because of others in some way.

> *One's life has value so long as one attributes value*
> *to the life of others, by means of love, friendship,*
> *and compassion.*—**Simone de Beauvoir**

> **Never underestimate**
> **the worth of others.**

Our Influence on Each Other

We gather and collect meaning from everything around us in ways and times beyond our knowing. When we appreciate that in randomness we receive the infusion of human possibilities, we get that everyone in that pot is important.

Throughout our lives, the contributions from both the formal and incidental made it too difficult to know the value of each. Yet each of us has had a significant influence on the lives of others. Every interaction, dialogue, support, discussion, or action contributed in ways we may never imagine.

When I undertook my practical teaching experience during my younger years, I was fortunate to be supervised by a qualified teacher who had some amazing perspectives on life. He had a marked influence on my growth as a person. He would never know the magnitude of his influence. It was something I have never forgotten.

There were many other small yet significant things that shaped me, some of which I recall in detail and others I have no recollection of.

An email I received typified the magnitude of this very point. It was about a teacher who began a classroom project titled, "Who you are makes a difference." Every child in the class heard from the teacher why that was so. It had such an impact. They wanted to share the concept with the community. They brought it to people from all walks of life, and the impact was overwhelming. For many, it was just what they needed to hear. Many of their lives were riddled with sadness and feelings of worthlessness, and such an act of kindness made a huge difference.

So in this life, we both receive and give. We are the consumer and the recipient. No matter what we give, it is important for overall growth.

What I gave others was my gift, and what they gave me was their gift. Gifts were often disguised and seen as problems or nuisances—the difficult child, the words I didn't want to hear, the sick family member, or the person I disliked. I realized those gifts brought me the opportunity to develop and find ways to be with them, focusing on tolerance, care, and acceptance.

I was beginning to see that everything was important in my life, no matter how much I did or didn't want it. All these things were necessary for me to develop as a person.

The value of a man should be seen in what he gives and not in what he is able to receive.—**Albert Einstein**

> **Never underestimate
> your worth to others.**

Sameness

And just how it is for us, it is for others.

In time, I came to see the sameness in us all. Our minds and bodies in their physiology and physical composition shared so much in common. This alone was a great reason to be compassionate.

We each felt the range of emotions possible from love and fear. We saw the spectrum of light and all it projected, manmade and natural. We heard the sounds and messages exposed to us in various modes—from our parents, teachers, leaders, friends, community, and world—and we experienced the ups and downs of life through our circumstances. We were likely to be in the same overwhelming state of wobbliness.

I became better at listening on this level. I could see that others, too, were affected by things in their world. When I took the time, I began to hear similar stories, similar traps, and similar challenges. It helped me realize I wasn't alone. We were all facing the same sorts of things.

More than ever, I felt everyone around me as the same. It seemed everyone was seeking. What were we all seeking? We might each answer differently, but it seemed that when I broke it down, there were many core similarities. And why wouldn't there be? We were all human. We each beat odds to be born at this time. That alone suggested something common between us.

I felt my eyes shift from judgement to appreciation. I hadn't been looking from the perspective of sameness. It helped me see so many wonderful things in others that I hadn't seen before. I was more able to feel their pain, notice their greatness, and understand them. It was how I became better at relating to some people who in the past I had found difficult.

From the outside, it appeared my tolerance had improved, but I realized it was more than that. Much of what others offered could remain undiscovered if I lost my way to relate to them. I understood the point of looking for the gifts—rather than noticing perceived flaws—in myself or others.

The only bond worth anything between human
beings is their humanness.—**Jesse Owens**

> **Focus on what is the same as you**
> **among what appears different.**

Difference

When we see difference as the problem, we are not able to see the value that difference brings.

It seemed difference was our biggest challenge. For as much as we were the same, we were different. Moments were unique, and that would ensure a depth of difference in us all.

I found difference brought me a new perspective and saved me from isolation. It was often the difference in opinion and ideas from others that spurred me to tackle new things. It helped me take on things in business that I was once closed to, such as social media and marketing. It helped me inject some spice in the way we celebrated family events and special occasions.

Difference inspired me to engage people I had once veered away from for many distorted reasons. I wasn't just trying to be friendlier, I genuinely wanted to discover more about them and their lives. It didn't matter who they were—if they were standing next to me in a line, or arriving as a client, or meeting me in a social setting. I became more and more curious. The talk was less about me and more about them. I spent time with others differently.

My curiosity led me to more conversations with my own father in the years before he died. I wanted to know more about his life, his stories, his views on life, his journey from Italy to Australia, his family. Sadly, however, many of his stories and insights will never be told.

My new awareness prompted me to glimpse the lives of others with so much more interest and curiosity. Their uniqueness and difference expanded what I saw possible for my own life.

While we have the gift of life, it seems to me the only tragedy is to allow part of us to die—whether it is our spirit, our creativity, or our glorious uniqueness.—**Gilda Radner**

> **See every difference**
> **as a gift.**

 Before moving on, you may want to:

- Imagine how it feels to live in the shoes of someone from a different country, situation, or age group.
- Find the gift within.

A Reflection of Each Other

Often what we see in others reflects an aspect of ourselves. At some point, we have been the very thing we love, hate, like, and dislike in others. Everything is on a sliding scale of oneness and appears different in different contexts.

I came to see how my values and perceptions had changed over time. Something I once described as good, bad, beautiful, ugly, right, or wrong only reflected how I saw and what I valued at that particular time. It was the reason I referred to my life before cancer as my "past life." That life seemed to be driven by a completely different person.

My cancer experience and the events around that time significantly changed the way I viewed things. I realized everything was relative to something. My challenge relative to my life before had things I saw as good shift to not so good and the not so good to good. The beautiful seemed not so beautiful, and the not so beautiful seemed beautiful.

My views and opinions of myself and others changed. The people I shared company with changed. The way I went about life changed. Things I had once been, seen, done, liked, and felt had shifted to something very different.

This change highlighted my capacity for the yin and yang. It was my life situation that influenced where I sat. Like a single ray of light that contained every colour, I, as a single human being, contained a potential for plenty. That was becoming clearer as I discovered things in myself that I didn't know existed.

As I looked out to those from other countries, at people who once seemed so different, I found they had the same potential. Everyone existed on the spectrum of oneness. How we presented at any given moment reflected what was prominent at that time: age, country, lifestyle, health, wealth, situation.

I realized that it was through the challenges I had experienced over the years that my "new self" had emerged, and that this was a good thing. I realized how valuable it was for me to continue to face things and expand. It was inevitable that I would face pain, but it was worth it.

When the new arrived in the shape of outside challenges—illness, bills, chores, business, relationships—I felt more equipped to face them. When the new arrived in challenges that I chose—for example, learning my first language, Italian—I felt more determined to face the pain, embarrassment, frustration, confusion, and uncertainty.

All difference in this world are of degree, and not of kind, because oneness is the secret of everything.—Swami Vivekananda

> **See others as a mirror to discover more about you.**

Creating Possibilities

When our experience is limited or heavily out of balance, we can only view from that lens.

I came to see that those who lived to the detriment of themselves, others, and the world were likely to be living from a limited perspective. Many appeared to be in situations where life was closing them into a world within their minds with stories—the ego stranglehold. For those who had experienced anger or brutality, fear or pain, resentment or jealousy, hatred or judgement, that could be how they saw the world. If someone hadn't been exposed to or involved with situations, people, or events that brought light or love, that option would seem less likely to be available to them.

This point was emphasized in *Les Miserables*, a movie I saw just recently. Jean Valjean, the main character of the movie, had his world turned upside down when a priest showed mercy and forgiveness after he stole silverware belonging to the church. The priest's love, blessings, and kindness changed Jean's view of the world, which he had previously only known as negative. From his new experience of kindness, he could no longer continue on his path of crime and anger. He turned himself around and brought light to his life and work.

In the past, I couldn't understand how people were unable to be or see better for their lives. How did people hurt others, commit awful crimes, deceive, manipulate, and do other wrongs? Until someone experienced or felt true kindness, love, or forgiveness, they couldn't live by it. The greatest gift in that situation would be the gift of kindness, forgiveness, and love.

When I received love and kindness during the time of my illness, I realized how beautiful it felt. That later influenced my own actions when caring for Steve and others in their time of illness. Before that, I didn't know how to care for someone during difficult times. It made sense how important it was to bring a glimpse of light to the lives of those in darkness, to give them the opportunity to feel and taste a new experience of the things that would help them in life, to be caring to show care, to be loving to show love, to be forgiving to show forgiveness, to be accepting to show acceptance. It was my intention to live by that in my work and life.

I saw with my own eyes the power that unconditional, genuine intent for support and love had on the lives of others. Sometimes it was all they needed to find their way. When negative behaviours of others were judged, abhorred, and criticized, it reinforced the experience of hate, criticism, and judgement that already existed in their troubled world. And what were we actually criticizing and judging? The actions of people troubled by a society and surroundings that we all had a role in creating.

The way to support a change in destructive behaviours and attitudes was to provide an experience of energy, care, love, and support. I felt strongly that it was the only way to bring love to our families, communities and world.

What you do speaks so loudly that I cannot hear
what you say.—**Ralph Waldo Emerson**

**Make it possible in
someone else's life.**

Receiving the message

In subtle ways our actions communicate our world.

At any one time, I represented an assimilation of all my learning and influences. When I began to look out at others from a more non-judgemental viewpoint, I saw that others—especially those who committed crimes and bad acts—were a testament to what was possible given their life situation. They offered valuable information. They were in a troubled state, and their actions communicated that.

I had never looked at it that way before. I had often just judged what came my way. I could hear my inner dialogue of *wrong, naughty, silly, unfair,* or whatever it was. I was caught up in the disappointment, frustration, and agitation of the action rather than what it represented or communicated.

It helped me see that I had done something similar with those close to me—Steve, my children, my family, and my friends. In time, I began to look more at their actions and talk as an expression of their world. That was their gift. They let me in. They let me know who they were.

When I opened up and expressed, I too shared things about myself. Receiving was a privilege. The message from my friends, my family, and all others was a privilege. It prompted a change in me—to take more notice of the message rather than judge the action. I felt my job was to listen. Many people were in trouble. They were struggling to find perspectives and approaches to keep them well and balanced. I felt more and more that was a major role for all of us—to find ways to support, nurture, and guide the ever-growing number of people who struggle.

An eye for any eye only ends up making the
*whole world blind.—**Mahatma Gandhi***

Just listen . . .

Interconnectedness

When we feel the interconnectedness between us and everything, we may begin to view ourselves on earth as a huge moving organism whose mission (like that of every other organism) is purely to survive as a whole.

I had moments where I glimpsed the intricate web of relationship between others and myself. I was connected not only to my immediate family and friends but to everything, in incidental ways that just were. I was connected by the universal forces that acted on me. In most moments, when I thought my life and body were separate from everything around me, I came to appreciate there was actually more to it.

My further reading on the matter made me realize that our bodies, homes, cars, furniture, and belongings—things I saw as solid objects—were actually all in motion. Their centres were atoms that consisted of a nucleus surrounded by electrons with charged particles in motion. No atom was a static thing. The frequency of the vibration of each atom determined whether it appeared still, solid, moving, or visible. Energy was always in motion—even my own outer shell that appeared solid was actually connecting with others from an energy perspective.

I'm not sure why, but I started to feel many subtle connections—through the oxygen (vegetation by-product) I breathed; through the carbon dioxide I expelled; through the natural cycles and rhythms of the Earth's orbit around the sun and the moon's orbit around the Earth; through the changing seasons, the high and low tides, the cycles of the moon. It somehow felt so incredible, the way we were all linked.

The indigenous people of the land had always known and respected this information. They used it for their survival; their fishing, planting, and hunting; and their culture, knowledge, understanding, and experience. This awareness was a gift to me. It helped me feel that I was never really alone. I had an immense connection with many elements around me, and when I was open to them, they offered support.

On many a lonely night during Steve's illness, the full moon was like a long-lost friend, and the stars against the blackened backdrop of a country sky brought an endless array of familiar faces. This whole sense of connection to nature helped strengthen my connection with people. I felt comforted when others were OK. The more under stress or in pain they were, the more it filtered into my being.

When my children struggled to find answers and perspectives with what they were facing, I felt it too. We were all in it together, and that seemed to expand my capacity for empathy. It also strengthened my resolve to maintain the framework of Self-Others-Earth (SOE). Doing anything for myself at the expense of others indirectly negated any positive. Doing for myself with consideration and benefit (not detriment) to others and the earth made much more sense.

Thousands of candles can be lighted from a single candle,
and the life of the candle will not shorten. Happiness
*never decreases by being shared.—****Buddha***

> **Feel the joy that joy
> brings to others.**

Before moving on, you may want to:

- Think about a time when you felt the energy field around another person when there was an instant connect or attraction. Feel how that came to be.

Energy Transformed

**When we think in terms of energy, we can find ways
to shift the balance of where that energy is focused
in our lives.**

Even my thoughts—the electric impulses running through my mind—were energy. All energy was in constant and perpetual movement, transforming into action, words, or emotion. From these, other transformations of energy rippled through.

Everything I experienced was imprinted in my mind and transformed in some way into my life. The energy of thought was received in my body and the bodies of others. This was evident in the way I sensed the mood and felt the plight of others. It was evident when I thought of a person just as he or she was contacting me, or when I discovered a friend was having the same thought at the same time in separate situations.

How often such examples presented! As I was writing this, I received a call from my dear friend who said she was in contemplation over ways to help with her stress when Chi Kung came into her mind. She contacted me, as it was something we had intended to do together a few years before. The thing was, that very morning the idea of Chi Kung came to me, and I decided to get back into the Friday morning sessions.

It was more than thoughts that had power. What I felt in my heart had even more power to manifest greatness. This had been proven over and again in different situations. I marvelled at a study that dated back to June 7 and July 30, 1993, led by a scientist, John Hagelin, in which several thousand people in Washington, DC, meditated twice a day for almost two months. The result found a correlation between the group meditation and the reduction in the crime rate during that period. It was hypothesised that from the silent space within those in the group practice, the electromagnetic field transmitted what was required.

On a smaller scale, I recall a time when I inherited my son's beagle, Bubbles. Bubbles the beagle was, to say the least, a hyperactive and mischievous two-year-old puppy when she arrived. It was at a time when I was looking for peace and freedom, and somehow she didn't fit the picture. Trouble was, she was special to my son, and I wasn't prepared to break their bond.

At first, Bubbles brought out the worst in me. I was resisting. I was trying to control things I couldn't. I couldn't stop her inquisitiveness, her playfulness, or her destructive mistakes. I could feel the angst in my body over it. Our relationship worsened. I was spending a lot of energy in the negativity of it. It was as though she knew how I felt.

Then one day, I decided the only way to resolve the situation was through my heart. I sat her down and looked deep into her eyes to a place where I saw a beautiful young lady who just wanted to be loved. She'd had a rough start to her life (she'd run into a moving car, jumped from a moving car, and escaped from home on several occasions), and she was seeking someone to guide her and be patient.

As I patted her beautiful multicoloured coat, I instantly felt gratitude pour from her. She quieted to a level I hadn't experienced before. She received the message from my heart as I felt hers. It was the turning point in our relationship. She is now a much-loved member of our family and gives us so much more—in fact, a story about *The Adventures of Bubbles the Beagle* could be a bestseller!

Empathy from my heart was the vehicle that transported me to the heart of others and the heart of things.

> *The best and most beautiful things in the world cannot be seen or even touched—they must be felt with the heart.*—**Helen Keller**

Bring intention from your heart and enjoy what you reap.

Listening Beyond the Logic of the Mind

With an appreciation of what lies beyond what we see, we are more open to the amazing connection between science and a higher intelligence. It can resurrect our faith in something beyond our body, mind, and spirit, and with that comes hope.

I enjoyed reading about the new science and evidence of a connection to a greater existence. There were revelations about the mind's potential and its connection through frequency with the super conscious that existed beyond our realm.

I found topics on quantum, plasma, and magnetic-field physics were a scientific interpretation of what I and so many people already knew and felt in their own way—there was communication and information from another source. Wisdom was far more than intellectual intelligence— what we refer to as IQ. I began to read more on spiritual intelligence, emotional intelligence, and heart intelligence, and it was beginning to make sense of different ways of functioning.

My ongoing personal work enhanced my desire and willingness to explore these topics without judgement, precedence, and relativity. It helped open my eyes when the magic of information, clues, coincidences, messages, and attractions felt so strong.

One example was the evening I arrived early for a workshop on EFT (Emotional Freedom Technique). I found myself in discussion with a doctor who was presenting a seminar on transfer factors in the same complex. I was meant to be with a friend, but because of a flare-up of fibromyalgia, she couldn't attend. Ironically, the doctor informed me that transfer factors worked wonders for people with fibromyalgia. That was the clue—I was meant to listen. As it turned out, they were not only useful for her, they were wonderful for me as well. I realized I had in fact been introduced to them in the past but hadn't chosen them at that point. My gut led me to know it was time to try them out.

I realized how the gut feeling that told me to get checked out with my health issue indirectly saved my life. The coincidences that arrived in my life were more than just coincidences. Padre Pio let me know that Dad was well cared for. The time of Sid's arrival, 22:44, let me know that Dad's energy was around. I began to trust the gut feelings and signs that in time helped me make sense of things.

When I found myself worrying, forcing, and controlling, I felt comforted by the magic that arrived in the form of subtle guides. They somehow always arrived. It was a personal language that arrived in a personal way.

It may help you to read, as I did, *Spiritual Intelligence: The Ultimate Intelligence* by Danah Zohar and Ian Marshall.

> *Great spirits have always encountered violent opposition*
> *from mediocre minds.*—**Albert Einstein**

> **Look to the coincidental and unusual for possible insights.**

CHAPTER 25

KEY FINDING 4—
LIVE IT HERE AND NOW

No matter what I discovered along the way, it was always about the "gap"—the "how" of bringing the knowing to the doing and being. I found that the journey I was embarking on enabled me to consciously apply my personal discoveries, and that got me closer to it. I also glimpsed moments where I felt nothing but being. Whether the feeling arrived naturally or whether I needed to pursue some constructive, healthy, and helpful ways, I recognized I was on the path to greater influence and a better feel for life.

Moments

When we see that it is from quality moments that we gain a quality life, then moments are all we need concern ourselves with.

I realized that if moments were my life, then it would be worthwhile that in some small way my vision and my true sense of self existed in them. That would mean that each moment, decision, talk, action, and approach would be aligning and moving me toward the very things I was striving for. I only had from now to the end of my life, so it made sense to live each day with traces of what I wanted for the next.

When I really thought about a moment, I realized there was a fine line between the past and future. It was both the future of one moment and the past of the next. No wonder it was easy to focus on the past (reflecting or ruminating) or focus on the future (creating or dreaming).

The gift I received when I got cancer was the connection I felt with the here and now. Get well and live right now. It helped me realize the time for anything was now. I had put things off in the past, waiting for them to arrive in the future. I realized living for that time jeopardized living. It was only in the here and now that I had to eat well, reduce stress, appreciate my days, heal my woes, find peace, and do some things I had wanted to achieve. I didn't have the time to wait.

I was fortunate my experience with the here and now brought another option of how to be with the moment. It meant from that point on, I had something else to choose. When my focus took me back to the past or away to the future, I would settle into my best here-and-now action and thought. Creating my future by living it in the present meant that each day I was planting the seeds of what I desired for my life. I was reflecting the life I was seeking.

It may help you to read, as I did, *The Power of Now: A Guide to Spiritual Enlightenment* by Eckhart Tolle.

> *What matters is to live in the present, live now, for every moment is now. It is your thoughts and acts of the moment that create your future. The outline of your future path already exists, for you created its pattern by your past.*—**Sai Baba**

> **Feel your vision for life
> in each breath.**

 Before moving on, you may want to ask yourself:

- How is life for me right now?
- Am I living the path to my future vision?
- Am I living with intentions, connections, and traces of action and energy for that which I envision?
- Do I realize that my dreams are on the road to my reality when I create small steps in that direction?

Bring Learning to the Moment

The more aware we become, the more we can choose to move from our traps and toward the life we desire. We are more open to notice "what is" and work with that to achieve in our lives.

I began to see that the more I learned and understood about creation, existence, myself, my relationships, my past, my ego, my drivers, and my vision, the better the quality of my experience in day-to-day moments would be. I became an active partner in the moment, with more insight into how to bring things back to a balance, a sense of joy and happiness, a sense of appreciation and hope, and a sense of love and compassion. These became my personal markers of success.

Another marker of success was my ability to more swiftly find my way to these balancing experiences. The more I learned about myself, the more I could identify my traps and be more aware of ways to settle myself down.

The new perspectives and approaches caused some of my old beliefs, habits, and rules to lessen their hold over me. I could move from blame, take responsibility, and let go of lots of things that weren't necessary to hold on to. I could challenge my thoughts, identify the emotion that may have sabotaged my moment, identify the nonsense logic I used to prove it, and admit to my actual self-serving intention in that moment.

These strategies were all on offer to free me from remaining in tension for subsequent moments and help me move on. I could snap out of things more easily (something I found difficult to do in the past). I brought something from within to see more clearly. I had ways to break the cycle, escape the entrenchment, and find clarity again.

The sooner I turned to my heart, where unconditional love resided, the more I brought forth my true intentions and cleared my clouded vision. My learning enabled me to get back to what I wanted rather than waste moments on what I didn't want.

> *There is only one corner of the universe you can be certain of improving, and that's your own self.*—**Aldous Huxley**

**Draw from the experience
of past wonders.**

Bring Appreciation to the Moment

No matter what happened, I appreciated the fact that I was in it and growing from it. I was more open to new perspectives. They had a big impact; they inspired and often shifted my perception of reality. They weren't just words in a phrase that sounded powerful. They *were* powerful. They had punch!

- "I am alive and privileged to experience life."
- "The past lives within me, and I live as a memory in the future."
- "Ups and downs are unfolding at the same moment."
- "All that is possible can exist in a moment."
- "It is but a moment and then there is the next."
- "Everything passes."
- "Nothing is permanent."

I appreciated that moments were the beginning of a creation, so I valued and treated them that way. They were potentially the beginning of something very amazing and very important in my life.

> *As we express our gratitude, we must never forget*
> *that the highest appreciation is not to utter words,*
> *but to live by them.*—**John F. Kennedy**

Find a message that has punch in your life!

Bring Stillness to the Moment

When I discovered more about the function of the brain, I came to train it in a way that minimized its sabotaging nature. I had approaches to settle my busy left brain, and I had strategies to manage the overemotional tendency of my right brain. I realized that often, it wasn't personal. It was something that just happened in the complexity of it all.

It was through the circuit breakers that I found the stillness and calm within.

In the midst of movement and chaos, keep
*stillness inside of you.—**Deepak Chopra***

> **Notice the pause between**
> **each breath.**

Bring the Senses to the Moment

When I was lost in my head—pulled into the traps of my brain—I remembered I had a body and jumped into my skin and connected with all that surrounded me. That approach enabled me to appreciate how my senses enhanced an experience.

The detail in what I saw, heard, smelled, tasted, and felt seemed to expand, and this alone brought something special to each moment. With eyes to see, I noticed the colour of a hot summer evening sky; with ears to hear, I noticed the subtle whistle of the trees that formed a backdrop to the chatter of birds in an early morning encounter; with a nose to smell, I noticed the scent of freshness of the herbs I used in my cooking; with a mouth to taste, I noticed the sweet, sour, tangy, and bitter elements to my food and felt the texture on my palate. I noticed crunchy, chewy, squishy, furry, tough textures.

It reminded me that life existed in the simplicity and beauty of what I could access through my senses. I allowed myself to live that life.

If we could see the miracle of a single flower clearly,
*our whole life would change.—**Buddha***

> **Close your eyes. Describe how**
> **you know you are alive.**

Bring Conscious Talk to the Moment

I found when I took note of what was happening in moments by talking it through, I kept myself more grounded to the here and now and to what was presenting—*I am driving to work, listening to music, thinking about the roadworks holding up traffic, getting agitated by reckless drivers, changing gears.*

When I could no longer hear the sound of present talk, I realized I had wandered off into a silent void where my mindlessness and stories lived. It was something to watch out for.

> *The key to success is to focus our conscious mind on things we desire, not things we fear.*—***Brian Tracy***

> **Talk what you see rather than what you think to break the cycle.**

Bring Conscious Awareness to Moments

When I noticed what I was noticing and where my attention was focused, I was in a much better position to catch the traps when they appeared: negative emotions, a recurring worry, a fear for the future, a false belief, an unhelpful habit. I had the chance to discover something else to do with it and redirect my attention elsewhere.

I tuned in more quickly and honestly to the signals, which were clues that I had been taken over by the traps.

A life lived of choice is a life of conscious action.
A life lived of chance is a life of unconscious
creation.—Neale Donald Walsch

Notice what you notice.

Bring the Unconditional to Moments

When in stillness and silence I found myself closer to the unconditional, I was open to seeing differently. I noticed the point of difference, the missing link, the opportunity, the detail, the layers, and the thing I hadn't seen before. I could somehow see the patterns that made sense of things, the creative solutions to problems, the new approach that worked better, and the many things that I later came to recognize as utter nonsense. I could often see what wasn't there and not see what was.

I remember a time when I had just bought milk, so I "knew" it was in the fridge. When I opened the fridge door to prepare my shopping list, I saw the milk, because I knew it should have been there. Unbeknownst to me, my son had used the milk the night before. My mind, however, created a picture of it as though it was still sitting there.

And the time I was looking for my keys, I looked in the same place over and over again. Nothing. Then somehow they seemed to just appear. Truth was, I was so busy rummaging I wasn't actually seeing clearly.

I realized that when I wanted to see things, I could. When I was on the lookout for a particular car, a particular sign, a reason for liking something, a reason for not liking something, whatever it was, I could find it. When I sought negative, I found negative. When I sought positive, I found positive. When I sought unusual, I found unusual. When I sought unconditional, I found unconditional—and unconditional was neither negative nor positive. It was more like an opportunity to see that many things in my life were actually time-consuming and unhelpful.

The unconditional helped me move toward better ways. In the clearness of the unconditional, many new routines and approaches appeared. I changed how I went about shopping, filing, cleaning, working, washing, cooking, socializing, engaging, communicating. After twenty years, my eyes opened up to a quicker, more effective way to peg my clothes on the line! I reaped the benefits, and life felt better for it.

I read about entrepreneurs who had become successful because of their ability to "see outside of the square." Steve Branson, for example, attributed his success to looking outside the realm of normal. The nuances led him to approach things differently, and that brought success.

> *Entrepreneurs are simply those who understand that there is little difference between obstacle and opportunity and are able to turn both to their advantage.*—**Niccolo Machiavell**

> **Look out with eyes
> that have no bias.**

Bring the Spirit of Humanness to the Moment

When I connected with the essence of my humanness, I felt the lightness of that moment. I was human, and while I may have *thought* I needed to do, say, and be—and *felt* I needed to do, say, and be—it was in fact an illusion.

It helped me see my life as a playing field to practice on. And play it was. In his book *A Whole New Mind*, Daniel H. Pink shares a quote from Dr. Lauren Artress, Episcopal priest and labyrinth pioneer: "We are not humans on a spiritual path, but spiritual beings on a human path." That started to make sense to me.

As a spiritual being, when I brought spirit to an experience, it felt like medicine. The spirit of lightness—humour, forgiveness, passion, beauty, and love—made life feel amazingly different. I laughed more, and things felt more vital, fresh, and vibrant, less serious and heavy. I realized that the essence of my spirit was always around when I needed it. I just needed to call upon it!

It may help you to read, as I did, *The Art of Happiness: A Handbook for Living* by the Dalai Lama and Howard C. Cutler.

> *I always try to balance the light with the heavy—a few tears of human spirit in the sequins and the fringes.*—**Bette Midler**

> **Whatever it is,**
> **play lovingly with it.**

Appreciate When Awareness Arrives

Awareness enables us to shift. Awareness arrives in its own time—it can't be forced upon us.

The choices I made were based on my awareness at the time. The more I chose a path of personal discovery and empowerment, the more it seemed my awareness expanded. But at any one time, I could only be as aware as my awareness allowed.

- If I thought I was aware but could do no other way, my awareness of how may not have allowed it.
- If I thought I was aware and knew how but didn't do, I may not have been aware of why.
- If I thought I was aware and could do and knew why, but still didn't do, I may not have been aware of other things about myself.
- If I thought I was aware of all of these but still didn't do, I may not have been aware of awareness itself.

I came to see that shifts in my awareness were reflected in how I experienced life, and the new and different I gravitated to. It reflected an ongoing process that was happening in its own time, in its own way—nothing more, nothing less. It couldn't have arrived any faster than the rate it arrived.

Knowing that, I could accept and be more forgiving of myself for my past ways. It helped me deal with feelings of regret when they arrived. Regret somehow didn't feel as uncomfortable. I began to use regret as more an indication that I had moved in my process—I had shifted into something different. And that was something to celebrate.

Regret didn't seem to last long enough to fester into guilt and shame; it passed through me more easily, and I was able to catch a pocket of gratitude for my growth and influence. My job was to nab regret as quickly as possible when it arrived. When I found myself regretful over something, such as slacking off on my exercise routines or eating poorly or speaking badly to someone or selecting easy options, it became my trigger to choose and create different actions that supported my true intention.

Despite the usually slow start, after a few mild and seemingly insignificant attempts, I could usually find my way. I'd reconnect with the five Tibetan rites routine or my basic chi kung set of movements or a healthier, more natural eating pattern. I found ways to face up to what I once avoided and the courage to return to my heart space, which brought me to a better tone and engagement with others.

As I watched the way I moved and reconnected with what I actually wanted, I realized I had really grown in my awareness of how to do it with love and respect.

Few are those who see with their own eyes and feel with their own hearts.—**Albert Einstein**

When awareness arrives in your life, do something with it.

The World—Our Reflection

When we recognize that the way we see the world, our life, our day, our moment is a reflection of the state of ourselves, we will know when to nurture ourselves and what to do.

How I saw the outside reflected my outlook and where I was at with things. When I felt well, energized, and positive, things tended to feel easier and I could place my attention on the positive aspect of things. When I felt less well, low in energy, and physically or emotionally stretched, things felt a lot harder.

It was from these internal states (such as anxiety, stress, or sadness) and physical states (such as fatigue, hunger, or weakness) that I began to learn about my limits and thresholds with this way of life. There were times when the old habits and patterns tended to re-emerge. I began to recognize the context—the times and situations—where my vulnerabilities, strengths, and limitations came to light.

It was all part of the process. Every life situation extended my cause for how to be true to myself, no matter who was watching and what was expected. I glimpsed times when I was no longer *trying to be* patient, tolerant, and accepting; I was *being* patient, tolerant, and accepting. *Trying to be* was replaced by *being*.

I began to feel more moments of just that—being. During those times, it seemed as though the world was so full and rich. Every corner brought something new. I realized that as I gained respect and wonder for my own life, my view on the world and its treasures also expanded.

It may help you to read, as I did, *Loving What Is: Four Questions That Can Change Your Life* by Byron Katie with Stephen Mitchell.

> *We see things not as they are, but as we are*
> *ourselves.—**H. M. Tomlinson***

**When you feel lost in life,
bring it back to a moment**

Trust

Have faith in what arrives.

My choice to take this road of discovery had me testing and trying difference, and from that came change. It was a very conscious approach at first. When my conscious attempts began to naturally infiltrate my day-to-day life, I realized I knew how to do it. It was like the unconscious competent state you enjoy when you finally drive a car without having to think about it.

It seemed the approach was integrated within me and had an intelligence of its own. I somehow knew when to take a breath, stop and silence, challenge my thoughts, nurture me or walk away and smell the roses. It helped me to cope and thrive in what I was in.

Not to say that I didn't find myself on the mindless and unaware path at times. When I realized I was out of sorts, I'd go back to some of my more conscious approaches to help me out. I would consciously infuse a breath, stop and silence, challenge my thoughts, and nurture me or walk away to smell the roses.

But whether it came naturally or whether it was under my conscious choice, it was all part of the process. It was an ongoing transformation. I trusted it was happening in a time and way that was meant to be, and for that I was able to accept where I was with it all. Sometimes here, sometimes there. I was on the path to a better me and a better life.

I trusted that everyone else was also on the path, albeit at different places and stages. Life on the path was not competitive. It was a process, in one's own time and way. For that, I found it possible to let go, forgive, and love myself and others for any mishaps along the way.

Adopt the pace of nature: her secret is patience.—**Ralph Waldo Emerson**

**Whatever arrives,
be grateful**

PART

In a Nutshell

This section provides some quick approaches to Find the Way:

- *Tune In*. Three steps to help with unnecessary patterns: identify, admit, decide.
- *Rebalance*. Two questions to help when stuck: Where am I now? How am I trapped?
- *Shift*. One acronym to help with ideas: PATIENCE.

Whether you decide to try it out or not is wholly up to you. Love and respect whatever you decide. Let self-nurturing be the path to everything else.

CHAPTER **26**

TUNE IN

Three Quick Steps

Identify

Admit

Decide

God grant me the serenity to accept things I cannot change,
The courage to change things I can, And the wisdom
*to know the difference.—**The Serenity Prayer***

Step 1: Identify—Without Attachment

Notice any vulnerabilities or pain in the context and content of your life—what, when, with whom, and where. Make an attempt identify:

- your qualities
- your values
- your emotions

- your thoughts
- your virtues
- your patterns
- your habits
- your wants
- your needs.

Listen, feel and see:

- I can . . .
- I do . . .
- I have . . .
- When . . .
- If . . .
- Where . . .
- I can't . . .
- I don't . . .
- I have not . . .
- When . . .
- If . . .
- Where . . .

Step 2: Admit—Without Judgement

Admit, however you perceive that to be:

- the good and the bad
- the wrong and the right
- the should and the should not
- the true and the false
- the possible and the impossible
- the confusing and the clear
- the black and the white
- the harsh and the gentle.

Step 3: Decide—with Action

It is your choice. Take ownership and accept the consequences.

- You could decide to just be aware.
- You could decide to debunk old ways.
- You could decide to find your heart.
- You could decide to develop more skills.
- You could decide to test and trial.
- You could decide to reflect.
- You could decide to be brave and courageous.
- You could decide to explore more.
- You could decide to seek support.
- You could decide to share your experience.
- You could decide to humour it.
- You could decide to love it.

Whatever you choose, the process is helping you to:

- Move along the continuum of possibilities.
- Be more of or less of.
- See that you too have traces of every quality in you.
- Be non-judgemental because of it.
- See the sameness in us all.
- Be compassionate and understanding and forgiving.
- Engage in difference.
- Feel and connect with your life.
- Get to know yourself.

CHAPTER 27

REBALANCE

Two Quick Questions

Where am I now?

How am I trapped?

Question 1: Where Am I Now?

Where is your energy and focus directed? Identify and admit.

Are you in your head?

- Thinking or analysing
- Stuck in the past or future
- Worrying, dreaming, telling stories, creating drama

Are you in your emotions?

- Feeling overwhelmed
- Feeling tense

- Holding your breath
- Overbreathing
- Heart racing
- Sweating

Are you in your body?

- Doing, doing, doing
- Multitasking
- On the run
- Idling

Are you in your talk?

- Talking over
- Talking nonsense
- Talking fast
- Talking non-stop
- Talking negatively
- Talking positively

Are you in your being?

- Attuned
- Listening
- Settled
- Clear
- Observant

Question 2: How Am I Trapped?

Where is your imbalance? Often it is too far left and a little right is needed. Identify and admit.

LEFT	RIGHT
Control Locked into the way it *should* be, routines, structure	**Flexibility** Open to new ways, seeing things when they arrive, prepared to shift
Time-bound Waiting, in a hurry, forcing, set plans, chasing the time, time frames	**Experience-based** Feeling, reading the play, integrating challenges with what arrives, observing
External Rewards Focused on the goal, status, title, money, possessions, winning	**Internal Rewards** Focused on the feelings, insights, satisfaction, comfort, peace, relationships, purpose
External Answers Strategies, protocols, rules, research, being told how, what, when, where.	**Internal Answers** Listening within; body, mind, spirit; knowing the self; following your own choice, way, responsibility
Overthinking Using logic and brain power to gather information to know and solve.	**Heart-based** Placing the problem in the heart to seek the solution, following the gut and intuition

LEFT	RIGHT
Single Focus Intense, overdoing, one-dimensional, focused	**Varied focus** Shift of focus based on moment-by-moment signals of need; fluid, flowing
Destructive Unaware, unproductive, worry, non-nurturing pleasure	**Nurturing/Constructive** Love, respect, acceptance for self, others, and the earth

CHAPTER **28**

SHIFT

The One Acronym

PATIENCE

Perspective

Awareness

Thoughts

Intention

Emotion

Nonsense

Clarity

Escape

The P in PATIENCE: Perspective

Look for other perspectives and watch the shift in your perception of reality. Be patient with it. Ask yourself:

- Has this ever appeared differently?
- How do others see it?
- What else could it be?

Try these exercises to expand your perspective:

- Look into the eyes of an old person until you can see his or her youth.
- Identify one new detail of an object you are familiar with.
- Imagine changing roles with another person you either know well or don't. Feel that person's world.
- Imagine seeing things from another time in history.
- See yourself—step outside and view yourself.
- Listen to stories from people who once were but now are.
- Immerse yourself and extract the wisdom and greatness from the writings of prophets.
- Select something you don't like and observe it until you are able to see something you like about it.
- Select someone you truly admire. Now remove that individual's title, trimmings, belongings, and assets. As he or she stands before you, describe what it is you admire.

The A in PATIENCE: Awareness

Be aware of where your attention is placed. Shift your attention and notice what you notice. Be patient with it. Ask yourself:

- Where is my attention right now?
- What is keeping me attached to it?
- What other things am I maybe not aware of?
- Where else could I place my attention right now?

As an exercise to expand awareness, place vigilant attention on a single object. Relax, be still, and experience silence. Be present to breath, touch, sounds, feel, sights. Notice:

- your body when you feel good.
- something you haven't noticed before.
- what makes it difficult or easy to focus.
- what anxious anticipation feels like in your body.
- the range of and swings of mind, body, and heart states in a day.
- what feedback you listen and don't listen to.
- your established physical routines and patterns.
- your common speech dialogues or patterns.
- what you believe about yourself and others.
- when you are aware that you are aware.

The T in PATIENCE: Thoughts

Thoughts are fleeting, changing phenomena, so be careful what you do with them. Be patient with them. Ask yourself:

- Is this thought worth following?
- How can I allow this thought to pass without following or becoming entrenched in it?
- What other thought can shift me to something that serves me better?

As an exercise to expand influence over thoughts, when thoughts arise, admit to yourself the intention behind the thought. Ask yourself what type of emotional response occurred in your body from that thought. Notice how much time you have spent in your thoughts. Take some time to:

- Inject purposeful thoughts of love and compassion into your mind space.
- Produce a disposal bin in your mind for unwanted thoughts and stories.
- Create a story with your mind's thoughts to align with your intended life mission.
- Listen with stillness in your body.
- Induce a daydreaming state to exit the thinking state and experience the difference.
- Use your senses without thinking or using language but rather feeling and appreciating.

The I in PATIENCE: Intention

Look to your true inner intention. Infuse integrity and love, and you will reap the rewards. Be patient with it. Ask yourself:

- What is fuelling my intention?
- What part of my ego is behind this?
- Can it nurture me, others, and the earth?

Try these exercises to expand your influence of intention:

- Create a vision for what you intend (with work, friendships, health, learning, exercise).
- Create a short intention to affirm your vision.
- Identify the patterns, behaviours, and attitudes you intend to release to allow this vision.
- State an intention about what you want for the day.
- Look to find each day.
- Do an act of kindness and compassion.
- Engage in a small step toward your vision.
- Repeat to yourself your intention.
- Note the impact of intention on the outcomes in your life.
- Notice what in you keeps your quality positive intentions alive.

The E in PATIENCE: Emotions

Notice if your emotion is driving your action. Allow the emotion without becoming entrenched in it or any story from it. Infuse empathy, and it will pass. Be patient with it. Ask yourself:

- What is the emotion?
- What is keeping me in the emotion?
- What is the emotion telling me?

Try these exercises to expand your influence over emotions:

- Identify an emotion as it arises. Note the thoughts and sensations in your body and the effects on behaviour and attitude. Become familiar with them.
- Cry for the things you are sad for.
- Smile broadly for the things you are happy for.
- Inform others of emotions you experience.
- Extract the information that your emotions bring.
- Cuddle a pet and absorb the love.
- Laugh out loud.
- Smile and notice what happens.
- Frown and notice what happens.
- Cry in a sad movie.
- Sing with joy.
- Dance with self-love.

The N in PATIENCE: Nonsense

Notice if it is a nonsense story that requires an immediate stop. Find another version and stick to that for a while. Be patient with it. Ask yourself:

- Have I made sure this is really true?
- Have I assumed, generalised, or distorted something to reach this conclusion?
- How can I be sure?

Try these exercises to expand your ability to identify nonsense:

- Identify what "true" means to you.
- Find a historical truth that has since been declared untrue.
- State the direct opposite of things appearing real to you.
- Imagine a future news headline of a present-day truth that was debunked.
- Find the fun, humour, or lightness in a difficult situation.
- Identify what part you resist most.
- Find someone who discovered a new truth and changed his or her life.
- Identify when a good became a bad or a bad became a good, or a pleasure became a pain and a pain became a pleasure.
- Identify times when you have displayed aspects of things you dislike in others.
- Discover what tells you "I can."
- Discover what tells you "I can't."
- Discover what tells you what to listen to.

The C in PATIENCE: Clarity

Check your clarity by applying a creative new slant, more communication, or more possibilities. Be patient with it. Ask yourself:

- How can I be sure?
- What else could it be?
- What does my intuition tell me?

Try these exercises to expand your clarity:

- State with clarity your reasons for a selection or choice.
- Engage in difference to expand your experience.
- Change a familiar routine or one that could do with a modification (an exercise routine, eating strategy, saving strategy). Note any gains or preference.
- Select three or four ingredients and explore how many ways they can be utilized in creative meal design. Explore as many ways as you can think of to use eggs, or come up with some different ways to enjoy apples.
- Seek an idea or alternative strategy to a current dilemma and test it in your life.
- Place a worry in a bubble to the right of you and then change its shape, size, and texture. What do you notice?
- Call on your intuition or instinct and notice the response.
- Breathe into your heart space and ask your heart what presents.
- Notice messages from your subconscious through "thoughts from nowhere," coincidences, dreams, or standout words or images.
- Ask for an answer and see what arrives.

The E in PATIENCE: Escape

You can engage something different at any time to escape. Remember, however, to be open to embrace, learn, and attempt. Be patient with it. Ask yourself:

- What can I do or say right now to feel better?
- What has worked before?
- What strengths can I draw from?

Try these exercises to expand circuit breakers and escapes:

- Identify the role of key people in your life, those you would call upon for light relief, deep discussion, new perspectives, action, support, fun, advice, mentoring, inspiration, information, or love.
- Practice a tension-release breathing technique, such as: inhale into your belly, exhale, and release.
- Learn energy tapping on relevant pressure points for relief, or use trigger points, self-massage, or gentle stretch.
- Develop a mantra that instantly brings you support ("Calm," "My best intention," "For the good," "Peace," "I can").
- Extract a positive purpose or learning from everything, no matter how small.
- State a new thing each day to be grateful for.
- Tell yourself how your strengths can help you out.
- Practice walking away and silence.
- Immerse yourself in nature.
- Express your thoughts by drawing, writing, or doodling.
- Feel you heart; find compassion and empathy.
- Move your body.

Appendix 1

Resources

This section offers resources including websites,
organisations and books related to the broad
range of topics I mentioned throughout.

We found it useful to contact a support organisation on cancer related issues. This site helped us;
http://www.cancercouncil.com.au/

Padre Pio was a significant figure in our lives. This site offers a little more about his life story;
http://padrepiodevotions.org/a-short-biography/

I found journaling to be an important part of my healing. This site offers some tips on how to journal;
http://www.createwritenow.com/how-to-write-a-journal-0/

I subscribed to many sites that presented a range of natural approaches for cancer. This is one of the sites;
http://www.cancerdefeated.com/

I found Meditation helped settle my mind and body. This site has some short meditations that I found useful;
http://www.withandrewjohnson.com/

I committed to the blood group diet. This site describes a little more about it;
http://www.dadamo.com/

My intuition developed over the years. This site describes ways to develop that;
http://www.soniachoquette.com/

I studied Life coaching. This site offers more about that;
http://www.coachfederation.org/

I studied and used EFT to help let go of challenging emotions, beliefs and thoughts. This site describes more about that;
http://www.thetappingsolution.com/about.php

I developed Rhythm of Life coaching. Here is the website link;
http://rhythmoflifecoaching.com.au/

I developed a Rhythm of Life coaching face book page. Here is the link;
https://www.facebook.com/pages/Rhythm-of-Life-Coaching/161817248021?ref=hl

I developed a personal program named *Find the way*. This page brings you to the help page where support is provided;
http://rhythmoflifecoaching.com.au/find-the-way/

I set up a Blog to inform friends and family about Steve's progress during his illness. This is the site;
www.blogger.com

I participated in an online writing course to learn more about writing a book. This links to the course:
http://www.andrewjobling.com.au/one-word-at-a-time/

I found it powerful to clean out various aspects of my life. This site offers more about that;
http://zenhabits.net/simple-living-manifesto-72-ideas-to-simplify-your-life/

I undertook regular Chi Kung sessions. This site describes more about that;
http://www.taichi.com.au/chikung.html

I mentioned a study by John Hagelin related to meditation. This site describes more about that;
http://hagelin.org/about.html

I undertook the 5 Tibetan rites. This site shows the 5 exercises;
http://www.youtube.com/watch?v=TJElLrpBetc

I mentioned Steve and I used Transfer Factors. This site provides more information;
http://www.4life.com/

I mentioned that I commenced volunteering. This innovative organisation prototyped a project titled 'weavers' that focused on caring for carers;
http://www.tacsi.org.au/

A Whole New Mind: Why Right-Brainers Will Rule the Future by Daniel H. Pink

Dying to Be Me: My Journey from Cancer, to Near Death, to True Healing by Anita Moorjani

Emotional Intelligence: Why It Can Matter More Than IQ by Daniel Goleman

Evolve Your Brain: the Science of Changing Your Mind by Joe Dispenza, DC

It's Not About the Bike: My Journey Back to Life by Lance Armstrong

Loving What Is: Four Questions That Can Change Your Life by Byron Katie with Stephen Mitchell

Prisoner of Belief: Exposing and Changing Beliefs That Control Your Life by Matthew McKay, PhD, and Patrick Fanning

Proof of Heaven: A Neurosurgeon's Journey into the Afterlife by Dr. Eben Alexander

Quantum Healing: Exploring the Frontiers of Mind/Body Medicine by Deepak Chopra, MD

Spiritual Intelligence: The Ultimate Intelligence by Danah Zohar and Ian Marshall

The Art of Happiness: A Handbook for Living by the Dalai Lama and Howard C. Cutler

The Attention Revolution: Unlocking the Power of the Focused Mind by B. Alan Wallace, PhD

The Body Quantum: The New Physics of Body, Mind, and Health by Fred Alan Wolf

The Kid Who Climbed Everest: The Incredible Story of a 23-Year-Old's Summit of Mt. Everest by Bear Grylls

The Long Walk by Slavomir Rawicz

The Power of Intention by Wayne W. Dyer

The Power of Now: A Guide to Spiritual Enlightenment by Eckhart Tolle

You Can Heal Your Life by Louise L. Hay

Appendix 2

Steve's Top
Eleven Recipes

1. Meatballs
2. Kaffir Lime Salmon with Sautéed Spinach and Oven-Roasted Potatoes
3. Chicken in White Wine on a Sweet-Potato Mash
4. Veal Coated with Fresh Breadcrumbs and Capsicum and Mushroom Sauce
5. Vegetable Lasagne
6. Curry Turkey Rissoles with Potato Salad
7. Vegetable and Cheese Omelette
8. Stuffed Zucchini
9. Lamb Fillet on Quinoa and Asian Salad
10. Green Vegetable Combo and Potato Bake
11. Anna's Yoghurt Cake

We really enjoyed these recipes and hope you do too.

Although not mentioned throughout the next section, it is worthwhile noting that each meal was prepared with the utmost attention to hygiene. I worked on clean benches, used clean utensils and avoided cross contamination of foods. I avoided physical contact with foods and wore latex gloves as a precaution. Where possible I used organic options and washed produce thoroughly in cold water with a little cider vinegar to support the elimination of residual chemicals.

You may need to substitute ingredients to suit your personal likes or food requirements.

Let me know how you go . . .

Meatballs

Ingredients

- Olive oil
- 2 garlic cloves
- Basil, a small handful
- 2 bottles of pasta sauce/tomato puree
- 2 cups chicken stock
- Spices—I throw some in to vary it up
- Mustard sauce, a big blob
- Sweet chilli sauce, a bigger blob
- 2 slices of bread (I used spelt)
- 1 kilogram mince (meat, poultry, or a combination)
- 2 small eggs, beaten
- Grated Parmesan, about a handful
- Fresh parsley, finely chopped for meatballs and less chopped for garnish
- Salt and pepper

Method

Prepare the sauce:

1. Place a little oil in a large saucepan. When heated, add the garlic and basil for a couple of minutes to flavour.
2. Add the pasta sauce and the chicken stock and bring to a boil, and then reduce heat.
3. Add the spices, mustard sauce, and chilli sauce.

Prepare the bread:

4. Give the bread a quick soak in a little water until all covered.
5. Squeeze the water from the bread until as much water as possible is drained.

Prepare the meatballs:

6. Place the mince in a large mixing bowl.
7. Add the beaten eggs, Parmesan, finely chopped parsley, salt, and pepper.
8. Add the squeezed-out bread slices.
9. Wearing latex gloves, knead the combined ingredients until all parts are fully combined into an even mixture.
10. Still wearing the gloves, place a small tablespoon of the mixture into the palm of your hand and roll with the other hand to form a ball. Place the meatball into the sauce mixture. Continue until all of the meat mixture has been used.
11. Keep the lid on the saucepan for about an hour for the meatballs to cook.
12. Remove the lid and continue to cook for another half hour to reduce the sauce and thicken.
13. Drain each meatball using a slotted spoon to transfer it to a heat-resistant bowl.

To finish:

Sprinkle with parsley garnish. Eat the meatballs with a green vegetable salad or garden salad, or add the remainder of the sauce to some cooked pasta and serve with the meatballs.

Kaffir Lime Salmon with Sautéed Spinach and Oven-Roasted Potatoes

Ingredients

- 1 potato per person
- Olive oil
- Salt and pepper
- 4 cloves garlic, crushed, skin on, plus more minced garlic as needed
- A few sprigs of rosemary
- 1 salmon fillet per person
- 1 tomato, sliced
- Grated ginger
- Crushed chilli
- ½ teaspoon of roughly chopped coriander per fillet
- Kaffir lime leaves
- Bunch of spinach
- Sea salt

Method

Prepare the potatoes:

1. Peel the potatoes and cut lengthways into quarters. Place on an oiled oven tray. Cover with oil, salt, and pepper.
2. Place the garlic cloves on the tray together with scattered sprigs of rosemary.
3. Cook the potatoes in a 180°C preheated oven until brown and crispy, about 45 minutes to 1 hour.

Prepare the salmon fillets:

4. Cut aluminium foil squares large enough to cover each of the salmon fillets, with a pocket of space left for steaming.
5. Place salmon on the foil and create a boat shape by scrunching the foil.
6. Place tomato slices along the salmon fillet. Sprinkle the ginger, some of the minced garlic, the chilli, coriander, salt, and pepper over the fillets. Drizzle oil on each fillet. Lie a couple of Kaffir lime leaves in each of the fillet parcels
7. Enclose the salmon parcel with the foil, leaving space for the fish to steam. Secure at the top with a scrunching action.
8. Place the parcels in an ovenproof dish and cook the salmon for approximately twenty minutes. Remove the dish from the oven.

Prepare the spinach:

9. Wash the spinach, drain, and roughly cut into pieces.
10. Place a small amount of water in a saucepan. Add the spinach and cook until tender. Drain the spinach.
11. Heat a small amount of oil and garlic over medium heat, and then add the drained spinach. Add sea salt and pepper and toss the spinach until well-coated.

To finish:

Place a salmon parcels on a plate. Open the foil seal of the parcel (stay clear from the release of steam). Serve with the sautéed spinach and roasted potatoes.

Chicken in White Wine on a Sweet-Potato Mash

Ingredients

- Flour, for dusting (I use spelt flour)
- Salt and pepper
- 2 chicken thighs per person (at least 6 for flavour)
- Olive oil
- 1 white onion, finely sliced in rings
- ¼ cup white wine (whatever you have)
- Chicken stock (enough to fully cover the chicken)
- ½ teaspoon mustard (optional)
- Sprig of rosemary (optional)
- 1 sweet potato
- 2 white potatoes
- Dash of milk
- Dash of butter
- Grated cheese (I use a mix of Parmesan, cheddar, and mozzarella)
- Parsley, chopped, for serving

Method

Prepare the chicken:

1. Place some flour, salt, and pepper in a freezer bag.
2. Add one chicken thigh at a time. Shake it in the bag until well-coated with flour. Remove it from the bag, shaking off any excess flour. Repeat with each thigh.
3. Heat the oil in a low frying pan that has a lid.
4. Place the thighs in the pan and turn once a light brown crispy outer has formed. Brown the reverse side of the chicken.

5. Cover the chicken with the onion. After a minute, add the white wine and cook for another minute. Then add the chicken stock, mustard, sprig of rosemary, salt, and pepper.

6. Cover with the lid and cook on low heat for approximately 30 minutes, until basically cooked through.

7. Remove the lid and simmer until the liquid has thickened slightly. Discard the sprig of rosemary.

Prepare the sweet-potato mash:

8. Peel the sweet potato and white potatoes. Cut into 2-centimeter cubes. Place in cold water in a microwave-safe large dish.

9. Cook the potatoes until they are very soft to mash. Drain and return to dish.

10. Add milk and butter. Mash with a potato masher. Add grated cheese, salt and pepper. Further mash the mixture and add more milk or butter if required.

To finish:

Place a large spoonful of sweet-potato mash on a plate. Place two thighs on the plate and cover both the chicken and the mash with a little of the onion sauce. Sprinkle with parsley. Serve with greens or salad

Veal Coated with Fresh Breadcrumbs and Capsicum and Mushroom Sauce

Ingredients

- 1 piece of sliced bread per slice of veal (I use wholemeal)
- Fresh Italian parsley (a small bunch), finely chopped
- Grated Parmesan (about a handful)
- Salt and pepper
- Cornflake crumbs (a handful)
- 2 small eggs
- Plain flour (I use spelt)
- Sliced veal, tenderised (1 or 2 slices per person, depending on size)
- Oil (I use olive oil)
- 1 red capsicum
- Basil (a small bunch)
- 1 Garlic clove minced
- 1 can chopped tomato
- 1 cup chicken stock
- 6 small mushrooms

Method

Prepare the veal:

1. Place the bread and ¾ of the parsley in food processor to form a crumb mixture. Place the crumbs on a large piece of waxed paper and add Parmesan, salt, pepper, and a sprinkle of cornflake crumbs.
2. Place the eggs in a shallow bowl with some salt and pepper and beat gently.
3. Place the flour on a large piece of waxed paper.

4. Coat each piece of veal with flour, gently patting excess away; egg, gently scraping excess away; and then the crumb mix, removing excess and pressing gently.
5. Leave the veal in the fridge for a couple of hours before cooking.
6. To cook, heat oil on medium heat. Add veal and cook each side until golden brown.

Prepare the sauce:

7. Place capsicum, basil, and garlic in the food processor until finely chopped
8. Heat oil in a small saucepan on medium heat. Add the capsicum mix to the heated oil and stir.
9. Place the canned tomato in the food processor to make a smooth sauce and then add to the heated capsicum mix.
10. Add the chicken stock and salt and pepper and cover. Heat until boiling.
11. Wash and cut mushrooms into thin slivers and add to the sauce. Return to a boil and then reduce heat
12. Remove lid and simmer to thicken before serving.

To finish:

Place a small amount of sauce over each veal cutlet and sprinkle with the remaining parsley. Serve with green salad or green vegetables.

Vegetable Lasagne

Ingredients

- Oil (I use olive oil)
- 1 onion, grated
- 2 cloves garlic, minced
- 1 kilogram mince (meat, poultry, or a combination)
- 1 carrot, grated
- 1 capsicum, grated
- 1 small red chilli (optional)
- 1 zucchini, grated
- Salt and pepper
- 1 can tomatoes
- Small bunch of basil
- 1 bottle tomato puree
- 4 cups chicken stock
- 1 small tub tomato paste
- 500 grams broccoli
- 500 grams low-fat ricotta
- 2 large handfuls of grated Parmesan
- 8 sheets of fresh lasagne noodles, or, for homemade pasta sheets, 2 cups of plain flour (I use spelt flour) with 1 egg and a dash of oil
- Mozzarella cheese

Method

Prepare the sauce:

1. Heat about 2 tablespoons of oil in a large saucepan. Add the onion and garlic.
2. Add the mince to the oil and mix through until its colour has changed. Add the carrot, capsicum, chilli and zucchini and add

305

to the mince mixture. Stir through the mince and add salt and pepper.

3. Place the canned tomatoes and the basil in a food processor until a smooth sauce has formed. Add to the mince mixture together with the tomato puree, chicken stock, and tomato paste.

4. Cover and cook sauce for at least 45 minutes. Uncover to thicken a little before using in the lasagne.

Prepare the ricotta mixture:

5. Steam the broccoli until soft. Place in the food processor until a paste-like texture has formed. Mix with the ricotta together with 1 handful of Parmesan cheese, salt, and pepper.

Prepare the pasta sheets:

6. *For homemade pasta:* Add sifted flour, egg, and a dash of oil into the food processor until a ball of dough has formed. Refrigerate for at least 1 hour. Knead dough on a floured board. Cut into 8 pieces and feed each piece into a spaghetti machine until it reaches the appropriate thickness. Lie each sheet on a floured flat surface until needed.

Preparing the lasagne:

7. Line a large lasagne dish with a small amount of the sauce mixture, and then place pasta sheets to cover the sauce. Top with mozzarella cheese and then more sauce mixture. Repeat the layering system. With one or two of the layers (depending on the amount of mixture), line the pasta sheet with the ricotta mixture instead of sauce before the next pasta sheet is laid. Place a generous amount of sauce on the final layer and sprinkle with a combination of mozzarella and Parmesan cheese.

8. Cover with foil and place in a 180°C preheated oven for about 45 minutes to 1 hour. Remove and let stand for a few minutes before cutting and serving.

To finish:

Add a small amount of extra sauce on lasagne slices if needed. Serve with a fresh green garden salad.

Curry Turkey Rissoles with Potato Salad

Ingredients

For rissoles:

- 1 cup baby peas
- 1 kilogram turkey mince
- 1 small bunch coriander
- 1 cup breadcrumbs (dried or fresh)
- 1 small container ricotta
- 1 small bunch spring onions
- 2 tablespoons curry paste
- A sprinkle of turmeric
- 1 small can light coconut milk
- Salt and pepper
- Oil (I use light olive oil for frying)
- Sweet chilli sauce

For salad:

- Potatoes (1 per person or a minimum of 6 large)
- Bay leaves
- 1 cup peas
- 3 eggs (or more for extra potatoes)
- Creamy egg mayonnaise, or, for homemade mayonnaise, 3 egg yolks, 2 tablespoons Dijon mustard, 2 tablespoons white wine vinegar, and 200 millilitres olive oil
- Dill, finely chopped
- 3 thinly chopped sweet-and-sour gherkins

Method

Prepare the rissoles:

1. Preheat oven to 180°C.
2. Cook and cool peas.
3. Place the turkey mince, the cooled peas, and all other ingredients except for the oil and sweet chilli sauce into a large bowl. Wearing latex kitchen gloves, mix all ingredients until fully combined.
4. Still wearing the gloves, form balls about the size of a small handful, using a rolling action in the palm of your hands. Flatten slightly to form the rissole.
5. Heat oil in a non stick pan, add rissoles and brown each side to a golden colour and then place into an oven dish. Baste each rissole with sweet chilli sauce and cook in the oven for approximately 15 minutes. Baste with more sauce halfway through cooking time.

Prepare the potato salad:

6. Boil potatoes in their jackets together with bay leaves until soft (use a skewer to test). Allow to cool.
7. Peel the thin layer of potato skin, cut the potatoes into small cubes, and place the cubes in a large bowl.
8. Cook the peas on the cooktop with a small amount of water. Allow to cool.
9. Place the eggs in a small saucepan covered with cold water. Bring to a boil and then cook for a further 5 minutes (for hard boil). Cool the eggs with running water and peel the shell. Cut the eggs into small pieces.
10. *If making your own mayonnaise*: Place the egg yolks in a blender with Dijon mustard and vinegar. Blend the ingredients. Keep

the blender on while you add the oil, drops at a time. Add salt and pepper to taste.

11. Assemble the salad by combining the peas, eggs, dill, gherkin, salt, and pepper. Add a large dollop of mayonnaise and mix until fully combined.

To finish:

Serve the rissoles with the potato salad and either fresh green beans or a fresh green garden salad.

Vegetable and Cheese Omelette

Ingredients

- 6 organic free-range eggs
- Small amount of light milk
- Salt and pepper
- Small tub of low-fat ricotta (optional)
- Small handful of mixed cheeses (Parmesan, mozzarella, tasty)
- Olive oil
- Small bunch of spring onion, thinly sliced
- 1 cup of peeled and grated sweet potato
- 3 tomatoes, thinly sliced
- Small bunch of baby spinach, washed
- Small handful of fresh chopped parsley

Method

1. Gently whisk the eggs, and then add the milk, salt, and pepper. Whisk a little more. Add the ricotta and other cheeses to the eggs and mix through. Set aside, remembering to give another quick whisk before pouring.
2. Place a little oil in a large round flat frying pan. Heat gently and then add the onion; cook until translucent. Add the sweet potato and stir through for a minute. Add tomato slices to cover the pan. Turn over the tomato slices once as they begin to change colour. Cover the mix with the baby spinach and allow to cook, giving it a gentle mix-through occasionally. Pour the egg mixture over the vegetables and allow to cook. Place the frying pan in the grill section of the oven to finish the cooking process.
3. Return the omelette to the stovetop and give it a gentle shake to release the omelette from the base.

4. Either serve the omelette directly from the frying pan or, if possible, place a large round serving plate over the omelette and flip the frying pan upside down to allow the omelette to fall onto the serving plate.

To finish:

Sprinkle the omelette with the parsley. Serve the omelette with a fresh garden salad or steamed fresh green vegetables.

Stuffed Zucchini

Ingredients

- Oil (I use olive oil)
- 1 Garlic clove minced
- 1 small chilli finely chopped
- Small handful basil chopped
- 500 grams beef mince (or other mince of your liking)
- 1 bottle tomato puree
- 1 cup chicken stock
- Salt and pepper
- 1 cup rice
- Mixed cheeses (Parmesan, mozzarella, tasty)
- 1 very large zucchini for every two people

Method

1. Place a little oil in a large saucepan. When heated, add garlic, chilli, and basil for a couple of minutes.
2. Add the mince and stir until colour has changed. Add the tomato puree, chicken stock, salt, and pepper. Cook sauce for approximately ½ hour.
3. Place the rice into 2½ cups of water and cook in microwave until water is absorbed.
4. Prepare a mixture of the cooked rice, some of the meat sauce (capturing as much of the meat as possible), some of the mixed cheeses, and salt and pepper.
5. Preheat the oven to 200°C.
6. Cut each zucchini in half lengthways. Scoop the seeds from the centre to create a deep well for the rice mixture. Spoon the mixture into the zucchini, pressing to secure it.

7. Cover the zucchini with a generous amount of sauce and cheese. Cover the tray with foil and cook for approximately 1 to 1 ½ hours, or until the zucchini is fully cooked through. Remove the tray from the oven and allow it to stand for a minute before serving.

To finish:

Place a stuffed zucchini half on a plate. Serve with fresh green beans, steamed broccoli, or your favourite side.

Lamb Fillet on Quinoa and Asian Salad

Ingredients

- 2 large lamb fillets
- Soy sauce
- Hoisin sauce
- Chinese five-spice powder
- Sprinkle of turmeric
- I crushed garlic
- Salt and pepper
- 1 cup organic quinoa
- 2 cups of chicken stock
- 50 grams roasted slivered almonds
- 1 small baby cos lettuce, washed, drained, and thinly sliced
- 2 Lebanese cucumbers, cut into small slivers
- 1 carrot, peeled and grated
- ½ red onion, thinly sliced
- 6 corn spears, cut into 1½-centimetre pieces
- Small handful of bean shoots
- 1 small bunch of coriander and mint
- Juice of 1 lime
- 2 tablespoons soy sauce
- 1 red chilli, finely chopped
- 1 tablespoon palm sugar or caster sugar

Method

Prepare the lamb:

1. Marinate the lamb in the soy, hoisin, five-spice powder, turmeric, crushed garlic, salt, and pepper. Refrigerate for a few hours.

2. Remove the lamb from the marinade and place it on an oven tray and cover with foil. Place in a 180 degree preheated oven for approximately 45 minutes (or until cooked through).
3. Set the lamb aside to cool. When cooled, cut into thin slices

Prepare the quinoa:

4. Place the quinoa into a sieve and rinse through. Place the quinoa into a small saucepan and cover with the chicken stock. Place on medium heat until the stock comes to the boil, and then reduce heat and cover. Allow for the stock to fully evaporate and the quinoa to soften completely.
5. Remove from the heat and allow to cool. Line the base of a large flat serving dish with the quinoa.

Prepare the salad:

6. Place the slivered almonds in a 150 degree heated oven and roast for a couple of minutes or until just changing colour. Remove from the oven and allow to cool.
7. Spread the lettuce on top of the quinoa. Spread the cucumber over the lettuce. Sprinkle a layer of carrot over the cucumber. Mix the onion and corn spears gently into the lettuce, ensuring an even blend of colour of all ingredients.
8. Gently place the bean shoots, coriander, mint, and almonds throughout the salad.
9. *Make the dressing:* Place the lime juice, soy sauce, chilli, and sugar in a blender and mix well. Gently toss with the salad.

To finish:

Place the lamb evenly over the salad on a serving platter. Bring to the table to self-serve.

Green Vegetable Combo and Potato Bake

Ingredients

For potato bake:

- 6 potatoes, peeled and sliced
- 1 sweet potato, peeled and sliced
- Mixed grated cheese (Parmesan, mozzarella, tasty)
- Salt and pepper
- 300 millilitres light cream or evaporated milk
- 2 cups chicken stock

For vegetable combo:

- Dash olive oil
- 2 cloves garlic, crushed
- 1 small red chilli, cut into slivers
- 3-centimetre piece of ginger, thickly sliced
- 2 handfuls green beans, trimmed
- 1 large head broccoli, cut into florets
- 2 celery stalks, thinly sliced
- 1 zucchini, cut into chunks
- ½ cup chicken stock
- 150 grams baby spinach

Method

Prepare potato bake:

1. Preheat oven to 180°C.
2. Layer an oven dish with potato slices and then sprinkle with grated cheese, salt, and pepper. Layer with sweet-potato slices

and then sprinkle with grated cheese, salt, and pepper. Continue layering, alternating potato and sweet-potato slices until all have been used.

3. Mix the cream with the chicken stock and pour over the potato layers. Top with more grated cheese. Cover with foil and bake in the preheated oven for about 1 hour or until nearly cooked. Remove the foil to finish cooking the potato and to brown the top layer and reduce any excess liquid. This may take approximately 20 minutes.

Prepare the vegetable combo:

4. Heat the oil gently in a large non-stick pan with a lid and add the garlic, chilli, and ginger. Stir quickly and then add the beans, broccoli, celery, and zucchini. Add the chicken stock and cover. Just before the vegetables are tender (approximately 15 minutes), add the baby spinach. After a couple of minutes remove the lid to reduce any excess liquid.

To finish:

Use these as a side dish to accompany grilled lean steak, chicken, or fish.

Anna's Yoghurt Cake

Ingredients

- 4 eggs
- 2 cups caster sugar
- 1 cup vegetable oil
- 1 teaspoon vanilla extract
- 500 grams traditional Greek-style natural yoghurt (I use Black Swan because it has a thicker texture)
- 4 cups self-raising flour (I use plain spelt flour with bicarbonate and baking powder)
- 700-gram jar pitted cherries (Morello if possible, but other fruits are good too)
- Icing sugar

Method

1. Preheat oven to 180°C. Line a 25-centimetre round springform tin.
2. Place the first five ingredients into a large bowl and combine using an electric mixer on medium speed.
3. Slowly add sifted flour to the bowl, mixing until combined well.
4. Drain the jar of cherries and add to the bowl, mixing through well.
5. Place the batter into the prepared cake tin and bake in the oven for approximately 45 minutes, or until cooked through.
6. Once removed from the oven, allow to cool and then release from the tin.

To finish:

Sprinkle with icing sugar and serve on its own or with cream and other fresh fruit.

Thank you for reading about our journey.
Feel free to contact me about any of the content.